OPINION WRITING

Also by Ruggero J. Aldisert

The Judicial Process: Text, Materials and Cases
(2d ed. 1996)

Logic for Lawyers: A Guide to Clear Legal Thinking
(3d ed. 1997)

Winning on Appeal: Better Briefs and Oral Argument
(2d ed. 2003)

Road to the Robes: A Federal Judge Recollects
Young Years & Early Times
(2005)

A Judge's Advice: 50 Years on the Bench
(2011)

Opinion Writing

THIRD EDITION

Ruggero J. Aldisert
Senior United States Circuit Judge,
Chief Judge Emeritus,
United States Court of Appeals for the Third Circuit

Carolina Academic Press
Durham, North Carolina

Library of Congress Cataloging-in-Publication Data

Aldisert, Ruggero J.
  Opinion writing / Ruggero J. Aldisert. -- 3rd ed.
    p. cm.
  Includes bibliographical references and index.
  ISBN 978-1-61163-123-4 (alk. paper)
  1. Legal composition. 2. Judicial opinions--United States.
I. Title.

KF250.A35 2012
808.06'634--dc23   2012018489

Carolina Academic Press
700 Kent Street
Durham, North Carolina 27701
Telephone (919) 489-7486
Fax (919) 493-5668
www.cap-press.com

Back cover photo from family collection
Cover design by Molly Gleason

Printed in the United States of America

2020 Printing

Dedication

To our judges, state and federal ...

When the Trevelyans and the Carlyles of another time come to write the social history of this period, they will write of how a handful of men and women managed, against all seeming odds, to hold back the night so eagerly awaited by the ignorant armies of many camps.

> Bernard J. Ward
> Professor of Law
> University of Texas
> Austin, TX

The dedicatee for this edition is again the late Professor Bernard J. Ward, who died on May 7, 1982. He and fellow professor, author and lawyer, the late Charles Alan Wright, who died on July 7, 2000, were each other's best friend. It was my special honor to have known both well. Each of them has been associated with my books—either as here, the object of a dedication, or as in the case of Charlie, author of a foreword. I have decided to amplify my dedication to Bernie at this time, because I am now able to make reference to Charlie's informal memorial piece entitled *The Wit and Wisdom of Bernie Ward*, 61 Tex. L. Rev. 13 (1982–1983). And in unabashed plagiarism, with Charlie, I say about Bernie that "There was not a law professor in the country who was admired by, and a friend of, so many federal judges."

> Bernie Ward was a man of many passions. He was fascinated by history, he enjoyed sports, he loved poetry, he appreciated feminine beauty [his wife, Elaine], he could be persuaded to enjoy a drop of some stimulating beverage, and he cared, deeply and passionately, about the federal courts. On all of these, and many other subjects, Bernie commented learnedly and eloquently.

61 Tex. L. Rev at 14. Our trails crossed at many circuit judicial conferences, where his speeches were the stuff of which true oratory emerged. More significant was my private time with him as friend-to-friend. We shared a particularly fine summer of 1972 when he and I served on the summer faculty at Texas, invited to teach there by Charlie Wright, who supervised the program. The three of us enjoyed many evenings in their homes, an experience that made solid our connection for so many years. The magnificence of Bernie's speech and expression was a joy, transmuting text into lyricism. Another anecdote is illustrative:

In 1957 the lower federal courts were "nearing the end of a republic-long era of dallying in the sun," Bernie thought. "Thereafter, with stunning suddenness the federal courts changed utterly, and a terrible beauty was born. Paradigm shifts were brought about by such things as *Monroe v. Pape*, large reapportionment decisions, the expansion of habeas corpus, and the 1964 Civil Rights Act and those that followed." Only a Bernie could say that "strange new little litigants were moving in massive numbers towards the federal Courts—blacks, women, schoolchildren, prisoners and employees." During the same turbulent and exhilarating time, I was teaching Federal Courts at the University of Pittsburgh School of Law, where I used Charlie's case book, and shared Bernie's quotations, and always felt at home with the masters.

—RJA

CONTENTS

PART ONE
THEORETICAL CONCEPTS UNDERLYING AN OPINION

PART THREE
WRITING STYLE

PART FOUR
CHECKLISTS

PREFACE TO THE
THIRD EDITION

Differences between this edition and the previous editions are fundamental. To be sure, all editions have been divided into four distinct sections: (1) theoretical concepts underlying a judicial opinion; (2) the anatomy of an opinion; (3) writing style; and (4) opinion writing checklists.

But this present volume is more than a teaching text. Instead, it takes both new and experienced judges by the hand and reveals to them step-by-step how to write a judicial opinion. It is immaterial whether that writer presides over a state or federal trial tribunal, appellate panel, administrative agency proceeding, private arbitration, or the United States Supreme Court. That writer can even be an excited law student who has just received news of an appointment as a law clerk to a judge. They can all find practical and valuable assistance from the pages that follow because I have been writing judicial opinions for over a half century as a trial and appellate judge at the state and federal levels and, at least since the mid-seventies, have been teaching the theory and technique of opinion writing to newly commissioned judges through specialized seminars, lectures and writings.

In over 50 years as a judge, I have been involved with thousands of opinions written by my colleagues and me. Moreover, I have been fortunate in past years to have been designated to serve as a visiting judge in a number of other Judicial Circuits—the Fifth, Seventh, Ninth (extensively), Tenth and Eleventh. My experience serving in the different U.S. Courts of Appeals—from Atlanta, Georgia to Seattle, Washington—has provided me a rare opportunity to acquire first-hand knowledge of the operation of the judicial process.

It is this learning that I want to pass along now. This edition is a combination teaching manual and compendium of information. It is more than "what"; it is "how."

The emphasis in this book is on appellate court opinions, but much of its contents apply also to opinions of trial judges, arbitrators, administrative law judges and agency review boards. Because tribunals of the first instance have certain unique characteristics and emphases, this edition seeks to fill a void present in previous editions. Separate treatment is necessary because trial and appellate opinions serve different functions. Trial court opinions are justificatory only—designed to explain the tribunal's decision. An opinion for an appellate court has a completely different purpose—the correction of errors of trial tribunals, and applying, examining and evaluating the law of the jurisdiction.

Part of any judicial education process is always the give-and-take of informal lunches with other judges. Before I took senior status, I enjoyed these events mainly in Pittsburgh and Philadelphia with federal colleagues. After I made the trip West in 1987, and settled in California, I was fortunate to be invited to join the "judges' table" (a corner table that was set aside a few years after World War II in the University Club of Santa Barbara). It was here where I made friendships with judges of the Superior Court of Santa Barbara County. These included William Gordon, now retired, and Ronald Stevens and Patrick McMahon, of happy memory. I am now the "old man" at the table, whose regulars include retired judges James Brown and James Slater, and sitting judges Denise de Bellefeuille, George Eskin, Donna Geck, and James Herman.

In writing this book, many of the observations regarding trial judges have been enriched by my lunch buddies, on both the criminal and civil sides of a modern-day California trial court. Each week seems to drive home the fundamental differences between my halcyon experience on a Pennsylvania trial court from 1961 to 1968 and the tasks facing today's trial judges, tasks that are both comprehensive and sophisticated. I acknowledge with much affection and respect the valuable contributions and insights of my friends at the "judges' table."

This is the first edition of this book that discusses at length the importance of administrative law judges. Depending on the case, ALJs might be required to resolve a dispute, make findings of fact, reach conclusions of law, explain the rationale behind a decision, satisfy supervisors or supervising judges that the case was properly decided, create a record for appeal, set precedent, persuade litigants that the law supports the decision, educate litigators and the public about the law, or even reprimand litigants for improper behavior. All of this, the ALJs must do within the constraints of too-little time, binding precedent, agency conventions, readers' limited attention span, personal schedules, court rules, and updated technology. This book aims to lend a hand in accomplishing these multifaceted tasks.

Also in this edition, other unsung heroes of the judicial process are finally given proper recognition. "Private court adjudication" is what arbitration is all about. In addition to the decision-making apparatus being private, arbitration is unique because the process is generally based on a contract—that controls the subsequent arbitration procedures, and the award is usually commercial in nature. We have dedicated an entire chapter to arbitration procedures and opinion writing.

Law clerks must understand that this book is for them, too. If a clerk does not have this book prior to starting in chambers, she should start reading this book on her first day on the job. This is an exercise that will serve the law clerk well in the months that follow. Because of their necessary importance in opinion writing, we present a chapter on the important role of law clerks.

Another dimension has been added to this edition—a series of checklists to assist the opinion writer. I have prepared these for all opinion writers. They are designed for photocopying so that writers may have copies of these checklists at their sides as their work progresses. Special forms have been prepared for appellate judges, trial judges, administrative law judges and arbitrators. They take three forms—general checklists, checklists to test opinions and checklists to shorten the opinion.

Any books on opinion writing are considered serious literature by common understanding, if not by definition. This book is no exception. Yet there are times when a dash of humor can be more effective than a page of multisyllabic prose. Although known for writing six serious books on the law, by nature I seek the humorous side of life. To this end, I have conceptualized a dozen or so relevant concepts and asked again a very talented professional editorial cartoonist Russell Hodin, of San Luis Obispo, California, to freshen these pages with wit and bubbling effervescence.[1]

Although I have emphasized the time, study, and special interests I have in opinion writing that propel the publication of this book, the end product is a collaboration. I have been especially fortunate to have had outstanding assistants in this process. Fifty generations of law clerks have assisted me since I first slipped into my robes in 1961.

For this edition, my sixth book on the law, I am especially grateful for the valuable contributions of two outstanding lawyers, who have added quality, polish and editorial sparkle to my manuscript. They are my 2011–2012 term clerks—Collin Wedel, of Stanford Law School, and Kristina Katz Cercone, of

---

1. Russell Hodin illustrated also my book, A JUDGE'S ADVICE: 50 YEARS ON THE BENCH (2011).

Harvard Law School. They demonstrated maturity beyond their years, and profound loyalty and dedication to the success of this comprehensive endeavor.

This is the second book to which my career law clerk, Grace Wendy Liu, has made valuable contributions. After primary and secondary education in Taiwan, she is a graduate of the University of California at Santa Barbara and holds a law degree from Pepperdine Law School.

* * *

Although I technically retired in 1987, since that time I continue to be a very active "senior" federal judge, and in addition, have written a number of books on the law including supplemental editions. This has involved incredible demands, expending valuable time that intrudes on the retirement time of my wife, Agatha, and me. As in the case of the other books, my wife has soldiered on with me and my writing. Thanks to her patience and encouragement, as well as excellent literary advice, our sixty years together have been extraordinarily rewarding.

RUGGERO J. ALDISERT
Senior United States Circuit Judge
U.S. Court of Appeals for the Third Circuit

Santa Barbara, California
2012

Preface to the Second Edition

The big difference in this new edition is more in format than in text, although we have made some additions. What you will read is very much the same, but occasionally a subject pops up in a different setting, or under a different format, and we have been generous in tweaking some of the text.

The major change, however, will be the extensive availability of this new edition. Anyone who wants a copy can now get one through my publisher, AuthorHouse, or through any of the leading online booksellers.

There was limited access to the first edition, which was provided exclusively to certain members of the judiciary. I was commissioned to write the book; thereafter it was distributed gratuitously. For many years, all federal judges—trial and appellate—received copies of *Opinion Writing* as they were commissioned, but only state appellate judges were included within the largess. Additionally, state and federal administrative judges, hearing officers, commissioners and private arbitrators—all of whom write judicial opinions—were not included. As the author, I have also received many inquiries as to its availability from law librarians, and many requests to them originated from former law clerks who, having had great familiarity with the book, wanted to continue its use.

The first edition's distribution was terminated a few years back by the company that had purchased my previous publisher. The new company was no longer interested in the free judge-distribution plan, which was a popular public service but hardly a profitable endeavor. I re-acquired the copyright in order to revise, publish and redistribute the book myself. I am pleased that a wider audience of professional opinion writers and students of the judicial process will now have immediate access to the second edition.

The new added text largely describes methodologies that have become popular since the early edition appeared in 1990, and is chiefly intended to address the malady of excessive writing in opinions. As suggested in Chapter One, too many of them have an ailment known as "law reviewitis," being over-written and over-footnoted, obese and sloppy, instead of clean and neat.

To cure the burgeoning problem of excessive citations, for instance, we start with a question you must ask every time you get the urge to put pen to paper, or fingers to keyboard: "Why am I citing this case in my opinion?" You may be citing the case for the purpose of its analogous material facts. You may be citing the case for reasoning that supports your theory. Or you may be interested only in the conclusion of the case and are citing it only to support the legal consequence attached to a detailed set of facts. Beyond these three reasons, hold off.

I also now highly endorse the use of the parenthetical, a modernly popular writing device that explains a cited case without contributing to an opinion's undue verbosity. Accompanying a citation with a parenthetical replaces un-necessarily long descriptions of cited cases, and instead achieves the objective of concise opinion writing by zeroing directly in to why you are citing the case and where the case fits into the theme or focus of your opinion.

Finally, I have included an expanded discussion of the importance of logi-cal reasoning in effectively stating the rationale of your opinion, a topic close to my heart. An understanding of basic formal logic is invaluable to excellent opinion writing (and to opinion reading comprehension).

I have been writing judicial opinions for almost 50 years (during my Com-mon Pleas Court judgeship of eight years, the Pennsylvania Supreme Court required trial judges to write an opinion in every case that was appealed; to play it safe, I wrote an opinion in every final judgment). I think I do not ex-aggerate to suggest that few, if any, judges today have had more experience when it comes to this phase of the judicial process. But I did not work alone. Almost 50 generations of law clerks, in my state trial court and federal appel-late experience, have served me faithfully and well. I am quick to acknowledge that I learned something from each of these energetic young men and women, talented graduates of America's fine law schools. I willingly acknowledge their unfailingly excellent contributions.

From this group I am especially grateful for four volunteer editors who as-sisted in this endeavor: Rita K. Lomio of the Harvard Law School and Anika Christine Stucky of the Oklahoma Law Center from 2007–2008; and Meehan Rasch of the UCLA School of Law and Matthew Bartlett of the University of California, Hastings College of the Law in 2008–2009. The latter two editors were charged with more responsibility and more extensive activity because of the earlier changes I had brought about from the first edition, but each of my four wonderful law clerks has left an indelible stamp on these chapters. As well, our book will leave its mark of permanency on them as they proceed into their careers. Ms. Rasch and Mr. Bartlett also coauthored with me a companion law review article to this book, entitled "Opinion Writing and Opinion Readers," which may be found in Volume 31, Page 1, of the Cardozo Law Review (Fall 2009). I also extend my appreciation to Jacqueline Phan, my judicial assistant and a graduate of the University of California at Santa Barbara, for her loyalty and dedication to these pages and their author.

Law books don't just "happen"; they take time and research. When the author is still very active on his court, this means substantial commitments to evenings and weekends at home. This is also the precious time of Agatha, my very wonderful wife and helpmate for almost 60 years, who is required to tolerate this intrusion into our time together. In accepting this effort with magnificent patience, Agatha continues to contribute, inspire and support me with love and affection, now into these many years.

RUGGERO J. ALDISERT
Senior United States Circuit Judge
U.S. Court of Appeals for the Third Circuit

Santa Barbara, California
2009

PREFACE TO THE FIRST EDITION

This book comes not from one person, but from many. My own ideas have been tested and refined over the years in a process where I have observed and absorbed the talents of others.

Because appellate judges, trial judges, administrative law judges, and government board or commission members—all of us—are professional writers, there is much from which to pick and choose in examining our writings. Moreover, what we write is as important as what we decide. This is so because a judge's opinion performs as well as explains. It is a performative utterance. In this respect, writings of the government's judicial branch are unique. Written explanations of decisions in the executive and legislative branches (and in the private sector) do not possess the power of judicial opinions. They possess neither the bite of precedent nor the authority of case law. The contents of this book are expansions of discussions held at the Senior Judge Seminars sponsored by the Institute of Judicial Administration at New York University in 1970–1971, 1973–1982 and 1985. They reflect also ideas discussed in seminars for newly appointed judges at the Federal Judicial Center in Washington, D.C., 1974–1980, 1982. I had the privilege to serve as discussion leader in "Opinion Writing" at many of these sessions. I acknowledge, therefore, an indebtedness to the judges of the highest courts of the state and federal judicial systems, who were members of the seminars. If you have a penchant for numbers, this is over 300 appellate judges from each of the 50 states, from all federal courts and from the Supreme Court of Canada and most Canadian provinces. In 1989, I counted 24 of the then state chief justices in that group.

I am indebted to the people at West Publishing Co. for encouragement, support and valuable assistance in the publication of this book.

Thirty generations of law clerks in the Common Pleas Court of Allegheny County, Pennsylvania (Pittsburgh) and the United States Court of Appeals for the Third Circuit served me faithfully and well. I am quick to acknowledge that I learned something from each of these energetic young men and women, talented graduates of America's fine law schools.

I thank my editor Oscar Shefler, world-class writer and friend of over 50 years. We first worked together from 1937 to 1941 on The Pitt News, student newspaper at the University of Pittsburgh. We are older and grayer now, but our juices still manage to run when a reworked phrase finally sounds just right. I also thank Catherine S. Hill, Anne Marie Finch and Susan Simmons Seemiller for exhaustive research and valuable editorial and substantive suggestions, and Susan von Frausing-Borch and Mary Ellen Staab for manuscript preparation.

Finally, I am grateful for the patience and good cheer of my wife, Agatha, who continues to inspire out here in California as much as she did in those many Pittsburgh years.

RUGGERO J. ALDISERT
Senior United States Circuit Judge

Santa Barbara, California
December 1990

About the Author

Ruggero J. Aldisert, Senior Circuit Judge of the U.S. Court of Appeals for the Third Circuit, received his B.A. and J.D. degrees from the University of Pittsburgh. Following college, he served for four years on active duty during World War II in the U.S. Marine Corps. His distinguished career on the bench began in 1961, when he was elected as a judge for the Court of Common Pleas of Allegheny County, Pennsylvania. In 1968, he was nominated by President Lyndon B. Johnson to serve on the U.S. Court of Appeals for the Third Circuit, where he remains today and where he served as Chief Judge from 1984 to 1986. In addition to a distinguished career on the bench, Judge Aldisert has also written numerous popular and influential books addressing legal writing issues.

For more than 20 years, from 1963 to 1986, Judge Aldisert was an adjunct professor at the University of Pittsburgh School of Law in Pittsburgh, Pennsylvania. He has been a visiting professor at Arizona State University, New York University, the University of Texas, the University of Virginia, and Augsburg University in Germany. He has lectured throughout the United States, and throughout the world, in such places as Canada, England, France, Germany, Italy, Poland, Croatia, and Serbia. He has also published more than 40 articles on the law.

Not only has Judge Aldisert advanced the cause of better legal writing in his capacity as judge, educator, and writer, he has also earned the respect of some of the most esteemed members of the legal community. In 2005, Aldisert became the first recipient of the "Distinguished Appellate Jurist Award," bestowed by the American Bar Association's Council of Appellate Lawyers. In 2008, Aldisert received the "Golden Pen Award" from the Legal Writing Institute for his "unwavering commitment to promote the use of clear language in his judicial opinions, in his books, and in his teaching." Former Associate Justice of the United States Supreme Court Harry A. Blackmun offered the following commentary in the foreword to Judge Aldisert's book The Judicial Process: Text, Materials and Cases:

> He loves the law. He yearns to know its history and its character or, to use the word he has employed effectively in this volume, its anatomy.

He has a persistent but most refreshing curiosity about the law. He wants to know what it is, why it is what it is, and how all of us who labor in its vineyard use or misuse it.

Introduction

This book is new. Its purpose is not. That purpose traces its ancestry to 1970, when I first attended the Institute of Judicial Administration's Senior Appellate Judges Seminar in New York. With some eight years under my belt as a Pennsylvania Common Pleas Court (trial) judge, I was then completing my second full year as a U.S. Circuit Court of Appeals judge. By that time, I realized I needed to know more about opinion writing.

This is not to say that I was a novice. Pennsylvania Common Pleas judges had to write an opinion in every case that came up for appeal. As a result, I prepared a written statement of reasons in every post-trial motion, as well as in pretrial motions to suppress evidence. Still, I was not comfortable with opinion writing, and was prompted to ask many questions of the seminar leaders and to record their comments most dutifully.

Who were the seminar leaders? It is no exaggeration to say they were judicial giants: Roger J. Traynor from California, Walter V. Schaefer from Illinois, John Minor Wisdom from Louisiana, Frank Kennison from New Hampshire, Samuel J. Roberts from Pennsylvania, Robert A. Leflar from Arkansas and Warren E. Burger from Washington, D.C.

More interested in theory than in style, I asked the discussion leaders to reconcile the lean, crisp approach of Justice Schaefer's Illinois Supreme Court—which, by rule, prohibited all those accursed footnotes—and the florid style of the U.S. Supreme Court—which (except for Hugo Black's writings) were cluttered with multiple citations and footnotes and separate opinions. I was told that there was no schoolbook answer, but the discussion leaders agreed that the sole purpose of the judicial opinion was to explain the decision and not to take on the character of a law review article.

I was invited back to the seminar as a faculty member in the following year and later accepted the task of discussion leader in "Opinion Writing."

By 1973, I had prepared a somewhat detailed outline for advance distribution to seminar members. Class discussions with newly selected judges of the highest state courts, Canada and the U.S. Courts of Appeals, however, prompted me to revise and make additions, and deletions. Each subsequent year brought further modifications. These continued even after I took out a copyright in 1979, driven by new insights gained in contacts with seminar colleagues and in discussions at the Federal Judicial Center's seminars for circuit judges.

It was a momentous time for me as I became more and more enthralled by the idea of writing a book on the subject. The wish was father to the execution as I took heart upon being assured that the advance of years had not lessened the processes of ongoing maturation and creativity; in fact, my experience added to the process.

In order to stimulate further discussion, I made an annual distribution of the newly revised outline to judges of the highest courts as well as participants in the Intermediate Appellate Judges Seminar. I must admit that my ego suffered not one bit when the feedback included such comments as "Your outline is the first thing I give to my clerks" and "When are you going to expand this into a book?" Harold Ross, late editor of *The New Yorker*, once wrote upon coming across an exceptional manuscript, "I am encouraged to go on." Borrowing the thought, I responded in the same manner to those comments.

At last, I was ready to start the job; this time fate intervened as I assumed the position of chairman of the Advisory Committee on Bankruptcy Rules. That post imposed great demands upon my schedule. When it ended, I slipped into the robes of Chief Judge of the U.S. Court of Appeals for the Third Circuit. The spirit remained willing to write the book, but the assignment left little or no time for extrajudicial activities.

Once I attained senior judge status, that excuse no longer served me. After all, nothing much engaged my hours except for sittings with my home court in Philadelphia and my lively calendars as a visiting judge with the Fifth, Ninth and Eleventh Circuits, and various committee assignments.

Like most people who take on the writer's craft as a secondary activity, I found that what counts is not so much the 24 hours of the day as the minutes left over. Too, I must confess that the duties listed in the paragraph above came more easily and allowed more discretion in the rationing of time than those involved when I served as the ranking officer of the Third Circuit.

Thus was born the book you now hold in your hands. It bears my name as author and the words are indeed mine, but the content is the result of interaction with about 300 senior appellate judges, including four justices of the U.S. Supreme Court, over a span of about 20 years.

The Book: How to Use It

The book is divided into four parts: Theoretical Concepts Underlying an Opinion; The Anatomy of an Opinion; Writing Style; and Opinion Writing Checklists. It may help if I set forth a few guidelines.

This book is for every judge at every level: local, state and federal; appellate and trial court judges; administrative law judges, hearing officers and members of the agency. It will be particularly helpful for all law clerks. The country's private judges—arbitrators—will also benefit from this edition. If you are not on this list, you may be excused from class. Otherwise, please attend.

Every judge, including this author, can profit by learning how to improve the work product. We are constantly surrounded by court attaches, law secretaries, law clerks and lawyers who "Your Honor" us to death. All of them agree that you, so far undiscovered, are the greatest master of English prose since Winston S. Churchill and the greatest opinion writer since Benjamin Nathan Cardozo. Remember, though, what the English divine Thomas Fuller said some three centuries ago: "He that praiseth publicly will slander privately." Let the content of this book help you to determine for yourself whether there is the remotest possibility of improvement in your splendid prose. In other words, at least read some parts of this book to see whether you are capable of exceeding heights.

At some time, I hope, you will read most of the book.

What you tackle first, and in what order you continue on to the rest of it, may depend upon how you classify yourself according to the following self-rating categories:

Experienced Trial and Appellate Judges

(Surely you are not one of those crotchety old dogs—we all know a few of them, don't we—the guys and gals who take refuge in the contention that they have been around too long to learn new tricks.)

Read the checklists in Part Four (Chapter 21 for trial judges and Chapters 18–20 for appellate judges). Then, if you think you can improve at least some of your writing habits, look at Part Two: Anatomy of an Opinion to see what interests you:

- Orientation paragraph
- Summary of issues

- Statement of facts
- Writing the reasons of decision

At this point, you may find time to read Part Three: Writing Style.

Having been beguiled into traveling this far, you may decide that you have made such an investment in effort that you might as well proceed to the end. It is not guaranteed, but what author has ever been free of that hope?

Trial Judges: New or Veteran

Read Chapter 13: "Opinions of Trial Courts and Hearing Tribunals" as well as Chapter 21: "Trial Court and Hearing Tribunal Checklists."

Administrative Law Judges: New or Veteran

Read Chapter 14: "Opinions of Administrative Law Judges" as well as Chapter 22: "Administrative Law Judges' Checklists."

Arbitrators: New or Veteran

Read Chapter 15: "Arbitration Procedures and Opinion Writing" as well as Chapter 23: "Arbitrators' Checklists."

All New Judges

Who are they? They are all judges with less than three years of experience.

My advice: start with page one and read the entire book. My guarantee: if you take my preachings to heart and apply them faithfully, you will not only write better opinions but win the undying respect of your peers in the profession.

Law Clerks

This book is for you. Start reading this book your very first day on the job. If there is anything you have trouble understanding, I will accept the blame and ask you to grant me exculpation by reading it again and again until you do understand it. This is an exercise that will serve you well as you rise in your chosen profession.

To those few of you who think you already know as much as your mentors have learned over the course of their careers, I commend these words of Mark Twain:

> When I was a boy of fourteen, my father was so ignorant I could hardly stand to have the old man around. But when I got to be twenty-one, I was astonished at how much the old man had learned in seven years.

PART ONE

THEORETICAL CONCEPTS UNDERLYING AN OPINION

CHAPTER ONE

WRITING JUDICIAL OPINIONS

§ 1.1 Overview:
The Increasing Importance of
Writing a Good Opinion

Our jurisprudence traditionally required a public statement of reasons to accompany decisions. As Professor Charles A. Miller once said, "The law is not majestic enough in the American system to endure for good but unexplained or unexplainable reason."[1] Our statements of reasons—judicial opinions—have improved dramatically since the days of the English jurist Sir John Fortescue, Lord Chief Justice of the King's Bench, who 500 years ago proclaimed: "Sir, the law is as I say it is, and so it has been laid down ever since the law began; and we have several set forms which are held as law, and so held and used for good reason, though we cannot at present remember that reason."[2]

Although we have come a long way from Lord Chief Justice Fortescue, we have a problem with judicial opinions, nonetheless. For several halcyon decades, judicial caseloads were small and the number of opinions published was minimal. In 1983, however, Justice Charles G. Douglas III of the New Hampshire Supreme Court observed a troubling exponential trend in the pace of published opinions. As he put it, "the number of opinions received by West in 1929 was the same number it received in 1964—some 35 years later. Yet the number has [almost] doubled to 54,104 in 1981 in just half that time!"[3] By the late 1980s, the production of state and federal opinions had plateaued at 60,000 published opinions per year, a total that—somewhat incredibly—has varied hardly at all over the last 20 years.

At first, given Justice Douglas's observations and the inarguable expansion of most courts' workloads over that period, this static number might seem surprising. Indeed, judges today are flooded with cases. In 2009 an average active judge

---

1. CHARLES A. MILLER, THE SUPREME COURT AND THE USES OF HISTORY 14 (1969).
2. *Id.* (citing DAVID MELLINKOFF, THE LANGUAGE OF THE LAW v (1963)).
3. Charles G. Douglas III, *How to Write a Concise Opinion*, 22 JUDGES' J. 4, 4 (1983).

on one of the twelve regional U.S. Courts of Appeals was responsible for deciding 640 cases and writing 156 opinions.[4] To put that number in perspective, consider that, in 1969—my first full year as a member of the U.S. Court of Appeals
for the Third Circuit—each judge on my court was responsible for deciding 90
cases per year and writing a for-publication opinion in one-third of them.

As courts have gotten busier, however, the pace of opinion publishing has
not been able to keep up with the rate of incoming cases. Faced with an avalanche of cases, state and federal judges dispose of an ever-expanding number of them using nonpublished opinions. Indeed, during the same 20-year
period in which the number of *published* opinions held steady, the number of
nonpublished opinions climbed and climbed and climbed, from nearly 75,000
in 1990 and to an astronomical zenith of over 200,000 in 2007 (*see* Figure 1).
The opinion-proliferation trend Justice Douglas foresaw turned out to be true,
albeit for nonpublished opinions only.

There are a number of explanations for this "paper storm," especially at the
appellate level. In the past, most state and federal courts had a specialized appellate
bar, experts in evaluating the prospects of relief on appeal. No such bar exists today,
even at the level of the Supreme Court. Every lawyer now believes that he or she
is competent to pursue and win an appeal. However, even though one may be
a good trial lawyer and know the rocky terrain of trial courtrooms, this does not
guarantee the ability to handle the slippery slopes of appellate advocacy. Experienced appellate judges sink into melancholy when they consider how shallow
is the preparation of some of the lawyers who crowd their dockets.

Moreover, we have undergone a profound change in the role of the lawyer-
client relationship. Many lawyers are no longer able to control, or even mod-
erate, the demands of emotion-laden clients. Often, professional advice and
wisdom are insufficient to curb the excesses of losing parties in law suits. Persons who would never dare to instruct a cardiovascular specialist on heart surgery have no qualms about instructing their lawyers on when and how to
prosecute appeals of highly technical cases. Such persons are everywhere. They
are not restricted to any economic or social class. Appellants are rich or poor,
from the east, west, north and south, scarred by adverse jury verdicts or an-
gered by judicial rulings. They are chief executive officers of multinational corporations who direct prestigious law firms on when to move and when not to
move. They are impecunious defendants in criminal cases represented by court-
appointed counsel who have nothing to lose by cluttering appellate dockets.
Some appellants rationalize their actions thus: "I got a raw deal. Hey, it's just

---

4. U.S. Courts, Federal Court Management Statistics-2009: Courts of Appeals—Judicial Caseload Profile, *available at* www.uscourts.gov/cgi-bin/cmsa2009.pl.

Figure 1. State & Federal Courts' Published & Nonpublished Opinions, by Year

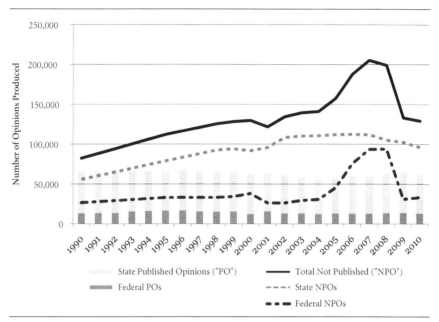

Note: Numbers derived from Westlaw's databases collecting state and federal opinions.

a crap game and maybe I'll be lucky." Most people think cases are tried on appeal *de novo*. They simply cannot recognize that courts of appeals have limited review powers.

Then there are the lawyers. Some accede to demands for appeal because they fear they may lose the client and earn reputations as "no-guts" lawyers. Others frankly and vulgarly retreat to a self-interested protective maneuver, taking appeals as calculated defenses against possible malpractice suits by clients for failure to exhaust all remedies.

Another factor is economics. Until about 50 years ago, taking an appeal required a substantial cash outlay. When I came to the bar, all appellate briefs and the entire record had to be professionally printed. This was a major expense. It constituted a financial barrier that discouraged some unnecessary appeals. Now appeals are available at discount prices. New court rules no longer require professional printing, which means that the office photocopy machine can grind out briefs at a minuscule fraction of the former cost. Electronically filed "e-briefs" are becoming more widely accepted. The rules now also allow the appellant to select those parts of the record necessary to support the brief. Appeal costs that used to run to thousands of pre-inflation dollars are now reduced, in most cases, to a few hundred dollars. In addition, what does an appellant stand to lose if the appeal costs are assessed against him or her? In the majority of cases, the only penalty is payment for the opponent's office-photocopied brief.

We cannot say that the increase of appeals is directly related to the increase of trial court filings. Proportionately, the increase of appeals during my career on the bench has been much higher. For example, in the federal system, district court filings increased by 219%, from 102,163 to 325,920, in the nearly four decades from 1968–2007. The number of appeals increased by 541%, from 9,116 to 58,410. Thus, appeals rose at a percentage rate of 322% higher than the rise in trial court filings.[5]

Yet an important circumstance cannot be ignored. People resort to the court system because the normal political process does not work the way they want it to. Elected legislators seem to be the last people in government willing to take a stand on issues that will arouse controversy back in the constituency. They know what happened to Senator Joseph Tydings of Maryland, who took a moral position on a rather innocuous gun-control issue—and paid for it with his political life when the National Rifle Association helped to knock his bid for re-election out of the ballot box. Such failures of the political process impel many aggrieved groups to turn first to the courts rather than viewing them as institutions of final resort.

People also flock to the courts in an attempt to make sense of the language of jurisprudence as enacted by today's legislatures, especially by Congress. Some legislators frequently incorporate intentional ambiguities into statutes, a practice animated by the demise of political patronage, lack of discipline in national political parties and the replacement of such discipline by the high-pressure influence of special-interest groups, political action committees and a network of demagogic hosts of radio talk shows. The Congressional eye is often focused not on the national interest or a particular public policy so much as it is on a very pragmatic consideration: How will the statutory language affect my constituency? Will I be hurt or helped by it? Can I get away back home with a half-adequate explanation?

As a result, statutory language is often *deliberately* enigmatic and unintelligible. Hammered out in committee compromise (or, more accurately, by committee staffs), it is often designed to mean all things to all people, with Congress recognizing that in the end the federal courts must interpret the statute. When an interpretation emerges from the courts, the legislator is in a

---

5. ANNUAL REPORTS, DIRECTOR OF THE ADMINISTRATIVE OFFICE OF THE U.S. COURTS, Tables 1969–2008.

position to tell complaining constituents that the problem with the bill was due not to the action of Congress, but to the action of federal judges in interpreting it. These factors of our political system undoubtedly contribute to the appellate caseload. Is case law churning and developing at the rate reflected by the increased number of appeals and opinions? Of course not. Our common law tradition requires unity of law throughout a jurisdiction and requires also the flexibility to incorporate legal precepts as they develop. Within this tradition is the concept of gradualness, with case law that advances cautiously and incrementally, in a system built by accretion from the resolution of specific problems. No one, not even the most fervent supporter of publication in every case, can seriously suggest that every one of these cases submitted for publication refines or defines the law or has precedential or institutional value. There is a need for a greater institutional inhibition against the paper storm, as I believe too many of the cases we hear result in a published opinion.

On the basis of 50 years' experience as a judge, with over 40 years as a federal appellate judge, I conclude that too many appeals are unnecessary. The metaphorical descendants of Don Quixote are out in full force tilting at windmills, seeking to overturn trial results that had been preordained from the moment the complaints were filed. Lest I be accused of undue cynicism, I rush to add that my views find comfort in the recorded seven years experience of the U.S. Courts of Appeals, which are courts of general jurisdiction with no discretionary power (except federal habeas corpus):

Table 1. Percentage of Cases Reversed on Appeal[6]

Nature of Proceeding	2004	2005	2006	2007	2008	2009	2010
All Appeals	8.4	10.0	8.7	8.4	8.3	9.6	8.4
Criminal	6.0	10.9	6.2	5.4	5.5	6.8	5.8
U.S. Prisoner Petitions	8.4	8.7	7.5	9.1	9.4	8.3	5.2
Other U.S. Civil	11.8	10.6	11.7	12.6	13.2	12.1	13.8
Private Prisoner Petitions	8.8	8.7	9.6	10.7	10.0	9.8	9.2
Other Private Civil	12.0	12.0	12.9	12.9	12.1	14.9	12.9
Bankruptcy	15.9	15.1	13.3	13.6	13.3	14.0	14.5
Administrative Appeals	5.4	6.3	7.9	6.3	6.3	7.8	6.8

The anomaly is evident: The number of appeals increase, but the likelihood of reversal decreases. So much for the chances of getting the trial court or ad-

---

6. Admin. Office of the U.S. Courts, 2001–2011 Statistical Tables for the Fed. Judiciary tbl. B-5, *available at* www.uscourts.gov/Statistics/FederalJudicialCaseloadStatistics.aspx. This table does not include data from the U.S. Court of Appeals for the Federal Circuit.

ministrative agency reversed when the case reaches the appellate court for decision on the merits.

Regardless of the reasons, at all levels of the state and federal judiciary, an ever-expanding number of nonpublished cases are being decided in reliance on an unchanging number of published opinions. Because published opinions issue in such a small percentage of resolved cases—in 2007, roughly 1 in 5 opinions was published—a published opinion carries far more weight than it once did. A good published opinion, therefore, can help many overworked judges quickly and cleanly resolve a similar case. A poorly crafted opinion, on the other hand, can create far-reaching, headache-inducing, deleterious ripples in the jurisprudential fabric, waylaying time-strapped judges even further.

I believe that too many opinions fall into the latter category. For years, I have been an avid opinion watcher. I use the word "watcher" advisedly because I have lacked the time to read opinions word for word except those of my own court and the U.S. Supreme Court. To be sure, over the years, I have meticulously examined sample opinions from student judges in my role as discussion leader in opinion-writing seminars. It might be more accurate to describe me as a full-fledged "opinion skimmer." As a hobby, or as some might say, "obsession," I like to skim opinions for style and form. I suppose that qualifies me for a title I have never seen before—opinion critic.

To be sure, we are fortunate to have a large number of good opinion writers in the federal and state court systems. Notwithstanding the complex nature of today's litigation, these opinion writers prove that a clear and cogent statement of reasons may easily explain the decision to the beleaguered reader who may be short of time and perhaps slow of comprehension. The work product of the excellent opinion writers, unfortunately, provides a stark contrast with that of their less-skilled colleagues.

The solution is not, obviously, for judges to simply publish their nonpublished opinions. Indeed, opinion production is surely one of those instances in which "less is more." Rather, to effectively confront the avalanche of cases, those opinions that are marked for publication should pass the test inspired by Roscoe Pound and the late Cardozo Professor of Jurisprudence at Columbia University, Harry Jones: (a) how thoughtfully and disinterestedly the court weighed the conflicts involved in the case and (b) how fair and durable its adjustment of the conflicts promises to be. The first factor goes to the "reasonableness" of the court's decision, the second to the logical validity of the reasoning.[7] To pass

---

7. *See* Harry W. Jones, *An Introduction to Jurisprudence*, 74 COLUM. L. REV. 1023, 1029 (1974); *see also* RUGGERO J. ALDISERT, LOGIC FOR LAWYERS: A GUIDE TO CLEAR LEGAL THINKING 4 (3d ed. 1997).

that test, I humbly recommend that judges follow the guidelines set forth in the pages that follow.

§ 1.2 Criticisms of Opinions

What, then, are the criticisms generally lodged against opinions written today? Here are some:

- They are too long.
- They are burdened with too many citations.
- They tend to ramble instead of clearly defining and discussing issues.
- They present lengthy and largely unnecessary discussion of the cases compared.
- They make unstructured references to other cases without indicating what facts in those cases are material or immaterial.
- They fail to set forth specific reasons for choosing one line of cases over others, saying, "We think that is the better view" and, "We prefer the majority view," without explaining why.
- They display acute "law reviewitis," being overwritten and overfootnoted, obese and sloppy instead of clean and neat. In these cases, the difference between well done and overdone is as apparent and catastrophic as in the case of roast beef.
- They often express a holding in terms that reflect factual scenarios not contained in the record. What we wind up with frequently resembles an artichoke that must be peeled off layer by layer in subsequent cases.
- They eschew those good, plain words and sentences that communicate rather than befuddle. I call this the IRS regulations syndrome; Orwell might have called it "lawspeak." Whatever we call it, there is much too much of it.
- They present too many published opinions—far too many—with no precedential or institutional value.

Certainly, some, but not all, of these criticisms are valid. Fortunately, they do not apply to all judges or to all opinions. Nevertheless, there is enough falling from grace to justify this book as a guide to avoid some of the most common pitfalls.

I do not represent that the book is the *sine qua non*. Far from it. All I represent, as I said in the Preface and Introduction, is that these observations reflect personal studies and experience, and the exchange and distillation of views with some 300 appellate judges of the highest state courts and a sizeable number of U.S. circuit judges taking part in seminars sponsored by the Institute of Judicial Administration at New York University and the Federal Judicial Center in Washington, D.C.

A judge is a professional writer. He or she must possess literary skills. If such skills are not natural, they *must* be acquired or learned. The judge must accomplish this himself or herself. If a judge wants to write clearly and cogently, with words parading before the reader in logical order, the judge must first *think* clearly and cogently, with thoughts laid out in neat rows. To do so is to demonstrate respect for the elements of reflective thinking and the rules of deductive and inductive logic. Any judge who is unwilling or unable to do this cannot perform his or her judicial duties properly.

I recommend that the appellate courts, merit commissions of the states and the U.S. Attorney General and the Office of the Counsel to the President make proper inquiries and necessary investigations to determine the writing abilities and—no less important—the self-discipline and work habits of those under consideration for judicial posts. This is an important recommendation because to describe for the reader the reasoning of the court is critical. Justice Felix Frankfurter once stated:

> Fragile as reason is and limited as law is as the expression of the institutionalized medium of reason, that's all we have standing between us and the tyranny of mere will and the cruelty of unbridled, unprincipled, undisciplined feeling.[8]

Obviously, choosing the most literate law clerk is not enough. It is the judge who makes decisions and then the judge who must explain those decisions. It is the judge who holds the commission. It is the judge whose name goes on the opinion. It is the judge who must assume 100 percent of the responsibility. The law clerk is an assistant, and only an assistant. The law clerk must help in research, in the drafting process and in expressing views of the law, but—and this is a big "but"—every sentence the law clerk writes in the opinion must be totally understood and endorsed by the opinion-writing judge. To delegate some writing responsibilities to a law clerk is more than proper; it is an absolute necessity in this litigious age. This delegation, however, is legitimate only to the extent that the judge accepts the submitted language, understands what has been written, agrees with it and is willing to stake a professional reputation on it.

---

8. As quoted in TIME, Sept. 7, 1962, at 15, on the occasion of Frankfurter's retirement as a U.S. Supreme Court Justice.

§1.3 The Purpose of an Opinion

A judicial opinion may be defined as a reasoned elaboration, publicly stated, that justifies a conclusion or decision. Its purpose is to set forth an explanation for a decision that adjudicates a live case or a controversy that has been presented before a court. This explanatory function of the opinion is paramount. In the common law tradition the court's ability to develop case law finds legitimacy only because the decision is accompanied by a publicly recorded statement of reasons.

Announcing a rule of law of the case is nothing but a byproduct of the court's adjudicative function. It is acceptable only because the public explanation sets forth the grounds for the decision. Without this explanation, commonly called the statement of reasons, the court's decision would merely resolve that particular dispute presented by parties to the court. Thus, in our tradition, the critical byproduct of the decision survives long after the dispute between the litigants has been resolved.

This byproduct promulgates a legal precept describing the legal consequence that flows from the adjudicative facts set forth in the opinion. It forms the bedrock of the common law doctrine of *stare decisis* because the consequence attached to the relevant or material facts becomes case law which is binding on all future cases that come before the court containing identical or similar facts. Case law possesses the same power and force as a legislative act until or unless subsequently changed by the court or modified by the legislature.

The judicial opinion is much more than a naked utterance. To use J.L. Austin's phrase, it becomes a "performative utterance"[9] because the *decision* that it explains performs as a declaration of law. I have chosen the italicized word deliberately. I have not said that the "opinion" performs; it is the "decision" that performs. Only the decision declared in the opinion has the force of law. The doctrine we respect is *stare decisis*; it is not *stare rationibus decidendi* or *stare rationes dictis*. Our tradition, elegantly stated, is *stare decisis et non quieta movere* (to stand by the decision and not disturb that which is settled).

Because courts tend to overwrite opinions, it may often be said that the "discussion outran the decision."[10] Thus, it should be understood that the decision of the case can be measured by the precise adjudicative facts that give rise to the rule of the case. "Two cases or decisions which are alike in all material respects, and precisely similar in all the circumstances affecting their determi-

---

9. J.L. Austin, Philosophical Papers 220–39 (1961).
10. Wells v. Garbutt, 30 N.E. 978, 979 (N.Y. 1892).

nation, are said to be or run 'on all fours' with each other, or, in the more ancient language of the law, the one is said to 'run upon four feet' with the other."[11]

To be sure, case law may survive and endure when the decision reflects desirable current public opinion or is congruent with contemporary community
moral standards even though, upon analysis, the case's stated reasons may
prove to have been fallacious or to be invalid because societal changes have intervened. Even recognizing this, I hasten to emphasize that the acceptability and
vitality of the decision are usually measured by the quality of the reasons that
originally supported it.

The stated reasons are the "why" of a decision. To repeat, the quality of a
decision is commensurate with the quality and logical force of the reasons that
support it. Even so, two other necessary ingredients go into the mix. These
may be called the "how": (a) the narration of adjudicative facts and (b) the
statement of the issue or issues framing the case for decision.

Adjudicative facts are those selected from the gross facts found by the fact
finder from the congeries of record evidence. Such facts are deemed necessary,
relevant and material to the particular issue(s) presented for decision. There is
an important reason why the facts set forth in an opinion should be selected
with care. This reason goes to the heart of *stare decisis*: like cases should be treated
alike. And because our tradition is fact-specific, it is critical that the concept of
"like cases" should refer to cases that contain like material or relevant facts.

The decision that emanates from the opinion, the case law, is used to inform,
guide and govern future private and public transactions. This future use of the
decision is a necessary product if we accept Holmes's definition, as I think we
should, that law is nothing more pretentious than a prediction of what the
courts will do in fact.[12] To put it another way, a quality opinion will predict how
similar factual scenarios will be treated. Sadly, however, it is thus that we sow
the seeds of recurring litigation.

If decision X results from the presence of facts A, B, C and D, what will be
the decision if fact D is not present in the subsequent case or if additional fact
E is present? This depends on several considerations. Does the writer of the
opinion under comparison consider stated facts A through D to be material
and absolutely essential to the decision, and that a different decision would
have been forthcoming had fact E been before the court? Or does the writer consider that judges in subsequent litigation will interpret the original opinion
and decide which of the various facts A, B, C and D are absolutely controlling?

---

11. HENRY CAMPBELL BLACK, THE LAW OF JUDICIAL PRECEDENTS 61 (1912).
12. Oliver Wendell Holmes, Jr., *The Path of the Law*, 10 HARV. L. REV. 457, 460–61
(1897).

* * *

This book concerns judicial explanation and description. I will explain the theoretical bases of judicial opinion writing and describe the mechanics of draftsmanship. I will discuss specific parts of an opinion: the orientation paragraphs, the factual narrative, the statement of issues, the discussion of those issues, the declaration of the holding and the explanation of the relief granted. I will make some suggestions on what to do and when in preparing these components. I will deal with writing style. I will suggest checklists for preparing and reviewing your work. Throughout, I will examine excerpts of published opinions to illustrate key points. I will even critique some of my own opinions, setting aside such vanity and prejudice as may survive after six decades at the bar and on the bench, with all the satisfactions and comeuppances encountered along the way.

Before we begin this discussion, we must first face certain threshold questions, examined here in Part One. Under what circumstances should full-blown, signed opinions be written and published? What are acceptable alternatives? Finally—prepare yourself for the unpardonable pun from the world of basketball—under what circumstances should we exercise the full court press?

CHAPTER TWO

To Write or Not to Write

§ 2.1 Overview

Before an opinion is written, some preliminary questions face the court: Should an opinion be written at all? If so, should it be precedential and therefore published? Should it be a signed opinion or per curiam? Should it be a nonprecedential opinion, filed in the record and made available to the public, but designed not to be cited or used as precedent and prepared solely for the benefit of the litigants and the trial court in order to explain the decision? Should the court simply issue a terse statement announcing its judgment?

Where there is an unqualified right to appeal, as in federal courts of appeals, the sheer volume of cases has forced most courts to depart from the practice of publishing an opinion in every case. A paper storm of blizzard force has made it virtually impossible to write full-blown opinions in all cases. Courts have instead resorted to substitutes. These may be stark one- or two-sentence judgment orders or memoranda dispositions, published per curiams, or unpublished opinions.

§ 2.2 To Publish or Not to Publish: That Is the Question

In 1969, my first full year as a member of a U.S. Court of Appeals for the Third Circuit, each appellate judge was responsible for deciding, on average, 93 cases per year. Today, however, each active judge on my court decides over 400 cases every 365 days.

The original, dramatic increase in the federal caseload can be traced to two Supreme Court cases that were decided in the 1960s, the effects of which were fully felt by the courts in the early 1970s. First, in 1961, the Supreme Court resurrected 42 U.S.C. § 1983 in *Monroe v. Pape*,[1] and, two years later, in *Fay v. Noia*,[2] the Court opened the habeas floodgates to federal court review of state criminal convictions. More recently, the U.S. Courts of Appeals have been inundated with sentencing and immigration appeals following the partial death of the U.S. Sentencing Guidelines in *United States v. Booker*,[3] and the massive influx of undocumented immigrants from Mexico, Central America, China and Indonesia. To handle the crushing caseload increases, the U.S. Courts of Appeals have implemented the use of memorandum opinions and judgment orders—truncated explanations for a decision with no institutional or precedential value.

Thus, it becomes important for a court to decide which cases merit published opinions, and which do not. My personal view tracks the framework articulated by the great Benjamin Cardozo in *The Nature of the Judicial Process*.[4] Cardozo distinguished three categories of cases. The first category, a majority of the docket, is comprised of those cases where "[t]he law and its application alike are plain."[5] Such cases "could not, with any semblance of reason, be decided in any way but one.... Such cases are predestined, so to speak, to affirmance without opinion."[6] I agree with Cardozo that such opinions do not merit even a nonprecedential opinion. Instead, a plain judgment order or citation to the district court opinion in the appendix is sufficient.

Cardozo's second category of cases, a "considerable percentage" of the docket, is comprised of those cases where "the rule of law is certain, and the application alone doubtful."[7] In such cases,

> [a] complicated record must be dissected, the narratives of witnesses, more or less incoherent and unintelligible, must be analyzed, to determine whether a given situation comes within one district or another upon the chart of rights and wrongs.... Often these cases ... provoke differences of opinion among judges. Jurisprudence remains untouched, however, regardless of the outcome.[8]

It is in this second category where I believe a nonprecedential opinion is sufficient. The rule of law is settled and the only question is whether the facts

---

1. 365 U.S. 167 (1961).
2. 372 U.S. 391 (1963).
3. 543 U.S. 220 (2005).
4. Benjamin N. Cardozo, The Nature of the Judicial Process (1921).
5. *Id.* at 164.
6. *Id.*
7. *Id.*
8. *Id.* at 164–65.

come within the rule. Such fact-oriented opinions do not add to our jurisprudence and thus do not require publication.

It is only in Cardozo's third and final category where an opinion for publication should be written. The final category, the remaining "percentage, not large indeed, and yet not so small as to be negligible," is comprised of cases "where a decision one way or the other, will count for the future, will advance or retard, sometimes much, sometimes little, the development of the law. These are the cases where the creative element in the judicial process finds its opportunity and power."[9] From such cases, each modestly articulating a narrow rule, emerge the principles which form the backbone of a court's jurisprudence.

The U.S. Courts of Appeals have articulated the considerations relevant to determination of whether an opinion should be published or not in a variety of ways. These articulations find themselves in the local rules and internal operating procedures ("I.O.P.s") of each federal appellate court. The impact of these rules, however, has been altered by a 2006 amendment to the Federal Rules of Appellate Procedure, which states:

Rule 32.1 Citing Judicial Opinions

(a) Citation permitted. A court may not prohibit or restrict the citation of federal judicial opinions, orders, judgments, or other written dispositions that have been:

(i) designated as "unpublished," "not for publication," or the like[.][10]

§ 2.3 Per Curiam Opinions

A published per curiam opinion is written when a case does not warrant a signed, published opinion. It fits somewhere between an unpublished or memorandum opinion and a full-blown signed, published opinion. We use a per curiam opinion when the rule of law and its application to relatively simple facts are clear, or when the law has been made clear by an appellate decision subsequent to the trial court's judgment. It may be used to reverse the trial court or deny the requested relief from or the enforcement of administrative agency action. It may be used also for affirming the trial court or granting relief from or enforcement of administrative action under circumstances where a signed opinion is unnecessary, but there is a need for some published state-

---

9. *Id.*
10. Fed. R. App. P. 32.

ment of the court's reasons. A per curiam opinion may be as brief as one or two sentences that cite a controlling precedent or adopt the published opinion of a lower court. The U.S. Supreme Court, for example, used truncated one- or two-sentence per curiams with citations in three segregation cases greatly extending the reach of the landmark *Brown v. Board of Education*.[11] Reprinted in their entirety, they state:

> *Mayor and City Council of Baltimore City v. Dawson*
> Appeal from the United States Court of Appeals for the Fourth Circuit.
>
> Facts and Opinion, *Lonesome v. Maxwell*, D.C., 123 F. Supp. 193; 4 Cir., 220 F.2d 386.
>
> Messrs. C. Ferdinand Sybert, Atty. Gen. of Maryland, Norman P. Ramsey, Deputy Atty. Gen., and Ambrose T. Hartman, Asst. Atty. Gen., for appellants.
>
> Messrs. Robert L. Carter, Thurgood Marshall and Jack Greenberg, for appellees.
>
> Nov. 7, 1955. *Per Curiam*. The Motion to affirm is granted and the judgment is affirmed. (Public beaches and bathhouses).[12]
>
> *Holmes v. City of Atlanta*
> On Petition for writ of certiorari to the United States Court of Appeals for the Fifth Circuit.
>
> Facts and Opinion, D.C., 124 F. Supp. 290; 5 Cir., 223 F.2d 93.
>
> Messrs. Robert L. Carter, Thurgood Marshall and E.E. Moore, for petitioners.
>
> Messrs. J. C. Murphy and Henry L. Bowden, for respondents.
>
> Nov. 7, 1955. *Per Curiam:* The petition for writ of certiorari is granted, the judgments both of the Court of Appeals and the District Court are vacated and the case is remanded to the District Court with directions to enter a decree for petitioners in conformity with *Mayor & City Council of Baltimore City* v. *Dawson*, 350 U.S. 877, 76 S.Ct. 133. (Municipal golf course).[13]
>
> *Gayle v. Browder and Owen v. Browder*
> Facts and Opinion, D.C., 142 F. Supp. 707.

---

11. 347 U.S. 483 (1954).
12. 350 U.S. 877 (1955).
13. 350 U.S. 879 (1955).

Nov. 13, 1956. *Per Curiam.* The motion to affirm is granted and the judgment is affirmed. *Brown v. Board of Education,* 347 U.S. 483; *Mayor and City Council of Baltimore* v. *Dawson,* 350 U.S. 877; *Holmes* v. *Atlanta,* 350 U.S. 879. (Buses).[14]

§ 2.4 Alternatives to Published Opinions

§ 2.4.1 The Judgment Order

Alternatives to a published or per curiam opinion take various forms. At one end of the spectrum is the judgment order. The Fifth Circuit pioneered the judgment order as a way of dealing with the avalanche of appeals:

> Rule 47.6 Affirmance Without Opinion
>
> The judgment or order may be affirmed or enforced without opinion when the court determines that an opinion would have no precedential value and that any one or more of the following circumstances exists and is dispositive of a matter submitted for decision: (1) that a judgment of the district court is based on findings of fact which are not clearly erroneous; (2) that the evidence in support of a jury verdict is not insufficient; (3) that the order of an administrative agency is supported by substantial evidence on the record as a whole; (4) in the case of a summary judgment, that no genuine issue of material fact has been properly raised by the appellant; and (5) no reversible error of law appears.
>
> In such case, the court may, in its discretion, enter either of the following orders: "AFFIRMED. See 5th Cir. R. 47.6." or "ENFORCED. See 5th Cir. R. 47.6."[15]

Similarly, the Third Circuit, my home Court, has developed the following suggested forms for judgment orders in a variety of contexts:

1. *Civil Cases*

JUDGMENT ORDER

After consideration of all contentions raised by appellant, it is

ADJUDGED AND ORDERED that the judgment of the district court be and is hereby affirmed.

---

14. 352 U.S. 903 (1956).
15. 5th Cir. R. 47.6.

Costs taxed against appellant.

2. *Criminal Cases*[16]

JUDGMENT ORDER

After considering the contentions raised by appellant, to-wit, that the court erred: (1) in refusing to charge on the testimony of an accomplice as requested by appellant; (2) in admitting hearsay testimony of a witness; and (3) in refusing to grant a motion of acquittal on the theory of insufficiency of evidence; it is

ADJUDGED AND ORDERED that the judgment of the district court be and is hereby affirmed.

3. *Lack of Jurisdiction*

JUDGMENT ORDER

After consideration of all contentions raised by the appellant and concluding that this court has no jurisdiction because the appeal is premature, *see Griggs v. Provident Consumer Discount Co.*, 459 U.S. 56 (1982), it is

ADJUDGED AND ORDERED that the appeal be and is hereby dismissed without prejudice to the filing of a timely appeal.

Costs taxed against appellant.[17]

§ 2.4.2 The Nonprecedential Opinion

The short nonprecedential or memorandum opinion constitutes the majority of opinions issued by the U.S. Courts of Appeals. It falls somewhere between the judgment order and the published opinion.

The philosophy of the U.S. Courts of Appeals is reflected in an Eleventh Circuit I.O.P.:

> Publication of Opinions. The policy of the court is: The unlimited proliferation of published opinions is undesirable because it tends to impair the development of the cohesive body of law. To meet this serious problem it is declared to be the basic policy of this court to ex-

---

16. A judgment order affirming the district court in a direct criminal appeal includes a statement of those issues raised by appellant and considered by the panel.

17. 3d Cɪʀ. I.O.P. Cʜ. 16.

ercise imaginative and innovative resourcefulness in fashioning new methods to increase judicial efficiency and reduce the volume of published opinions. Judges of this court will exercise appropriate discipline to reduce the length of opinions by the use of those techniques which result in brevity without sacrifice of quality.[18]

Similarly, the Ninth Circuit extends this advice to visiting judges:

If a panel decides not to publish its disposition (memorandum), every effort should be made to shorten the disposition. Consistent with the objective of informing parties of the Court's reasoning, the disposition *should include*: (1) Statement of the Court's reason(s) for accepting or rejecting appellant's contention(s), with appropriate citations; and (2) statement of the result. The disposition may but *need not contain*: (3) statement of the nature and posture of the case; and (4) statement of appellant's contention(s) on appeal.[19]

In practice, most of these courts frown on setting forth facts in a nonprecedential opinion. In the Third Circuit, a nonprecedential opinion carries the boilerplate statement: "Because we write only for the parties who are familiar with the facts, the procedural history and the contentions presented, we will not recite them except as necessary to the discussion."

§ 2.5 Opinion Writing Guidelines

The type of opinion to be prepared depends upon what appellate review purpose is served by the opinion. Purposes of appellate review are threefold:

- *The review-for-correctness function.* This ensures that substantial justice was done.
- *The institutional function.* This provides a judicial mechanism for the progressive development of the law in the common law tradition. It is concerned with articulating and applying constitutional principles, authoritative interpretation of statutes and the formulation of policy.
- *The uniformity function.* This ensures uniform administration of justice throughout the jurisdiction.

---

18. 11th Cir. R. 36, I.O.P. 5.
19. 9th Cir. Manual for Visiting Judges.

Thus, a published opinion, classified as precedential, is generally not required where the court's decision is error-correcting and the court decision affirms the judgment or denies a petition for review of the administrative agency order. The reverse is not true. Where the opinion either reverses the trial court judgment or grants review, it may qualify as a "slam dunk" because the law is clear and application of facts thereto are also plain, and a published opinion is therefore unnecessary.

A signed or per curiam opinion should be published in all cases that contribute to the progressive development of the law. However, you must distinguish between those cases requiring interpretation and those simply requiring application of existing interpretation to new facts. The latter may not contribute to the progress of the law. If it does not, it should be disposed of by memorandum opinion or judgment order.

§ 2.6 Readership

You must always be aware of the audience for whom you write. Who makes up the audience for judicial opinions? This is a very deceptive question, because how you answer depends upon how you approach the purpose of an opinion. If you analyze the broad spectrum of possible ultimate consumers, you may end up with the advice that the opinion writer is communicating to all kinds of consumers. If this be so, the opinion should take the form of a papal encyclical, capable of covering the subject in minute detail within the four corners of an elaborate essay, an essay that can, in and of itself, discuss the entire breadth of the legal issues involved.

Some judges write this way and I think they are wrong. They are confusing an opinion, which is a statement of reasons explaining to the litigants why and how the decision was reached, with law review articles, *Corpus Juris Secundum* segments, tomes, and endowed lectures delivered to audiences of professionals at law schools, university assemblies, bar meetings or judicial conferences.

§ 2.6.1 Primary Consumers

The purpose of a judicial opinion is to tell the participants in the lawsuit why the court acted the way it did. Drawing upon an analogy to marketing strategy, the opinion should first address a primary market. There are two discrete sectors of the primary market for judicial opinions. One sector consists of the actual participants before the court and, in cases before an appellate court, the tribunal of the first instance whose judgment or order is being criticized or upheld. These participants have an all-pervasive interest. The other sector is the court as an institution. Thus, the opinion writer must at all times consider the effect the opinion will have on the court as an institution charged with responsibilities for setting precedent and for defining law.

These two sectors form the audience in the primary market. Writing should be directed to them. The opinion writer must focus on these mutually interested primary readers at all times in order to make as certain as possible that they understand the contents of the written communication precisely as the writer intends. What the audience receives should be exactly what the writer has sent. To achieve this, certain requisites demand our attention.

First, the polestar should be: Will the lay parties to the lawsuit understand what is being said? "Lay parties" do not mean the public at large; the broad spectrum of society will often be unfamiliar with the context, the terms of art, and the usages or customs of the transaction that gave rise to the litigation. The lay parties to the litigation, though, understand those elements. They will understand your decision if your explanation is, as it must be, clear, logical, unambiguous and free of what has been called the *lingua franca* of the legal profession—gobbledygook. All is lost if the parties do not know why you did what you did. It is one thing to lose a case; not to understand why compounds the loss. Mehler summed it up in a single sentence:

> [T]he gulf that often separates sender and receiver [of communications], spanned at best by a bridge of signs and symbols, is sought to be narrowed yet further so that ultimately the intended communication may have the same meaning, or approximately the same meaning, for those on the left bank as those on the right.[20]

If your explanation is clear to "lay parties," it should be clear to your colleagues on the court. However, in writing your opinion for the parties, you must also consider your duty to the court as an institution. The late Professor Sir Neil MacCormick discusses this duty in terms of the "three C's."[21] His "three C's" are consequence, consistency and coherence. To consider consequence, the opinion writer must keep in mind that the case holding not only applies to the present case, but will apply also to future circumstances that incorporate identical or similar facts. The opinion should not serve as a special supersaver airplane ticket, good only from this place to that place, only on this date and only at this hour.

The opinion must also be consistent with valid and binding legal precepts of the legal system. It must be coherent with an intelligible value or policy and

---

20. Irving M. Mehler, Effective Legal Communication 3 (1975).
21. *See* Neil MacCormick, Legal Reasoning and Legal Theory 100–28 (1978).

not measured by a random set of norms. Respect for MacCormick's consequence, consistency and coherence will satisfy the institutional demands of the multi-judge court of which the opinion writer is a member. The opinion writer, for the purposes of the case, is the designated representative or spokesperson for the court.

In sum, the writer must at all times keep in mind how intelligible the opinion is to the two important sectors of the product's primary market; he or she should at all times consider the parties to the lawsuit and his or her colleagues on the court. This requires constant concentration on maximum effective communication.

The late U.S. Circuit Judge John C. Godbold of the Eleventh Circuit has advised lawyers to sharpen communication skills: "It is not enough that counsel understands perfectly what he is saying in his written and spoken words. All is in vain unless the court understands."[22]

Judge Godbold's advice is also good for judges. It is not enough that the judge understands perfectly what is being written, it is essential that the reader does, too. A sentence by Daniel Webster comes to mind, "The power of clear statement is the great power of the bar."[23]

§ 2.6.2 Secondary Markets

Certainly, there are also important secondary markets for judicial opinions. They must not be ignored, but their interests are subordinate to those of primary market consumers. These markets may be far removed in space and time from the instant case, but if you write well enough for the primary consumers, the secondary ones will also reap the same cognitive benefits.

What and who are these secondary consumers? They vary. Some are institutions in the same judicial hierarchy, some at a higher rung, some may be lower. The highest court of the jurisdiction may be called upon to examine carefully the explanations of trial and intermediate court decisions. The court or agency in which the litigation originates studies them for future direction and seeks materials that will form the grounds for future decisions. Other secondary markets, of course, embrace the lawyers, who look for predictions as to the course of future decisions; still others represent the persons and insti-

---

22. John C. Godbold, *Twenty Pages and Twenty Minutes—Effective Advocacy on Appeal*, 30 Sw. L.J. 801, 803 (1976). Judge Godbold occupied the unique position of having served as the Chief Judge of the Courts of Appeals for the Fifth and Eleventh Circuits. He also served as the Director of the Federal Judicial Center in Washington, D.C.

23. Ronald J. Waicukauski et al., The Winning Argument 124 (2001).

tutions in the court's jurisdiction who seek reasonable guidance for conducting themselves in accordance with the demands of the social order.

Law school faculties and students also seek the opinions as study tools and research materials. So, too, depending on the subject matter, do state legislators and academics, among them political scientists, philosophers, sociologists, behaviorists and historians.

Representatives of the print and electronic media are among the instant readers, but it is my observation that they usually give more attention to minor magistrate proceedings and sensational courtroom trials than to appellate court opinions, except those that emanate from the U.S. Supreme Court. When the media occasionally do report opinions, the courts' statements are subject to merciless editing or compressed to 60-second TV or radio sound bites garbled by supercilious blow-dried, self-styled experts in all matters planetary (I can empathize with William Lamb, who wrote, "I wish I was as cocksure of anything as Tom Macaulay is of everything."[24]).

Ultimate consumers may be the bench and bar of other jurisdictions, the staff, counsel and Assembly of the American Law Institute, committees of federal and state legislators and authors of popular and professional comment.

The bottom line: write for the primary market. The secondary market is important, but not as important as (a) the participants in the case whose rights, claims, demands and defenses have been defined and refined and (b) the court as an institution.

Let the secondary market come along for the ride, but keep it out of the driver's seat.

---

24. Encarta Book of Quotations 634 (Bill Swainson & Anne H. Soukhanov eds., 2000).

CHAPTER THREE

REACHING AND JUSTIFYING THE DECISION: A DISTINCTION WITH A DIFFERENCE

§ 3.1 Overview

The opinion writer has the paramount task of thoughtfully and disinterestedly weighing the conflicts inherent in a controversy. Before one word is written, it is necessary to isolate the precise contours of the dispute. Even before this exercise begins, the opinion writer must understand the meaning of "law" in order to grasp the breadth, and therefore the scope, of the legal precepts to be discussed. This understanding is highly critical. To analyze putative precedents in the argument, it is important to determine whether the precept under consideration is a legal rule, principle or doctrine.

§ 3.2 Rules, Principles and Doctrines

The distinction between a legal rule and a legal principle is hazy, if not evanescent. Most often it matters little whether the law is described as a rule or as a principle. The difference becomes crystal clear and essential when a court decides to jettison a previous holding. We say that the holding is then "overruled." I have yet to hear that a case has been "over principled." Principles are thus the most immutable aspects of the law.

When we talk generally about the law of a certain discipline or jurisdiction, we refer to a number of legal precepts, more or less defined, coming within the rubric of Jeremy Bentham's notion of law as an aggregate of standards of conduct, or the sum total of a number of individual laws taken together. Thus we speak of the law of contracts, torts, crimes and antitrust as definable components of what we call "law."

We may view law also in the abstract, in the sense of how we adjust relations and apply, in an orderly fashion, a politically organized society's force. This notion appears in the popular phrase "law and order."

Then, too, we may view law in the sense of a body of philosophical, political and ethical ideas as to the end of law, and as to what legal precepts should be reflecting an idea. Moreover, this conception of the law embraces the tradition that these precepts may be reshaped and given new content or application, and that such matters form the basic study of jurisprudence. Roscoe Pound said it best, "The law must be stable, but it must not stand still."[1]

Still another view of law is what Pound described as "a body of traditional ideas as to how legal precepts should be interpreted and applied and causes decided, and a traditional technique of developing and applying legal precepts whereby these precepts are eked out, extended, restricted, and adapted to the exigencies of administration of justice."[2] In this sense, law is the study of judicial process: how do we choose starting points for legal reasoning; how do we evaluate the intrinsic merits of competing legal principles; how do we select among various interpretations of statute or judicial precept? Socrates was probably not the first to discover that the way to pin down the truth is to ask, ask and ask.

The judicial process is a study of ideas by which the courts decide to extend one precept by analogy while restricting another to the narrow bounds of its four corners. A study of the judicial process is a study of how courts resolve the yin and yang of the law: the law must be stable, yet it cannot stand still. It is a study of judicial decision making, as it actually takes place, or as the judges and practitioners hold it *ought* to take place. To energize the mechanics or dynamics of judicial opinions, however, the opinion writer must first come to grips with varying dimensions of legal precepts.

A legal precept may take several forms. It may be described as the law's statement of a standard of conduct. In Pound's formulation, legal precepts compose "the body of authoritative materials, and the authoritative gradation of the materials, wherein judges are to find the grounds of decision, counselors the basis of assured prediction as to the course of decision, and individuals reasonable guidance toward conducting themselves in accordance with the demands of the social order."[3]

---

1. Roscoe Pound, An Introduction to the Philosophy of Law (1922).

2. Roscoe Pound, *The Theory of Judicial Decision I*, 36 Harv. L. Rev. 641, 645 (1923).

3. Roscoe Pound, *Hierarchy of Sources and Forms in Different Sources of Law*, 7 Tul. L. Rev. 475, 476 (1933).

Legal precepts may be perceived as a hierarchy of various standards of conduct, expressed in ascending order from the very specific to the very general. In the common law tradition, they derive from case law, statutes, administrative regulations, constitutions and treaties. They are classified by their degree of generality.

§ 3.2.1 Rules

At the bottom of the hierarchy is the rule, a normative proposition making a certain legal result depend upon a certain situation involving a narrow range of facts. At common law, the sources of decision are rules of law in the narrow sense—rules of specific cases, "precepts attaching a definite detailed legal consequence to a definite, detailed state of facts."[4] These precepts provide "fairly concrete guides for decision geared to narrow categories of behavior and prescribing narrow patterns of conduct."[5] The common law "creeps from point to point, testing each step,"[6] like an ice skater on a half-frozen pond, and is most characteristically a system built by gradual accretion from the resolution of specific problems. Holmes noted that the great growth of the common law came about incrementally.[7] The courts fashioned *principles* from a number of *rules* of decision, in a process characterized by experimentation. At common law, rules of case law are treated not as final truths, "but as working hypotheses, continually retested in those great laboratories of the law, the courts of justice."[8] The common law has been described as "the byzantine beauty," a method of "reaching what instinctively seem the right results in a series of cases, and only later (if at all) enunciating the principle that explains the pattern—a sort of connect-the-dots exercise."[9]

Legal logic and legal reasoning are absolutes in this exercise. "Connecting the dots" is but a shorthand way to describe inductive reasoning. The "dots" represent holdings of individual cases, each announcing a specific consequence for a detailed set of facts. They are "connected" for a special purpose: to fash-

---

4. *Id.* at 482.

5. Graham Hughes, *Rules, Policy and Decision Making*, 77 Yale L.J. 411, 419 (1968).

6. Alfred North Whitehead, Adventures of Ideas 25 (1956).

7. Oliver Wendell Holmes, Jr., *The Path of the Law*, 10 Harv. L. Rev. 457, 468 (1897).

8. Munroe Smith, Jurisprudence 21 (1909).

9. John Hart Ely, *The Supreme Court 1977 Term, Forward: On Discovering Fundamental Values*, 92 Harv. L. Rev. 5, 32 (1978) (citing Anthony G. Amsterdam, *Perspectives on the Fourth Amendment*, 58 Minn. L. Rev. 349, 351–52 (1974)); *see also* Thurman Arnold, *Professor Hart's Theology*, 73 Harv. L. Rev. 1298, 1311–12 (1960); Oliver Wendell Holmes, Jr., *Codes, and the Arrangement of the Law*, 44 Harv. L. Rev. 725, 725 (1931).

ion broader precepts by techniques of induction. These techniques include the use of analogy, where resemblances are meticulously compared and special instances of like situations are enumerated.

§ 3.2.2 Principles

Precepts that are broader than narrow rules are called legal principles. Covering a broader range of facts, they are assembled from publicly stated reasons for publicly stated rules in previously decided cases. Formulation of a principle is a gradual process, shaped from actual incidents in social, economic and political experience. It is a process in which countervailing rights are challenged, evaluated, synthesized and adjudicated on a case-by-case basis in the context of an adversary proceeding before a fact finder in a court of law. For every common law rule there is a publicly stated reason, the *ratio decidendi*. And for each principle that slowly emerges, there is a solid base of individual rules from particular cases and from publicly stated reasons that support the decisions in those cases.

For example, consider the development of the principle "all oral conveyances of real estate are invalid." It came about by the process of inductive generalization through enumerated instances of cases announcing a legal rule.

> A's oral conveyance of real estate is invalid.
> B's oral conveyance of real estate is invalid.
> C's oral conveyance of real estate is invalid
>
> ....
>
> Z's oral conveyance of real estate is invalid.
> *Therefore*, all oral conveyances of real estate are invalid.

Principles in the law appear in statutes as well. I think I am safe in suggesting that most statutes promulgate precepts that are broader than those that emerge from a single case. Instances are myriad, but consider, for example, the laconic declaration of federal antitrust law in the Sherman Act:

> Every contract, combination in the form of trust or otherwise, or conspiracy, in restraint of trade or commerce among the several States, or with foreign nations, is hereby declared to be illegal.[10]

> Every person who shall monopolize, or attempt to monopolize, or combine or conspire with any other person or persons, to monopo-

---

10. 15 U.S.C. § 1.

lize any part of the trade or commerce among the several States, or with foreign nations, shall be deemed guilty of a misdemeanor....[11]

Upon these two sentences, old in years and broad in force, are engrafted countless volumes of reported cases, treatises and professional articles describing modern antitrust law in America. For over a century, thousands of judicial opinions have interpreted and applied these two statutorily created principles to the fact-specific scenarios presented to the courts.

§ 3.2.3 Doctrine

From broad principles, there is an even larger, more encompassing legal precept—the doctrine. Simply stated, a doctrine is a very broad principle. It may be a collection of rules and principles or a systematic fitting-together of rules, principles and conceptions in logically inter-dependent schemes.

Does it really make a difference in the scheme of things whether we attach a proper label—rule, principle or doctrine—to a particular legal precept? I think it does. It is important that a judge know not only the various precepts in his arsenal, but also the weight, history, import and malleability of each. In short, a judge must have the tools, and know what they are and how to use them.

§ 3.3 Two Processes: Decision Making and Decision Justifying

I now shift gears to introduce a concept not widely acknowledged, or even recognized—the distinction between making a decision and justifying it. We are indebted to Professor Richard A. Wasserstrom's analysis: "[T]he phrase 'judicial decision process' is, I submit, capable in itself of denoting two quite different procedures, neither of which has been as yet been carefully isolated or described."[12] There is what Wasserstrom describes as the "process of discovery," the manner in which a decision or conclusion is reached.[13] I call this the

---

11. 15 U.S.C. § 2. A 1974 amendment, *see* Pub. L. No. 93-528, substituted "felony" for "misdemeanor."

12. RICHARD A. WASSERSTROM, THE JUDICIAL DECISION: TOWARD A THEORY OF LEGAL JUSTIFICATION 25 (1961).

13. *Id.* at 25–27.

"decision-making process." At the trial court level, a single judge goes it alone, but on a multi-judge court, this two-step process must be a collegial function that takes place at the decision conference following oral argument or the submission of briefs. It is either followed by, or performed simultaneously with, the "process of justification," which inquires whether a decision or conclusion is justifiable.[14] I call this the "decision-justifying process."

§ 3.3.1 The Difference between "Hot" and "Cold"

In the appellate court context, the ideal model takes place in a "hot" court. This is a court that has received briefs weeks in advance of submission, giving the judges time to read and study them, thus, allowing them to make detailed analyses, perform substantial research and reduce that research to authoritative bench memoranda prior to the date of submission. It is a court on which the judge has an intelligent, informal understanding of the oral argument to come. It is a court that makes it possible for judges to participate in dialogue with counsel in open session.

It has been my experience that prior preparation leads to a better understanding among the judges. This tends to create a more ordered and formalized decision conference. The judges "are on the same page." The decision is made, the opinion is assigned and the opinion writer is given marching orders that reflect an outline of issues the opinion will take up. Under such circumstances, the writer can expect no surprises when his or her draft makes the rounds for approval, and the non-writing judges should expect no surprises from the draft. It has also been my experience in having sat as a judge on six of the eleven regional U.S. Courts of Appeals that this advanced preparation reflects the practice in most federal appellate courts today.

Often, though, the practice does not follow the ideal. Many courts are "cold," that is, a court where the judges have not had the opportunity to read briefs and the record in advance or to participate in a pre-argument study of the briefs or research of the law. It is a system that deprives the judge of critical law clerk research prior to oral argument. Felix Frankfurter espoused this practice, saying that he did not wish to be distracted from the oral argument of counsel. Justice Frankfurter attracted few if any disciples to his one-arm-tied-behind-the-back bizarre practice of no advance preparation. Most "cold" courts today result from crushing calendars and antiquated scheduling of briefs. They

---

14. *Id.*

are forced into this unfortunate practice; they do not voluntarily choose to operate this way.

§ 3.3.2 Where Decisions Are Made

At the appellate level, the two-step process of "decision making" and "decision justifying" takes place at the decision conference following arguments. At the decision conference in all appellate courts there may be total agreement or agreement on certain issues only, rather than unanimity. Naturally, there may be stated disagreement on the choice, interpretation or application of the law. Some members of the court may be unready; when called upon in conference, they may respond that they are "*dubitante*" (doubtful). Certain judges may be thoroughly prepared to make a commitment. Others may simply not be ready. Some may have entered the oral argument thoroughly prepared, but may become troubled after listening to argument (A friend once told me, "I understood this until you explained it to me."). This produces hesitation, the cause of which may have been excellent argument from one side. At other times, the argument may have been so dreadful that the judge is inclined to re-examine a studied approach previously reached by chambers' research and discussion. One who hesitates is lost, goes the old saw, but so is one who plunges blindly ahead along a fixed path. As James Thurber said, "He who hesitates is sometimes saved."[15]

When the participants are unready or cannot reach unanimity, the conference may not produce a consensus. At other times, only a very fragile consensus will emerge. Here, the conference reaches only the most tentative impressions, and the opinion-writing judge is given the chore of internal advocacy and instructed to write the opinion with the ultimate goal of persuading the other members of the court to accept his or her point of view.

When the writer proceeds into the task, a conflict often appears between what I call justice *in personam* (justice for the parties to the suit) and justice *in rem* (the courts' institutional responsibility respecting consequences, consistency and coherence). The opinion writer may report back that the decision made at conference "just won't wash." More than a few of us have heard the plaintive refrain that goes something like this: "Here is the result we want, but I'm not sure that we can reach it without doing violence to highly respectable authority."

Whatever the formality or lack of formality in the decision-making process, it is clear that the opinion writer always has a unique and important responsibility to accommodate the twin concepts of justice *in personam* and justice *in*

---

15. JAMES THURBER, *The Glass in the Field*, *in* THE THURBER CARNIVAL 263, 263 (1945).

rem. What is equally important, as I attempt to demonstrate in depth later, is that the public explanation for the decision must always conform to canons of logical order and be free from formal or material fallacies.

Because I have strong feelings on the necessity for Holmes's "predictability" in the law, or Karl Llewellyn's "reckonability," I believe that public justification of a decision must also track what took place generally in the private decision-making process at conference. If there is no congruence between the processes of decision making and decision justifying, predictability and reckonability may go down the tube.

How can trial judges find the grounds of decision? How can persons (individual, corporate or the body politic) find reasonable guidance toward conducting themselves in accordance with the demands of the social, economic and political order? How can all of this come about unless the public explanation of the manner by which a decision is reached describes how in fact it was actually reached by the judges in private? To be sure, the conference discussion will be skeletal. It will seize the high grounds and tread the low valleys. Intermediate terrain and slippery slopes will not be attempted. It is to the opinion writer that the decision conference allocates authority and competence to develop subsidiary details, to create a structured logical order for the court, and to polish it in accepted form. The broad strokes of collegial agreement, however, should always be present both in reaching the decision at conference and in justifying it publicly in the opinion. There should be collective agreement on the choice of the controlling legal precept where precepts compete, or on the interpretation of the controlling precept that has been selected, or on how what has been selected and interpreted may be properly applied to the findings of the fact finder.

The decision makers should agree on the specifics of analogy. They should agree on the material and relevant facts of the putative precedent. They should agree on whether the facts in the case at bar make a difference. When judges cannot agree at conference on what facts are relevant, a concurring or dissenting opinion may be forthcoming.

§ 3.4 Idiosyncrasies of Appellate Courts: The Pre-Decision Opinion Assignment

The ideal "hot" court method of making the decision and agreeing upon the contours of the opinion is sometimes thwarted by the internal procedure of many appellate courts, which assign an opinion to a single judge before argument, before conference and before decision. This procedure is designed to insure impartiality. Whatever protection to the impartial assignment ideal this may possibly produce, these procedures could be properly utilized *after* the decision is made and not *before*. Such pre-argument division may also be a response to the need for a judge to monitor all correspondence and motions associated with a case before argument. Even then, however, pre-argument assignment for the purposes of monitoring pre-argument case development can be separated from pre-argument assignment for the purposes of writing an opinion.

When the assignment is made prior to decision, the system encourages one-judge decisions and one-judge opinions. It has the unfortunate tendency to encourage individual judges in a multi-judge court to concentrate only on the cases assigned to them, and conversely, to give too much deference, consciously or unconsciously, to the judge who has been assigned the opinion. This is a fertile field for a one-person opinion to emerge from a multi-judge court.

I strongly disagree with this practice. It militates against the desirable concept of total multi-judge participation in both the decision-making and decision-justifying processes. I am surprised that organized bar groups in states that follow this practice have not objected. I am also surprised that court reform and improvement organizations have ignored the problem.

§ 3.5 Five Recurring Questions

The decision-making and decision-justifying processes are most important in Cardozo's third category of cases where neither the rule nor its application is clear. It is these cases "where a decision one way or another, will count for the future, will advance or retard, sometimes much, sometimes little, the development of law."[16] In such cases, the court faces a series of recurring questions:

1. When confronted with competing statutes or constitutional clauses, which should prevail (and *why*)?
2. Which of several competing legal precepts should prevail (and *why*)?
3. Should we extend one precept by analogy while restricting another to its four corners (and *why*)?
4. Should we meet the question of statutory construction in the abstract (and *why*)? What is the legislative intent (and how do we divine it)?
5. Is an element of a previous decision binding precedent or dictum (and *why*)?

---

16. BENJAMIN CARDOZO, THE NATURE OF THE JUDICIAL PROCESS 165 (1921).

THE FIVE RECURRING QUESTIONS KEEP
POPPING UP AGAIN AND AGAIN.

Which questions to address depends on the precise conflict at issue. The earlier the decision makers and the opinion writers zero in on the precise conflict between the parties, the more structured the decision-making conference will be, the more precise the outline of the opinion will appear, and the more tightly drafted the opinion will be.

CHAPTER FOUR

JUDICIAL DECLARATION OF PUBLIC POLICY

§ 4.1 Overview

No discussion of opinion writing theory can be complete without a reference to judicially declared public policy.[1]

Recent criticism of judges—whether as lawmakers or as interpreters of constitutional or statutory text—has been particularly strong where judges base decisions on public policy considerations. Such decisions generate controversy on grounds both political and institutional. Public policy issues more readily inspire the familiar labels of "liberal," "conservative," "strict constructionists" or "a Bork-type." They provoke criticism from social, economic and political perspectives. Some critics argue from an institutional perspective, contending that articulating policies for the public interest is the task of state and national legislatures rather than federal or state judiciaries. Depending upon the viewpoint of the critic, judges who seek to advance the common good expressly through policy making are pilloried as either "activists" or "traditionalists." This controversial aspect of judicial responsibilities demonstrates the interplay in the trichotomy of legal philosophy, jurisprudence and jurisprudential temperament.

Roger J. Traynor admonished us not to "be misled by the half-truth that policy is a matter for [only] the legislators to decide."[2] The courts are continually called upon to weigh considerations of public policy when adding to the

---

1. Some portions of this chapter originally appeared in Ruggero J. Aldisert, *The Role of Courts in Contemporary Society*, 38 U. Pitt. L. Rev. 437 (1977), and in Ruggero J. Aldisert, *Philosophy, Jurisprudence and Jurisprudential Temperament of Federal Judges*, 20 Ind. L. Rev. 453 (1987). An extended discussion of the issues in this chapter can be found in Ruggero J. Aldisert, Essay, *Judicial Declaration of Public Policy*, 10 J. App. Prac. & Process 229 (2009).

2. Roger J. Traynor, *Reasoning in a Circle of Law*, 56 Va. L. Rev. 739, 749 (1970).

content of the common law, when filling in statutory gaps left by an inattentive, divided or politically sensitive legislature and when applying constitutional precepts to changing and novel circumstances. In all these aspects of the judicial process, considerations of public policy may be compelling or even decisive. David A. J. Richards emphasized the same point, noting that policy considerations underpin even the threshold doctrines of justiciability:

> [T]he proper ends of adjudication surely at least sometimes include policies. For example, the many discretionary rules of standing, ripeness, mootness, and the like clearly rest in part on policies of conserving judicial resources, a social policy of maximum output from limited inputs. Even aside from the problematics of the proper weight of principle and policy in understanding these rules, many cases of adjudication on the merits clearly invoke policies, as in many instances of statutory construction. Even where there is no clear legislative intent, courts invoke policy considerations *sua sponte* in order to effectuate a sensible legislative result; the burgeoning area of federal common law is one example.[3]

These American authorities have rejected sentiments voiced by English judges of an earlier era: that "public policy is a very unruly horse and when once you get astride it you never know where it will carry you,"[4] and that judges are more to be trusted as interpreters of the law than as expounders of public policy.[5] More recent United Kingdom jurists do not follow the teachings of the earlier era. The venerable Lord Denning has applied the modern view in his discussion of the measure of damages in a tort case:

> At bottom, I think the question of recovering economic loss is one of policy. Whenever the courts draw a line to mark out the bounds of duty, they do it as a matter of policy so as to limit the responsibility of the defendant. Whenever the courts set bounds to the damages recoverable—saying that they are, or are not, too remote—they do it as a matter of policy so as to limit the liability of the defendant.[6]

---

3. David A. J. Richards, *Rules, Policies, and Neutral Principles: The Search for Legitimacy in Common Law and Constitutional Adjudication*, 11 Ga. L. Rev. 1069, 1097–98 (1977) (footnotes omitted).

4. Richardson v. Mellish, (1824) 130 Eng. Rep. 294, 303.

5. *In re* Mirams, (1891) 1 Q.B. 594, 595.

6. Spartan Steel & Alloys Ltd. v. Martin & Co., (1973) 1 Q.B. 27.

James D. Hopkins of the appellate division of the New York Supreme Court was similarly realistic in declaring that among the several devices available as bases for decisions—such as maxims, doctrines, precedents and statutes—public policy is primary. The other grounds for a judicial decision must yield to the declaration of public policy once that policy is ascertained.[7]

Although much of the controversy concerning judicial implementation of public policy is of recent vintage, the practice itself is longstanding and well established in common law adjudication. As early as 1881, Holmes wrote:

> The very considerations which judges most rarely mention, and always with an apology, are the secret root from which the law draws all the juices of life. I mean, of course, considerations of what is expedient to the community concerned. Every important principle which is developed by litigation is in fact and at bottom the result of more or less definitely understood views of public policy; most generally, to be sure, under our practice and traditions, the unconscious result of instinctive preferences and inarticulate convictions, but none the less traceable to views of public policy in the last analysis.[8]

Notwithstanding the importance of these considerations to judicial decision making, it is well to remember that judges are far more constrained than legislators in fashioning or declaring public policy. Former Yale Law School Dean Harry H. Wellington offers the thoughtful suggestion "that when a court justifies a common law (as distinguished from a statutory or constitutional) rule with a policy, it is proceeding in a fashion recognized as legitimate only if two conditions are met: The policy must be widely regarded as socially desirable and it must be relatively neutral."[9] This poses an obvious question: How may—indeed, how can—a court determine whether a policy is socially desirable? Wellington recommended that, in fashioning common law on public policy grounds, the courts first look:

> to the corpus of law—decisional, enacted, and constitutional—to determine whether relevant policies have received legal recognition....
>
>   ....

---

7. James D. Hopkins, *Public Policy and the Formation of a Rule of Law*, 37 Brook. L. Rev. 323 (1971).

8. Oliver Wendell Holmes, Jr., The Common Law 35–36 (1881).

9. Harry H. Wellington, *Common Law Rules and Constitutional Double Standards: Some Notes on Adjudication*, 83 Yale L.J. 221, 236 (1973).

In determining the extent of a policy's social desirability, a court should examine such things as political platforms, and take seriously—for this purpose—campaign promises and political speeches. The media is a source of evidence and so too are public opinion polls. Books and articles in professional journals, legislative hearings and reports, and the reports of special committees and institutes are all evidence.[10]

The sound requirement of neutrality extends to constitutional and statutory interpretation as well as common law adjudication. The principle of neutrality demands that judges, who are intentionally shielded from the pressures of interest groups by the structure of American government, should not justify their rulings by accepting the demands of one interest group at the expense of another that is not party to the litigation.[11] Herbert Wechsler bore the brunt of much criticism—unfounded and undeserved—for his 1959 Holmes lecture at Harvard.[12] Commenting in 1975 on that criticism, he reasserted the importance of his principle:

> The central thought is surely that the principle once formulated must be tested by the adequacy of its derivation from its sources and its implications with respect to other situations that the principle, if evenly applied, will comprehend. Unless those implications are acceptable the principle surely must be reformulated or withdrawn.[13]

This, I suggest, is but the jurisprudential expression of Immanuel Kant's categorical imperative: "[A]ct according to the maxim that can make itself at the same time a universal law."[14] (Some, on the other hand, subscribe to George Bernard Shaw's advice: "Do not do unto others as you would they should do unto you. Their tastes may not be the same.")[15]

---

10. *Id.* at 236–37.

11. *Id.* at 238.

12. Herbert Wechsler, *Toward Neutral Principles of Constitutional Law*, 73 Harv. L. Rev. 1 (1959).

13. Herbert Wechsler, *Remarks at Federal Appellate Judges' Conference*, Federal Judicial Center, Washington, D.C. (March 12, 1975), *reprinted in* Ruggero J. Aldisert, The Judicial Process 630–31 (2d ed. 1996).

14. Immanuel Kant, Groundwork of the Metaphysics of Morals 101–02 (Mary Gregor & Jens Timmermann trans. 2011) (1785).

15. George Bernard Shaw, Man and Superman: A Comedy and a Philosophy (1903), *reprinted in* Maxims for Revolutionists 227 (1965).

The essence of neutrality is the quality of evenhandedness, a recognition that whatever influence special interests may have in legislative decision making, the imposition of special burdens or favors on a particular group has no place in adjudication—no place, that is, absent special, principled reasons for being there. Special-interest decision making is for only the legislative branch, which has perfected the act; statutes are the products of a series of marginal adjustments and compromises among various semi-independent groups.[16] Politics is the art of the possible; legislation is the art of accommodation. The possible is conditioned by the ballot box. Modern legislators seem to accommodate only the perceived desires of the parochial constituencies whose members elect or support them, setting aside any consideration of what is preferable for the entire population of the state or nation. Even within their own electorates, they often fail to equate numbers with influence, being mindful of John Gardner's warning that minorities punish, but majorities seldom protect.

The judiciary is not equally restrained by, or susceptible to, the interests of electorates confined within relatively small legislative districts, nor does it have available to it the legislature's opportunities for largess. Judges can learn what is widely regarded as being desirable by identifying, isolating and then weighing the same factors legislators would take into account—and then, when it is proper to do so, ignoring those factors. Because they can, with courage and dignity, eschew parochial and partisan factors, they are able to make their decisions on fairly neutral bases of principles and rights.

Assuming the essential element of neutrality, we must turn now to a broader canvas of the relevant factors that relate to policy declaration. How is the judge to ascertain the public interest—the "common morality of society"[17]—and the policies that will advance it? Indeed, as U.S. Supreme Court Justice Stephen Breyer has cautioned, any judicial approach "based upon common values" is bound to be precarious. For, although "[t]hose values are themselves found in the Constitution.... [and] do not change.... [,] circumstances do change.

---

16. *See* MARTIN SHAPIRO, FREEDOM OF SPEECH: THE SUPREME COURT AND JUDICIAL REVIEW 29 (1966).

17. Eugene V. Rostow, *The Enforcement of Morals*, 1960 CAMBRIDGE L.J. 174, 196 (1960). Rostow described this common morality as:

>   a blend of custom and conviction, of reason and feeling, of experience and prejudice.... [I]n the life of the law, especially in a common law country, the customs, the common views, and the habitual patterns of the people's behaviour properly count for much.... All movements of law reform seek to carry out certain social judgments as to what is fair and just in the conduct of society.

Id. at 197.

And the constitutional job of [a] judge is to apply those permanent values to ever-changing circumstances."[18]

Proposing a solution to this conundrum, Wolfgang Friedman believed it necessary to identify the collective judgment in terms of basic norms of the community's life. He suggested that a primary source of information would be the general state of contemporary legislative policy, but argued also that the judge should turn to the state of organization in the society in which he lived, make note of the groupings and pulls of the major social forces of his society, be aware of society's pluralistic aspects and recognize the state of modern science.[19] H.L.A. Hart, too, discussed the importance of ascertaining the conventional morality of an actual social group, referring to "standards of conduct which are widely shared in a particular society, and are to be contrasted with the moral principles or moral ideals which may govern an individual's life, but which he does not share with any considerable number of those with whom he lives."[20]

This is perhaps the most critical aspect of our inquiry. The judge must screen out personal bias, passion and prejudice, and attempt always to distinguish between a personal cultivated taste and the general notions of moral obligation. Such standards of conduct reflect an obligation to respect rules of society. They are, in Hart's formulation, primary rules of obligation because of "the serious social pressure by which they are supported, and by the considerable sacrifice of individual interest or inclination which compliance with them involves."[21] Wellington said that the way in which one learns about the conventional morality of society "is to live in it, become sensitive to it, experience widely, read extensively, and ruminate, reflect, and analyze situations that seem to call moral obligations into play."[22]

The line of inquiry proposed by Rostow, Friedman, Hart, Breyer, and others is similar to that proposed by Wellington to determine what is "socially desirable" for common law adjudication. The attempt to base a decision on social consensus, however, is fraught with peril and, in the interpretation of constitutional precepts, may be inappropriate.[23] In the words of Justice Breyer:

---

18. Stephen J. Breyer, *Making Our Democracy Work: The Yale Lectures*, 120 YALE L.J. 1999, 2015 (2011)

19. Wolfgang Friedman, *Legal Philosophy and Judicial Lawmaking*, 61 COLUM. L. REV. 821, 843–45 (1961).

20. H.L.A. HART, THE CONCEPT OF LAW 165 (1961).

21. *Id.*

22. Harry H. Wellington, *Common Law Rules and Constitutional Double Standards: Some Notes on Adjudication*, 83 YALE L.J. 221, 165 (1973).

23. Louis Jaffe once inquired:

How does one isolate and discover a consensus on a question so abstruse as the

Many Americans—too many—believe that Supreme Court Justices act like junior varsity politicians, at least when they decide important cases. But that cannot be right. To decide cases via politics would undermine the very objective of judicial review.... [J]udges are not very good politicians. If you want confirmation, consider Dred Scott.... [T]he only affirmative claim I have heard said about the case is that its author, Chief Justice Taney, thought it might prevent the Civil War.... [H]e was certainly wrong.... [T]here are good reasons here why judges should not hold their fingers up to political winds to see which way they blow. And, in my experience, the Justices do not do so. They do not base their decisions on politics—in any ordinary sense of that word.

....

Still,.... many do believe that the Justices simply decide to write into the law whatever they think in general is good. But a system based upon a general subjective idea of the "good" will not work much better than a system based upon "politics." Nine judges, nine hundred judges, might well have nine, nine hundred, different views of what is good. A legal system resting on those subjective views, among many other failings, would lack stability. The law would change with each new appointment; the system would prove unworkable; and the public would lose confidence.[24]

A classic example of judges mistaking the public consensus is the position perennially espoused by Justices William J. Brennan Jr. and Thurgood Marshall in death penalty cases. Their concurring opinions in *Furman v. Georgia*[25]

---

existence of a fundamental right? The public may value a right and yet not believe it to be fundamental. The public may hold that the rights of parents are fundamental and yet have no view whether they include sending a child to a private school. There may be a profound ambiguity in the public conscience; it may profess to entertain a traditional ideal but be reluctant to act upon it. In such a situation might we not say that the judge will be free to follow either the traditional ideal or the existing practice, depending upon the reaction of his own conscience? And in many cases will it not be true that there has been no general thinking on the issue?

Louis L. Jaffe, *Was Brandeis an Activist? The Search for Intermediate Premises*, 80 Harv. L. Rev. 986, 994 (1967).

24. Stephen J. Breyer, *Making Our Democracy Work: The Yale Lectures*, 120 Yale L.J. 1999, 2012–13 (2011).

25. 408 U.S. 238 (1972).

argued that the death penalty was unconstitutional "cruel and unusual punishment" because it was out of step with contemporary community values.[26]
The rush of state legislatures to impose the death penalty since the Justices'
1972 statements shows the unmistakability of community reaction that stands
in complete opposition to these statements.[27] The tendency of judges to find
society's values in their own is a constant danger. Much adjudication in the
federal courts, especially in constitutional interpretations based on concepts
of public policy, moral standards and public welfare, is little more than the
conscious or unconscious imposition of certain judges' personal values. Many
of us who purport to be objective in identifying community values, and who
are indeed sincere about it, are actually intent on attaining immediate social
ends that we personally see as moral imperatives.[28]

---

26. *Id.* at 295–300 (Brennan, J., concurring); *id.* at 360–69 (Marshall, J., concurring).

27. In the 1990 edition of this book, I noted that a Gallup Poll taken in November 1985
disclosed that three out of four Americans favored the death penalty, 17% opposed it, and
8% were undecided. NEW YORK TIMES, Nov. 18, 1985, at 20, col. 3. Analysis of a Gallup
Poll taken in October 2011 notes that although 61% of Americans are still in favor of the
death penalty for a murder conviction, over the years support for the sentence of life without parole as an alternative to the death penalty has steadily increased. When the Gallup
question provides the respondent with an explicit alternative to the death penalty ("life imprisonment, with absolutely no possibility of parole"), support for the death penalty typically has registered in the 47% to 54% range. *See* Frank Newport, *In U.S., Support for Death
Penalty Falls to 39-Year Low*, GALLUP NEWS SERVICE, Oct. 13, 2011, *available at*
www.gallup.com/poll/ 150089/support-death-penalty-falls-year-low.aspx.

28. For an example of this phenomenon, consider the Supreme Court's First Amendment jurisprudence, in which the Justices' perceptions of settled "community values" frequently conflict. *Compare* Brown v. Entm't Merchs. Ass'n, 131 S. Ct. 2729, 2736, 2737 n.4
(2011) (noting, in the context of a California ban on sales to children of violent video games,
that a state should not be able to "restrict the ideas to which children are exposed," and that
"[c]rudely violent video games, tawdry TV shows, and cheap novels and magazines are no
less forms of speech than The Divine Comedy"), *and id.* at 2742 (Alito, J., concurring)
(writing that a state *does* have the power to limit children's access to the "potentially serious social problem" of violent video games, but concurring in the result because the statute
at issue was too vague), *with id.* at 2752 (Thomas, J., dissenting) (contending that states
have every right to restrict access to objectionable content because " 'the freedom of speech,'
as originally understood, does not include a right to speak to minors (or a right of minors
to access speech) without going through the minors' parents or guardians"), *and id.* at
2761–71 (Breyer, J., dissenting) (arguing that the physical activity involved in video-game-
playing, the increasing absence of parents from the home, the realism of modern video
games, and neuroscientific research showing increased violence among violent-video-game
players, when combined, permit the statute to pass strict scrutiny because of the state's
overriding interest in "helping parents make a choice" about how to properly educate their
children).

Adherence to the principle of neutrality in judicial decision making provides a check against the temptation to substitute personal for social values.[29] Similarly, a consideration of the first principles of legal philosophy may place a particular issue of public concern in a broader, more principled context and may force us to recognize any inconsistencies between our intuitive moral values and the more general philosophy of law to which we may subscribe.[30] An important component of our jurisprudential temperament is the threshold at which judges are willing to act in disregard or contravention of prevailing social norms, the extent to which they are willing to confront the "antimajoritarian difficulty."[31] In those instances in which social consensus is asserted as an ap-

---

29. Professor Kent Greenawalt has observed:
Serious moral choices typically involve some conflict between an action that would serve one's narrow self-interest and an action that would satisfy responsibilities toward others. The dangers of bias are extreme; either we value too highly our own interest or over-compensate and undervalue it. The discipline of imagining similar situations in which we are not involved or play a different role more nearly enables us to place appropriate values on competing considerations.
Kent Greenawalt, *The Enduring Significance of Neutral Principles*, 78 Colum. L. Rev. 982, 997 (1978).

30. The search for general principles can also affect our judgment in another way. We may discover that some of our intuitive moral views are not consistent with other intuitive views or with generalized principles to which we subscribe. As we test our intuitive reactions to particular situations against our accepted principles, both may give a little, until we arrive at what John Rawls calls a "reflective equilibrium," in which our sense of right for particular issues matches our principles.
Id.

31. Professor Laurence Tribe contends this problem is inherent in constitutional government: Whether imposed by unelected judges or by elected officials conscientious and daring enough to defy popular will in order to do what they believe the Constitution requires, choices to ignore the majority's inclinations in the name of a higher source of law invariably raise questions of legitimacy in a nation that traces power to the people's will.... In its most basic form, the question in such cases is why a nation that rests legality on the consent of the governed would choose to constitute its political life in terms of commitments to an original agreement— made by the people, binding on their children, and deliberately structured so as to be difficult to change. Since that question would arise, albeit less dramatically, even without the institution of judicial review, its answer must be sought at a level more fundamental than is customary in discussions of why judges, appointed for life, should wield great power. For even without such judges, it must be stressed, lawmakers and administrators sworn to uphold the Constitution must from time to time ask themselves, if they take their oath seriously, why its message should be heeded over the voices of their constituents.
Laurence Tribe, American Constitutional Law 10 (2d ed. 1988).

propriate basis for judicial declarations of public policy, how should a judge reconcile what Lon Fuller called the "inner voice of conscience"[32] with prevailing community standards?

§ 4.2 Where There Is No Consensus for Public Policy

In seeking an answer, I first distinguish between circumstances where there is a consensus and those where there is not. We should agree that free societies will change because it is their nature to do so. New ideas can gather strength in the social or intellectual marketplace and achieve the consensus. When these ideas are admitted and so absorbed, the legal system should expand to hold them. Conversely, the legal system should contract to squeeze out old policies that have lost the consensus they once held. The expansion or contraction of the legal system to reach these goals is what we call judicially declared public policy. So perceived, social consensus demands sympathy from the court. Where the legislature has not acted in accordance with changing social policies and seemingly does not so intend to act, the courts have not only the authority, but possibly the duty, to keep pace with the change in consensus. Individual legislators then function in only one direction: to ensure their own re-election with the kind of Darwinian instinct that tells animals they must fight to preserve their genetic stocks. The prevailing tendency among most legislators is to avoid a vote on any controversial issue likely to produce differences in opinion back home in the constituencies.

Richard Neely, a former justice of the West Virginia Supreme Court, and a former state legislator, is more blunt:

> [A] legislature is *designed* to do nothing, with the emphasis appropriately placed on the word "designed." The value of an institution whose primary attribute is inertia to politicians who wish to keep their jobs is that a majority of bills will die from inactivity; that then permits legislators to be "in favor" of a great deal of legislation without ever being required to vote on it. When constituents seek to hold a legislator responsible for the failure of a particular bill, he can say, plausibly, that it was assigned to a committee on which he did not serve and that he was unable to shake the bill out of that committee. If he has foreseen

---

32. Lon L. Fuller, *Positivism and Fidelity to Law—A Reply to Professor Hart*, 71 Harv. L. Rev. 630, 635 (1958).

positive constituent interest, he can produce letters from the committee chairman in answer to his excited pleas to report the legislation to the floor; correspondence of this sort is the stock in trade of legislators. Notwithstanding the earnest correspondence, it is quite possible that when the legislator and committee chairman were having a drink before dinner, the legislator indicated his personal desire to kill the bill in spite of the facade of excited correspondence.[33]

This does not mean that the judge must act only when public opinion reflects a majoritarian viewpoint, or even a plurality viewpoint. Had the Supreme Court waited for public consensus we might never have had *Brown v. Board of Education*;[34] in 1954 there was no national consensus for the compulsory integration of the public school system. This was one of those times that call for judicial intervention—or more properly, judicial operation—in advance of the consensus, which the judge may therefore properly outrun. In doing so, however, he or she must tread delicately.

§ 4.3 Four Concerns to Be Addressed

I suggest that judges must address the following concerns:

- Judges must convey the distinct impression and appearance of impartiality.
- Judges must, in fact, be impartial and independent in both the decision-making process and the process of justification.
- Judges must fulfill the obligations of neutrality and the obligations of both justice *in rem*, socially desirable because it is based on some preeminent moral principle, and justice *in personam*, justice for both the parties to the suit.
- Judges must identify and evaluate the relevant private, social, public and governmental interests. These must be not only evaluated, but compared, accepted, rejected, tailored, adjusted and, if necessary, subjected to judicial compromise.

Judges must cleave to the first principle of the reasoning process, which starts the march to the specific conclusion (or declaration of public policy): It must be a concept universally held and uniformly respected. It must be related to at least one of what I have described as supereminent principles of the law:

---

33. Richard Neely, How Courts Govern America 55 (1981).
34. 349 U.S. 294 (1955).

creating and protecting property interests; creating and protecting the interest of liberties; fulfilling promises; redressing losses caused by breach or fault; and punishing those who wrong the public.[35]

§ 4.4 Weighing of Interests

More often than not, however, the distillation of public policy derives from a sub-process of the judicial process now popularly known as "balancing interests." This requires, I repeat, that competing interests be identified and categorized as individual, public and social. The result should be a reasoned accommodation of those interests. Determining appropriate public policy plays a prominent role in contemporary adjudication, with a seemingly inexhaustible inventory of social interests pressing upon jurists for attention.

Pound recognized that in the common law we have been wont to speak of social interests under the name of "public policy," but he emphasized that the extent to which this technique may be considered valid depends, in the first instance, on whether all relevant identifiable interests are placed on the scale.

The extent to which the technique of "balancing interests" may be considered valid hinges on identifying all the interests. The expression "balancing interests" is useful, perhaps, but seriously misleading. It implies that the subject matter of the judicial process is somehow *quantifiable*. It is not subject to such quantification, notwithstanding the itch in this computer age to put numbers to every phenomenon. The best that can be hoped is that all the interests at stake in a case are *identifiable*. Having identified the interests at stake, judges can at least consider them, as I doubt that they can ever really be "balanced." A reasoned accommodation of the competing interests and the resolution of their conflicts—the judges' priorities, if you will—will be durable and acceptable to the extent that such accommodation and resolution are regarded and accepted as fair. Before the accommodation takes place, however, like types of interests must be identified. As there are fruits and fruits, e.g., apples and oranges, so are there interests and interests.[36]

Although courts frequently use the expression "interests," there is little judicial explanation of the word. This is very unusual. For myself, I have gone through an evolving process that now leads me to define an interest as a social

---

35. Adapted from Ruggero J. Aldisert, *The House of the Law*, 19 Loy. L.A. L. Rev. 755 (1985).

36. *See* Ruggero J. Aldisert, The Judicial Process 315, 479–80, 523–25, 601–11 (1976).

fact, factor or phenomenon reflected by a claim, demand or desire that human beings, either individually or as groups, seek to satisfy and that has been recognized as socially valid by authoritative decision makers in society.[37] All current judicial decisions involve a recognition, stated or unstated, of certain interests; most decisions involve a weighing of competing interests that have been unquestionably identified and recognized.

We then get to the question of how judges identify the groupings of behavior and values that will influence their decisions. Gmelin contended that "[t]he whole of the judicial function ... [involves] the subjective sense of justice inherent in the judge, guided by an effective weighing of the interests of the parties ... and in weighing conflicting interests, the interest that is better founded in reason and more worthy of protection should be helped to achieve victory."[38] Other than by an exercise of a threshold value judgment on certain factual phenomena, either in the record or in the judge's experience, I can find no other point at which judicial decision making can begin. This threshold judgment continues to color a judge's thinking as he or she gropes toward a decision in the case.

Once judges designate an interest, they then make a value judgment as to whether it is worthy of protection. If that is the tentative inclination, they summon relevant precepts that command a definite legal consequence. If specific rules in the narrow sense are found wanting, the judges range further to the generalized precept of legal principle or a still more abstract precept known as a doctrine or dogma. If rules of law, principles or legal doctrines fail to provide an answer, the courts then look to a moral principle and make a judgment as to whether it should be converted into a legal precept.[39] Where a satisfactory legal precept is then found or articulated on the basis of these facts, the courts have wrapped legal protection around the designated social facts or factors.

I believe this accurately characterizes the anatomy of the judicial decisional process. I believe also that a critical component of the process is the interest identified or favored by a given judge in a given court reaching a particular result in a particular case.

---

37. Compare my earlier formulation in *id.* at 616.

38. Georg Gmelin, *Sociological Method*, trans. in 9 Mod. Legal Phil. Series 131 (quoted in Benjamin Cardozo, The Nature of the Judicial Process 73–74 (1921)).

39. Examples of this process in constitutional law are plentiful. *See* Roe v. Wade, 410 U.S. 113 (1973); Griswold v. Connecticut, 381 U.S. 479 (1965); Fay v. Noia, 372 U.S. 391 (1963); Monroe v. Pape, 365 U.S. 167 (1961). The classic example in state tort law is the adoption of Restatement (Second) of Torts §402A (1965) (strict products liability); *see also* Ruggero J. Aldisert, *The Nature of the Judicial Process: Revisited*, 49 Cinn. L. Rev. 1, 39–40 (1980).

One primary responsibility of the advocate is the identification of the interests being weighed today by the courts. This, alas, often does not take place. Too often, briefs simply recite the various leading cases and attempt to bring the particular dispute within the boundaries of the decisions thought to be controlling. They address too briefly, if at all, the interests implicated in the decision. Such briefs are of little aid to the court. To be a success, Justice Brandeis wrote in his notebook, a lawyer must "[k]now not only the specific case, but the whole subject.... Know not only those facts which bear on direct controversy, but know all the facts and laws that surround."[40]

Referring to his notable survey of social interests, in a magnificent abstraction of the nature and ends of law, Pound said:

> Looked at functionally, the law is an attempt to satisfy, to reconcile, to harmonize, to adjust these overlapping and often conflicting claims and demands, either through securing them directly and immediately, or through securing certain individual interests, so as to give effect to the greatest total of interests or to the interests that weigh most in our civilization, with the least sacrifice of the scheme of interests as a whole.[41]

The process derives from the German jurist Rudolf von Jhering, who designated the method as *Interessenjurisprudenz*, a jurisprudence of interests.[42] Under this method of dispute resolution, according to Chester James Antieau, the court identifies the opposed societal interests, reconciles them if possible and, if reconciliation is not possible, rules that one societal interest under the circumstances must prevail over another, with an explanation of why this is so.[43] The process is very much at work today in many aspects of adjudication, especially in tort and constitutional law.[44]

I believe that judges today do consider the pragmatic effects of alternative courses of decision. They attempt to accommodate the social needs of all who would be affected by their decisions, irrespective of whether those affected

---

40. *Quoted in* Marlin O. Urofsky, Louis D. Brandeis and the Progressive Tradition 6 (1981).

41. Roscoe Pound, *A Survey of Social Interests*, 57 Harv. L. Rev. 1, 39 (1943).

42. Rudolph von Jhering, Der Zweck Im Recht (1904) [Law as Means to an End].

43. Chester James Antieau, *The Jurisprudence of Interests as a Method of Constitutional Adjudication*, 27 Case W. Res. L. Rev. 823, 829 (1977).

44. *But see* Louis Henkin, *Infallibility Under Law: Constitutional Balancing*, 78 Colum. L. Rev. 1022 (1978). For examples of how competing interests are weighed and reconciled in two antitrust cases, see *Tose v. First Pennsylvania Bank, N.A.*, 648 F.2d 879 (3d Cir. 1981), and *Unger v. Dunkin Donuts of America, Inc.*, 531 F.2d 1211 (3d Cir. 1976).

were the litigants before them. They look to the general state of contemporary legislative policy and the felt needs of the society—insofar as they can discern those needs in an increasingly pluralistic society. They consider economic forces, scientific developments and identifiable expressions of public opinion. To be sure, this decisional process has deontological as well as axiological overtones. It bears a remarkable resemblance to classic natural law.[45]

We have now completed Part One, the Theoretical Concepts Underlying an Opinion. We descend herewith from the clouds and enter the shop to address the nuts and bolts of opinion writing.

---

45. Ruggero J. Aldisert, *The Role of the Courts in Contemporary Society*, 38 U. PITT. L. REV. 445 (1977).

PART TWO

THE ANATOMY OF AN OPINION

CHAPTER FIVE

THE OUTLINE OF YOUR OPINION

§ 5.1 Overview

In the pages that follow in this chapter we discuss the separate parts of the opinion. This outline is *not* comprehensive, and is designed only to give a bird's eye view of what we will discuss in detail in the chapters that follow.

First, it must be noted that I write from the perspective of an appellate judge. Thus, the pages that follow focus primarily on the parts of an appellate opinion. But, as detailed more thoroughly in Chapters 13–15, this information can easily be employed by trial judges, administrative law judges and arbitrators.

Second, keep the following maxims in mind as you prepare, write and rewrite your opinion:

- An opinion is defined as a reasoned elaboration, publicly stated, that justifies a conclusion or decision. Its purpose is to set forth an explanation for the decision that adjudicates a live case or controversy.
- The Roscoe Pound-Harry Jones test of a good opinion: (a) how thoughtfully and disinterestedly the court weighed the conflicts involved in the case and (b) how fair and durable its adjustment of the conflicts promises to be.

The first part of this test goes to the "reasonableness" of the decision in the sense of being fair and just; the second, to the validity of the reasoning.

§ 5.2 Five Parts Necessary for an Appellate Opinion

These five parts form the structure of every well-written opinion. Each is absolutely essential. They are not new to the art of persuasive discourse, for they can be traced to Greco-Roman rhetoric. Examine the following table for a summary of each element:

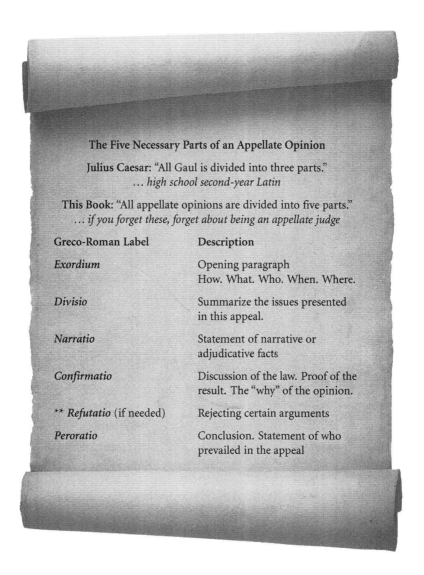

The Five Necessary Parts of an Appellate Opinion

Julius Caesar: "All Gaul is divided into three parts."
... high school second-year Latin

This Book: "All appellate opinions are divided into five parts."
... if you forget these, forget about being an appellate judge

Greco-Roman Label	Description
Exordium	Opening paragraph. How. What. Who. When. Where.
Divisio	Summarize the issues presented in this appeal.
Narratio	Statement of narrative or adjudicative facts
Confirmatio	Discussion of the law. Proof of the result. The "why" of the opinion.
** *Refutatio* (if needed)	Rejecting certain arguments
Peroratio	Conclusion. Statement of who prevailed in the appeal

§ 5.3 The Orientation Paragraph(s)[1]

The purpose of the orientation paragraph(s) is to set the stage for the discussion to follow. "It tells the reader at once whether he should begin thinking about contract law, tort law, criminal law or some other area in the vast field of jurisprudence."[2] It "establishes at the outset the roles of the plaintiff and defendant as appellant or appellee."[3] And, "[i]t may also supply other essential information. For example, [the orientation paragraph] can inform a reader as to whether there was a jury trial and, if so, whether the judgment follows the verdict."[4]

§ 5.4 Statement of Jurisdiction[5]

Does your court have jurisdiction to hear the appeal? Not a word should be written on the substantive merits of a case until you answer this question in the affirmative.

Federal appellate judges have an additional burden. They must also ascertain whether the trial court had jurisdiction to entertain the case. Unlike their state counterparts, federal courts have limited jurisdiction. They may hear cases based only on diversity of citizenship (with the requisite amount in controversy) or federal questions. Unlike most appellate issues placed in contention, the question of jurisdiction may be raised at any time either by the court *sua sponte* or by one of the parties.

§ 5.5 Summary of Issues to Be Discussed[6]

As a general rule, you should set forth the statement of all the issues very early in the opinion. The reason is obvious: You are giving the reader a preview of what the opinion will discuss. There are times, though, when you do not want to give the same dignity to each and every issue.

---

1. This topic will be discussed in greater detail in Chapter 7.
2. FREDERICK G. HAMLEY, INTERNAL OPERATING PROCEDURES OF APPELLATE COURTS 29–37 (1961), *reprinted in* ROBERT A. LEFLAR, APPELLATE JUDICIAL OPINIONS 172 (1974).
3. *Id.*
4. *Id.*
5. This topic will be discussed in greater detail in Chapter 6.
6. This topic will be discussed in greater detail in Chapter 8.

The summary of issues is prepared after preliminary research has been completed and the decision has been made as to what points the opinion will cover. Hours of opinion writing and opinion circulating may be saved if there can be a collegial agreement at the decision conference as to what issues the opinion should discuss.

Where in the opinion do we place the statement of issues? I believe the statement usually should precede the narration of the facts.

§ 5.6 Standards of Review[7]

Standards of review are critically important in appellate decision making. In large part, they determine the power of the lens through which the appellate court may examine a particular issue in a case.

The appellate process reduces itself to limited types of review, such as: review of the sufficiency of the evidence to meet the required burden of persuasion at the trial level; review of the exercise of discretion; and plenary review of the choice, interpretation and application of the controlling legal precepts. The Federal Rules of Appellate Procedure require a statement of the applicable standard of review for each argument presented in the briefs. A clear understanding of the scope of review for each point in a brief should be a minimum requirement for any proposed standard of advocacy competence.

§ 5.7 Write the Facts[8]

In addition to ruling in favor of a party in a dispute, judicial opinions have a byproduct that the common law tradition elevates to the status of a legal precept. This generally takes the form of a legal rule, which we have previously described as a detailed legal consequence attached to a detailed set of facts. Thus, the facts set forth in an opinion are more than merely informative. This being so, it is necessary to use care in selecting what facts you set forth. For this reason, I offer two suggestions:

- Never write the facts first; do not begin writing the facts until you have decided what issues you will address.
- Write tersely; tailor the statement of the facts to fit only the issues raised

---

7. This topic will be discussed in greater detail in Chapter 6.
8. This topic will be discussed in greater detail in Chapter 9.

Therefore, the facts should be stated as tightly as possible and confined to those material to the issues that will be discussed.

§ 5.8 Stating Reasons for the Decision[9]

We come now to the core of our subject, to the opinion's sinew and muscle and fiber, as we describe the process of stating reasons for the decision. This is the *ratio decidendi,* the *how* and *why* we have reached the decision. It is said that the judicial process is divided into two separate parts. The first is the process of discovery—reaching the decision. The second is the process of justification—writing a public explanation that justifies the decision we have made. It is here that the major criticisms are directed against our opinions. It is here that all of us must buckle down to demonstrate superior writing and explanatory skills.

§ 5.9 Disposition[10]

The opinion writer has an obligation to the reviewing courts and to the litigants to articulate clearly the action taken by the reviewing court. When the judgment or order is affirmed, this task is simple. An even greater necessity to clarify exists, however, when the judgment is reversed, vacated and remanded, or modified in some manner. The task in this instance is much more complicated.

Often it is enough to say, "The judgment of the trial court will be vacated and the cause remanded for further proceedings in accordance with the foregoing." This is appropriate only when there has been a clear-cut ruling on a discrete issue—most often the issue is evidentiary, procedural or pertaining to jury instructions.

Where the judgment is "vacated and the cause remanded for further proceedings," the trial tribunal is obligated to undertake further consideration of the case. The opinion writer should clearly and systematically set forth exactly what consideration is expected. If additional consideration of a legal issue is expected because the trial court should have addressed the issue in the first instance, the appellate court must be very clear in its directions.

---

9. This topic will be discussed in greater detail in Chapter 10.
10. This topic will be discussed in greater detail in Chapter 10.

CHAPTER SIX

Jurisdiction and Standards of Review

§6.1 Overview

Does your court have jurisdiction? Not a word should be written on the substantive merits of a case until you answer this question in the affirmative.

Federal appellate judges have an additional burden. They must also ascertain whether the trial court had jurisdiction to entertain the case. Unlike their state counterparts, federal courts have limited jurisdiction. They may hear cases based only on diversity of citizenship (with the requisite amount in controversy) or federal questions. Unlike most appellate issues placed in contention, the question of jurisdiction may be raised at any time either by the court *sua sponte* or by one of the parties.

§6.2 Subject Matter Jurisdiction Checklist

The judge should prepare a jurisdiction checklist for each case. This checklist is important for not only the judge but also the law clerks. Because law clerks serve on a short-term basis, a written checklist teaches them the first order of business. The following checklist should be employed by appellate courts to determine subject matter jurisdiction:

- ❑ Original proceedings jurisdiction.
- ❑ Interlocutory orders for which an appeal is permitted by rule or statute, *e.g.*, 28 U.S.C. §1292.
- ❑ All final judgments.
- ❑ For those courts adhering to Rule 54(b), Federal Rules of Civil Procedure, Judgment Upon Multiple Claims or Involving Multiple Parties, being certain to count the number of parties and claims below to

determine whether the trial court disposed of *all claims* of *all parties.* Otherwise, there is no final judgment.

§ 6.3 Issue Preservation for Review

In the appellate context, another early warning flag cautions against unnecessary consideration of the merits. The judge must determine whether the issue now presented on appeal was presented to the trial court for ruling so as to preserve the issue for appeal. This is the essence of the common law tradition that requires questions and objections to be timely presented at the trial or hearing in order to permit an adversary to respond by testimony or argument, thereby giving the trial court or administrative agency the opportunity to make appropriate rulings in the context of a trial setting. Appellate determination of reversible error is based on the presence of three interrelated circumstances that are present in the trial tribunal:

- specific rulings, acts or omissions by the trial tribunal constituting trial error;
- which are properly suggested to the tribunal by counsel; and
- which are accompanied by a recommended appropriate course of action in the trial tribunal.

When all three elements are present, the issue has been properly preserved for review by the appellate court.

Generally speaking, if the issue was not first presented to the trial judge or administrative agency, the reviewing court will not notice or consider it. A limited exception exists, however, known as "plain error," to permit the reviewing court to consider an issue not presented to the trial court. To qualify as plain error, it must have affected substantial rights by prejudicially altering the outcome of the trial court proceedings. If such is the case, the reviewing court then has discretion to correct this error only if it seriously affects the fairness, integrity or public reputation of judicial proceedings. Justice Hugo Black explained the purpose of the general rule:

> Ordinarily an appellate court does not give consideration to issues not raised below. For our procedural scheme contemplates that parties shall come to issue in the trial forum vested with authority to determine questions of fact. This is essential in order that parties may have the opportunity to offer all the evidence they believe relevant to the issues that the trial tribunal alone is competent to decide; it is equally essential in order that litigants may not be surprised on appeal by final decision there of issues upon which they have had no opportunity to

introduce evidence. And the basic reasons which support this general principle applicable to trial courts make it equally desirable that parties should have an opportunity to offer evidence on the general issues involved in the less formal proceedings before administrative agencies that have been entrusted with the responsibility of fact finding.[1]

§6.4 Standard of Review

Standards of review are critically important in appellate decision making. In large part, they determine the power of the lens through which the appellate court may examine a particular issue in a case.

The appellate process reduces itself to limited types of review, such as: review of the sufficiency of the evidence to meet the required burden of persuasion at the trial level; review of the exercise of discretion; and plenary review of the choice, interpretation and application of the controlling legal precepts. The Federal Rules of Appellate Procedure require a statement of the applicable standard of review for each argument presented in the briefs.[2] A clear understanding of the scope of review for each point in a brief should be a minimum requirement for any proposed standard of advocacy competence. I say this because I have seen competent lawyers completely nonplussed when we asked them to state the standard of review. A psychological block seems to crush those who refuse to recognize that trial tribunals' fact-finding processes can fast-freeze evidence into rigid and unchangeable facts. It makes no sense for lawyers to dress up a closing speech to a jury in the form of a brief to an appellate court that simply repeats the trial lawyer's recitation of a litigant's best *evidence* instead of addressing the *facts* found by the fact finder.

Everyone is entitled to a day in court. More often than not, however, and notwithstanding access to tiers of appellate review, this means only one "day" (or one trial) in court, for it is on that one "day" that the fact finder determines the facts and that the trial court exercises discretion and makes rulings of law. These initial determinations for the most part are final and binding, irrespective of impressive appellate briefs, thick volumes of records or eloquent argument. This reality of the judicial process is an aspect of the law lost upon most laypersons and many lawyers. The truth, though, is that most trial court decisions are set in a quick-hardening jurisprudential cement and will be subject to an extremely limited scope of appellate review.

---

1. Hormel v. Helvering, 312 U.S. 552, 556 (1941); *see also* Newark Evening Ledger v. United States, 539 F.2d 929, 932 (3d Cir. 1976).

2. Fed. R. App. P. 28(a)(9)(B).

§6.5 The Fact Finder

When the controversy concerns facts, findings are ordinarily permanent. Practical and philosophical impediments prevent us from displacing the fact finder's resolution of conflicting evidence. Fact finding is the province of the trial tribunal, be it a court or an administrative agency. The skill of a trial advocate is measured by the ability to persuade the fact finder to convert congeries of testimony and evidence into adjudicative facts. The fact finder may be a jury, a judge, a hearing examiner or administrative law judge and the board to which he or she reports. Trial advocacy, which deals with fact-based persuasion, calls for skills completely different from appellate advocacy, which requires legal precept persuasion.

There is the familiar story of the baseball umpire who said: "Ball or strike? Why, they ain't nothin' till I call 'em." The same is true of testimony. Even though the witness's testimony is a "factual" narrative, the oral testimony is not "fact"; it "ain't nothin'" until the fact finder calls it. Until a finding is made, or legally conceded by the adversary, the evidence is not elevated to the jurisprudential dignity of "fact."

THE EVIDENCE AIN'T NOTHIN' 'TIL
THE FACT FINDER CALLS IT A FACT

HOW DO YOU CALL BALLS AND STRIKES?

I CALLS 'EM AS I SEES 'EM!

I CALL 'EM AS THEY ARE!

HELL, THEY AIN'T NOTHIN' 'TIL I CALL 'EM!

AND THAT'S A FACT, JACK!

The fact finder is the sole judge of credibility, and is free to accept or reject even uncontradicted oral testimony.[3] Without regard to the number of rungs an appellant may climb up the appellate ladder, if minimal evidentiary quanta have been satisfied, the American tradition generally does not permit a reviewing court to disturb findings of fact.

§ 6.6 Three Categories of Facts

For a proper understanding of the procedures involved in review of fact finding, it is necessary to segregate three distinct and fundamental concepts: basic facts, inferred facts and ultimate facts.

The importance of distinguishing among these three types of facts is reflected in the various standards of judicial review. When the court sitting as fact finder identifies the basic facts and the facts permissibly inferred therefrom, neither may be disturbed on review unless they are deemed clearly erroneous.[4] "[A] review of ultimate facts," on the other hand, "entails an examination for legal error of the legal components of those findings."[5]

§ 6.6.1 Basic and Inferred Facts

Basic facts are the historical and narrative accounts elicited from the evidence accepted from eye or earwitnesses at trial, admitted by stipulation or not denied in responsive pleadings.

Evidence that is inferred from basic facts, rather than being direct, is often called circumstantial. Inferences of fact are permitted only when, and to the extent that, logic and human experience indicate a probability that certain consequences can and do follow from the basic events or conditions.[6]

---

3. Nanty Glo v. Am. Surety Co., 163 A. 523 (Pa. 1932); *see also* Sartor v. Ark. Natural Gas Corp., 321 U.S. 620 (1944); NBO Indus. Treadway Cos. v. Brunswick Corp., 523 F.2d 262 (3d Cir. 1975); Rhoades, Inc. v. United Air Lines, Inc., 340 F.2d 481, 486 (3d Cir. 1965).

4. Fed. R. Civ. P. 52(a)(6); *see also* United States v. U.S. Gypsum Co., 333 U.S. 364, 394 (1948).

5. Smith v. Harris, 644 F.2d 985, 990 (3d Cir. 1981) (Aldisert, J., concurring); *see also* Universal Minerals, Inc. v. C.A. Hughes & Co., 669 F.2d 98, 102–03 (3d Cir. 1981) (providing an extensive discussion of the distinction between review of basic and inferred facts on the one hand and of ultimate facts on the other).

6. *See, e.g.,* Edward J. Sweeney & Sons, Inc. v. Texaco, Inc., 637 F.2d 105, 116 (3d Cir. 1980).

§6.6.2 Ultimate Facts (Mixed Questions of Fact and Law)

We must distinguish an inferred fact from an "ultimate fact." An ultimate fact is a mixture of fact and legal precept. No legal precept is used in drawing permissible factual inferences—one set of facts inferred from another.

We usually express an ultimate fact in the language of a standard that has been enunciated by case law or by statute; e.g., an actor's conduct was negligent or the injury occurred in the course of employment or the rate is reasonable or the company has refused to bargain collectively. "The ultimate finding is a conclusion of law or at least a determination of a mixed question of law and fact."[7]

§6.7 Fact Finding: Who Does It, and Under What Conditions?

It is always the responsibility of the fact finder—jury, judge or administrative agency—to find the narrative or historical facts and to draw proper inferences therefrom. Often the fact finder must also go further and determine the ultimate facts as well, on the basis of the court's instruction in a jury case or on the basis of a proper application of a legal precept in a non-jury trial or agency hearing. The fact finder always operates within the acknowledged limitations of any judicial process.

Narrative or historical data are, at best, imperfect re-enactments of the actual events. They are constructed from the perceptions of witnesses. The most we can hope for is that the witnesses be not only honest but reasonably accurate in both perception and recollection. Inferred facts, best described as circumstantial evidence, are equally important. Professor Stebbing observes that inference "may be defined as a mental process in which a thinker passes from the apprehension of something given, the datum, to something, the conclusion, related in a certain way to the datum, and accepted only because the datum has been accepted."[8] Thus, inference is a process where the thinker passes from one proposition to another that is connected with the former in some way. But for the passage to be valid, it must be made according to the laws of logic that permit a reasonable movement from one proposition to another.

---

7. Helvering v. Tex-Penn Oil Co., 300 U.S. 481, 491 (1937).
8. L.S. Stebbing, A Modern Introduction to Logic 211–12 (6th ed. 1948).

Inference, then, is "any passing from knowledge to new knowledge."[9] The passage may not be mere speculation, intuition, or guessing. The key to a logical inference is the reasonable probability that the conclusion flows from the evidentiary datum because of past experiences in human affairs. For example, a nickel-plated revolver was used in the bank holdup by a ski-masked robber who got away with $10,000 in marked money. A nickel-plated revolver, a ski-mask, and $10,000 in marked money is found in the apartment of Dirty Dan, its sole occupant. The inference is permissible that our friend Dan was the bank robber.

The ultimate desire in adjudication is that fact finders be honest, intelligent and fair in evaluating the evidence presented. What the judicial process affords is a time-tested mechanism that seeks to fashion a courtroom reconstruction of what actually occurred. It is not perfection in all cases, but it does serve as a reasonable facsimile in most cases.

Once basic facts have been found, they are seldom dislodged. The trial lawyer's skill, therefore, is measured by the ability to persuade the fact finder of basic facts. The appellate advocate's skill is measured in part by the ability to convince the court that a given "fact" is not a "basic" fact, but an "ultimate" fact, so that he or she may argue the law portion of the ultimate fact.

This follows because the appellate court, and indeed the trial court in a post-trial context, may review only an erroneous legal interpretation given in the court's instructions to the jury, or a legal error by the fact finder in bench trials. The review is limited to the choice, interpretation or application of the legal precept. A review of an ultimate fact may not disturb its basic fact component in this mixed question of law and fact, but it is fair for an appellate court to review the "law" segment of the ultimate fact. This means that review is available when there is insufficient evidence to sustain the requirements of the legal precept upon which the ultimate fact is premised. For example, in a review of a finding of negligence in an automobile case, the evidence of speed, location of vehicles and direction of travel is historical or narrative. This is the "basic" fact component of the "ultimate" fact of negligence. It is not reviewable in jury trials and is subject to extremely limited review in bench trials.

§ 6.8 Who Found the Facts?

An important consideration of consequence in reviewing findings of fact is whether the facts were found by a judge, jury or administrative agency. The

---

9. Joseph Gerard Brennan, A Handbook of Logic 1 (1957).

nature of the fact finder will determine the scope of the appellate court's scrutiny.

The Seventh Amendment has controlling force in federal jury cases:

> In Suits at common law, where the value in controversy shall exceed twenty dollars, the right of trial by jury shall be preserved, and no fact tried by a jury shall be otherwise re-examined in any Court of the United States, than according to the rules of the common law.[10]

Most state constitutions have similar provisions guaranteeing trial by jury.[11] So long as there is some evidence from which the jury could arrive at the finding by a process of reasoning, the jury's finding of fact will not be disturbed. This, of course, is a different issue than the quantum of evidence necessary to sustain the various burdens of proof in civil and criminal cases.[12]

Facts found by a judge alone need a stronger evidentiary base. The findings, under federal rules and in those states adhering to Rule 52(a) of the Federal Rules of Civil Procedure, shall not be set aside "unless clearly erroneous, and the reviewing court must give due regard to the trial court's opportunity to judge the witnesses' credibility."[13] "Clearly erroneous" has been interpreted to mean that a reviewing court can upset a finding of fact, even if there is evidence to support the finding, only if the court is left with "the definite and firm conviction that a mistake has been committed."[14] This has been interpreted by the U.S. Court of Appeals for the Third Circuit to mean that the appellate court must accept the factual determination of the fact finder unless that determination "either (1) is completely devoid of minimum evidentiary support displaying some hue of credibility, or (2) bears no rational relationship to the supportive evidentiary data."[15]

Because the fact finder is given an opportunity to observe the demeanor of witnesses, it is generally the rule "that a fact finder's determination of credibility is not subject to appellate review."[16] Conversely, however, in cases in which the trial judge decides a fact issue on written or documentary evidence, some reviewing courts previously adopted the view that "we are as able as [the judge] to determine credibility, and so we may disregard his finding."[17] Many courts

---

10. U.S. Const. amend. VII.

11. *See, e.g.,* Pa. Const. art. I, §6; N.J. Const. art. I, §9; Del. Const. art. I, §4.

12. *See, e.g.,* Jackson v. Virginia, 443 U.S. 307 (1979).

13. Fed. R. Civ. P. 52(a)(6).

14. United States v. U.S. Gypsum Co., 333 U.S. 364, 395 (1948).

15. Krasnov v. Dinan, 465 F.2d 1298, 1302 (3d Cir. 1972).

16. *See, e.g.,* Virgin Islands v. Gereau, 502 F.2d 914, 921 (3d Cir. 1974).

17. Orvis v. Higgins, 180 F.2d 537, 539 (2d Cir. 1950).

and thoughtful commentators, however, concluded otherwise.[18] The question was finally resolved by Congressional approval of the amendment to Rule 52(a) of the Federal Rules of Civil Procedure, suggested by the Federal Advisory Committee on Civil Rules. The rule now reads that "[f]indings of fact, whether based on oral or other evidence, must not be set aside unless clearly erroneous, and the reviewing court must give due regard to the trial court's opportunity to judge the witnesses' credibility."[19]

In some state systems, it is necessary to inquire about and understand the stability given to facts found by a chancellor in equity. Historically, these facts were subject to a broad review in equity, but some jurisdictions, like Pennsylvania, give the same effect to a chancellor's findings as a jury verdict when they are affirmed at a post-trial motion.[20] In past years, Pennsylvania had an unusual practice in which exceptions to a chancellor's decree nisi as to both findings of fact and conclusions of law had to be considered by a multi-judge *en banc* panel before a final decree was entered. Under that practice, the facts found by the chancellor approved by the *en banc* court had the efficacy of a jury verdict.

§6.8.1 Fact Finding: Jury or Judge?

It is critical that the reviewing court understands the strictures that deny or severely limit its authority to disturb (1) narrative or historical facts and (2) permissible inferred facts. As we have observed, when the jury has found such facts, no review is generally available. Although a reviewing court may re-examine a determination of an ultimate fact, its review is limited to the legal component of that ultimate fact. The part of the ultimate fact consisting of historical or narrative facts, or inferences therefrom, is subject to either no review or limited review. For example, in *Universal Minerals, Inc. v. C.A. Hughes & Co.*,[21] the question was whether there had been an abandonment of a pile of culm (refuse from a coal mine). The court explained that abandonment is not a question of narrative or historical fact, but of ultimate fact, a determination of a mixed question of law and fact. The court explained:

> In reviewing the ultimate determination of abandonment, as an appellate court, we are therefore not limited by the "clearly erroneous"

---

18. *See, e.g.*, Lundgren v. Freeman, 307 F.2d 104 (9th Cir. 1962); Charles Alan Wright, *The Doubtful Omniscience of Appellate Courts*, 41 Minn. L. Rev. 751 (1957).
19. Fed. R. Civ. P. 52(a).
20. Schwartz v. Urban Redev. Auth., 206 A.2d 789 (Pa. Super. Ct. 1965).
21. 669 F.2d 98 (3d Cir. 1981).

standard, … but must employ a mixed standard of review. We must accept the trial court's findings of historical or narrative facts unless they are clearly erroneous, but we must exercise a plenary review of the trial court's choice and interpretation of legal precepts and its application of those precepts to the historical facts. *See United States v. United States Gypsum Co.*, 333 U.S. at 394, 68 S.Ct. at 541; *Smith v. Harris*, 644 F.2d at 990 (Aldisert, J., concurring); *cf. Cuyler v. Sullivan*, 446 U.S. 335, 34l–42, 100 S.Ct.1708, 1714–15, 64 L.Ed.2d 333 (1980) (review of mixed determinations of fact and law on federal habeas corpus). Thus we separate the distinct factual and legal elements of the trial court's determination of an ultimate fact and apply the appropriate standard to each component.[22]

We use the same approach when we review a jury's findings on a mixed question, but the distinction is more easily understood in that context because of the strict division of competence between the jury and the trial court and because of the intercession of the Seventh Amendment. If, for example, a jury finds that a party has abandoned an interest in property, we review the court's jury instructions to determine whether it erred in its explanation of the law; if we find no error, we examine the record to determine whether the evidence was sufficient to justify someone of reasonable mind in drawing the factual inferences underlying the conclusion.

§ 6.8.2 Fact Finding: Administrative Agencies

The reviewing court may not set aside the findings of administrative agencies unless they are "unsupported by substantial evidence" in light of the whole record.[23] What, however, is substantial evidence? For some time, recourse has been made to a U.S. Supreme Court statement by Chief Justice Hughes: "Substantial evidence is more than a mere scintilla. It means such relevant evidence as a reasonable mind might accept as adequate to support a conclusion."[24] A later statement clarified further:

> [Substantial evidence] means evidence which is substantial, that is, affording a substantial basis of fact from which the fact in issue can be

---

22. *Id.* at 103 (footnote omitted).

23. 5 U.S.C. § 706(2)(E); *see also* Beth Isr. Hosp. v. NLRB, 437 U.S. 483 (1978); Universal Camera Corp. v. NLRB, 340 U.S. 474 (1951); 4 KENNETH CULP DAVIS, ADMINISTRATIVE LAW TREATISE chs. 29–30 (1958 & Supp. 1976).

24. Consol. Edison Co. v. NLRB, 305 U.S. 197, 229 (1938).

reasonably inferred.... [I]t must be enough to justify, if the trial were to a jury, a refusal to direct a verdict when the conclusion sought to be drawn from it is one of fact for the jury.[25]

By 1988, the Supreme Court was prepared to say:

We are not, however, dealing with a field of law that provides no guidance in this matter. Judicial review of agency action, the field at issue here, regularly proceeds under the rubric of "substantial evidence" set forth in the Administrative Procedure Act, 5 U.S.C. §706(2)(E). That phrase does not mean a large or considerable amount of evidence, but rather "such relevant evidence as a reasonable mind might accept as adequate to support a conclusion."[26]

In the review of administrative agency proceedings, as in the review of judicial fact finding, the question of credibility is for the administrative law judge to determine. This conflict may have an important bearing on whether there is substantial evidence where the agency has not accepted the determinations of credibility of the administrative law judge who has had the opportunity to listen to the live witnesses and observe their comportment and demeanor.

§6.9 A Comparison: Common Law and Civil Law Traditions

The nonreviewability of facts found by a court of the first instance or an administrative agency is peculiar to the common law tradition. Civil law tradition permits review of facts through the courts of the second instance. Thus, new evidence can be taken and the evidence below re-examined in the various appeals courts, e.g., the French *cour d'appel*, the German and Austrian *landesgerichthof* and the Italian *corte d'appello*. Beyond the court of the second instance, the appeal to the final court is restricted to matters of law only — in France, a *pourvoi en cassation*; in Germany and Austria, a *Revision;* and in Italy, an *appello*.[27] Similarly, there is generous review of facts in appeals from administrative agencies to the specialized courts.

---

25. NLRB v. Colum. Enameling & Stamping Co., 306 U.S. 292, 299–300 (1939).

26. Pierce v. Underwood, 487 U.S. 552, 563 (1988) (quoting Consol. Edison Co., 305 U.S. at 229).

27. *See* Ruggero J. Aldisert, *Rambling Through Continental Legal Systems*, 31 U. Pitt. L. Rev. 1 (1982).

§ 6.10 Excerpts from Court Opinions

Statements of Review Standards

This is an appeal from a judgment of sentence for receiving stolen property. Appellant argues that the evidence was insufficient and that trial counsel was ineffective. Finding these arguments without merit, we affirm.

The test of sufficiency is whether, after viewing the evidence in the light most favorable to the Commonwealth, and then drawing all reasonable inferences favorable to the Commonwealth, the trier of fact could find that every element of the crime charged had been proved beyond a reasonable doubt.[28]

———

Since both appeals question the chancellor's findings of fact and conclusions of law, approved by a court en banc, the standard of review consists of the following:

[T]he findings of fact of the chancellor who heard the testimony without a jury, approved by a court en banc, are entitled to the weight of a jury's verdict; that such findings are controlling and that the court's decree should not be reversed unless it appears that the court abused its discretion or that the court's findings lack evidentiary support or that the court capriciously disbelieved the evidence. The chancellor's findings are especially binding where they are based upon the credibility of the witnesses....

However, the chancellor's "conclusions whether of law or ultimate fact are no more than his reasoning from the underlying facts and are reviewable," especially "where the underlying facts themselves are not *in esse* but are matters of inference and deduction".... Furthermore, a chancellor's findings of fact, even though approved by a court *en banc*, need not be accepted as conclusive if there is no evidence to support them or if they are based on an inference erroneously taken ... or where the evidence, in order to prevail, must be clear, precise and indubitable or must meet some other prescribed standard.[29]

———

28. Commonwealth v. Byers, 467 A.2d 9, 10 (Pa. Super. Ct. 1983).
29. *In re* Estate of Agostini, 457 A.2d 861, 863 (Pa. Super. Ct. 1983).

[T]he factual findings of the Commission regarding that issue, if supported by substantial evidence, are conclusive. This effectively limits the scope of our review....[30]

Appellant first contends that the trial court erred in failing to grant a demurrer at the close of the Commonwealth's case. Because appellant's counsel did not rest following the adverse ruling on the demurrer but instead presented a case in defense, a challenge to the correctness of this ruling on appeal can be considered only as a challenge to the sufficiency of the evidence as a whole.... The verdict winner is entitled to the benefit of all reasonable inferences upon which a jury might have relied, and resolution of factual conflicts will not be disturbed on appeal so long as there is support in the record for the verdict.[31]

§6.11 Review of the Exercise of Discretion

It is unfortunate that in our jurisprudence, several distinct meanings have been attributed to the word "discretion." Bouvier's Law Dictionary defines discretion as "[t]hat part of the judicial function which decides questions arising in the trial of a cause, according to the particular circumstances of each case, and as to which the judgment of the court is uncontrolled by fixed rules of law" and "[t]he power exercised by courts to determine questions to which no strict rule of law is applicable but which, from their nature, and the circumstances of the case, are controlled by the personal judgment of the court."[32]

Jurisprudents have given other meanings to the term, all of which utilize a broad concept of choice but not in the narrower sense we use today. They speak of "strong" or "primary" discretion to describe the freedom to choose a legal norm, in the sense of choosing a legal precept as the starting point of legal reasoning. In this sense, this would describe a judge's exercise of a value judgment.

In discussing the review of the exercise of discretion today, judges and members of the legal profession refer to what Hart and Sacks described as "the power

---

30. Capital Funds, Inc. v. SEC, 348 F.2d 582, 585 (8th Cir. 1965).

31. Commonwealth v. Olds, 469 A.2d 1072, 1074 (Pa. Super. Ct. 1983).

32. BOUVIER'S LAW DICTIONARY 884 (3d rev., 8th ed. 1914).

to choose between two or more courses of action each of which is thought of as permissible."[33] In this discussion I do the same.

Review of discretion is one of the most troublesome aspects of the judicial process. Knowing simply that one is invested with discretion does not tell much. The crucial inquiry, necessarily, is the extent of the discretionary power conferred. The scope of review ranges from rigid limitations, similar to the limited scrutiny of fact-finding determinations, to the extensive review permitted in the review of legal precepts. Language used by appellate courts in review of discretion is unfortunate; often there is sheer hypocrisy in the process. This is best illustrated when an appellate court pontificates that it cannot substitute its discretion for that of the trial court, then proceeds immediately to do just that. Byron comes to mind: "And whispering 'I will ne'er consent'— consented."[34]

An excellent formulation of how to determine the presence of an abuse is found in the following statement: "Discretion is abused when the judicial action is arbitrary, fanciful or unreasonable or where no reasonable man [or woman] would take the view adopted by the trial court."[35]

§ 6.12 Excerpts from Court Opinions

Review of the Exercise of Discretion

Our cases make it clear that an application for a change of venue is addressed to the sound discretion of the trial court, whose exercise of discretion will not be disturbed by an appellate court in the absence of an abuse of discretion.[36]

Appellants claim that the trial court erred in not permitting rebuttal testimony by an expert witness ... Appellee's expert had testified that a prior accident on the same motorcycle was not causally related to the accident in question. Appellants wished to have their expert rebut this with testimony about undetectable damage. The trial

---

33. Henry M. Hart, Jr. & Albert M. Sacks, The Legal Process 144 (1994).

34. Byron, Don Juan, Canto I, St. 117.

35. Golden Gate Hotel Ass'n v. San Francisco, 18 F.3d 1482, 1485 (9th Cir. 1994) (internal quotation marks and citation omitted).

36. Commonwealth v. Romanelli, 485 A.2d 795, 801 (Pa. Super. Ct. 1984).

court and the *en banc* court held that this was inadmissible, as the proffered rebuttal testimony had not been revealed in discovery....

The admission of rebuttal evidence is normally within the discretion of the trial judge.... Even if the trial court erred in this matter—and we do not hold that it did—the excluded testimony was not so critical as to warrant a new trial. The grant or refusal of a new trial by the lower court will not be reversed by this Court in the absence of a clear abuse of discretion or an error of law which controlled the outcome of the case....[37]

———————

In this appeal by the government, brought pursuant to 18 U.S.C. §3731, we are asked to decide whether the district court abused its discretion when it precluded a key government witness from testifying at trial in a criminal case as a sanction for the government's failure to turn over to the defendant certain exculpatory evidence prior to trial. We hold that although the government withheld materially exculpatory evidence in direct violation of a valid district court order, it was an abuse of discretion for the district court to issue a preclusion order based on a violation of *Brady v. Maryland*, 373 U.S. 83, 83 S.Ct. 1194, 10 L.Ed.2d 215 (1963), because the defendant was not prejudiced by the government's nondisclosure.[38]

§6.13 Review of Questions of Law

When it comes to the review of the trial court's determination of the appropriate legal precept, the appellate courts are given the freest of reins. If review of fact finding is at the nadir of the appellate function, the examination of the trial court's selection and interpretation of legal precepts is the zenith. On a legal question, the appellate court is not restricted by the limited review of discretion or by the division of judicial labors which protects findings of fact in the common law tradition and under the constitutions of the various sovereignties. Generally speaking, the appellate court is free to examine *de novo* all aspects of legal precepts—the choice of the controlling precept by the trial tribunal, the interpretation thereof and the application of the precept to the findings of fact.

A reviewing court's function is to determine whether a trial court committed a mistake of sufficient magnitude to require that its judgment be reversed

———————

37. Matsko v. Harley Davidson Motor Co., 473 A.2d 155, 161 (Pa. Super. Ct. 1984).
38. United States v. Starusko, 729 F.2d 256, 257 (3d Cir. 1984).

or vacated. Putting aside those jurisdictions in which appellate courts must search the record for error, the reviewing court's role is inexorably intertwined with the performance of the advocates. An appellate court may, under certain conditions, consider matters *sua sponte* but, generally, when an appellate court considers questions raised by an appellant alleging error, it relies upon the issues set forth by the advocates. The broadest scope of judicial review extends to pure questions of law. Here, review is plenary and the role of the appellant's lawyer is to persuade the reviewing court that the tribunal of the first instance has erred in choosing a legal precept, interpreting that precept or applying that precept.

§ 6.14 Excerpts from Court Opinions

De Novo or Plenary

The standard of review is familiar. Summary judgment may be granted only if no genuine issue of material fact exists. Rule 56(c), F. R. Civ. P.; *Goodman v. Mead Johnson & Co.*, 584 F.2d 566, 573 (3d Cir. 1976), *cert. denied*, 429 U.S. 1038 97 S. Ct. 732, 50 L.Ed.2d 78 (1977). An issue is "genuine" only if the evidence is such that a reasonable jury could find for the nonmoving party. *Anderson v. Liberty Lobby, Inc.*, 477 U.S. 242, 106 S. Ct. 2505, 2509, 91 L.Ed.2d 202 (1986). At the summary judgment stage, "the judge's function is not himself to weigh the evidence and determine the truth of the matter, but to determine whether there is a genuine issue for trial." *Id.*, 106 S. Ct. at 2510. On review, this court applies the same test that the district court should have adopted. *Dunn v. Gannett New York Newspapers, Inc.*, 833 F.2d 446, 449 (3d Cir. 1987).[39]

Rule 52(a) broadly requires that findings of fact not be set aside unless clearly erroneous. It does not make exceptions or purport to exclude certain categories of factual findings from the obligation of a court of appeals to accept a district court's findings unless clearly erroneous. It does not divide facts into categories; in particular, it does not divide findings of fact into those that deal with "ultimate" and those that deal with "subsidiary" facts.

---

39. Floyd v. Lykes Bros. S.S. Co., 844 F.2d 1044, 1045 (3d Cir. 1988).

The Rule does not apply to conclusions of law. The Court of Appeals, therefore, was quite right in saying that if a district court's findings rest on an erroneous view of the law, they may be set aside on that basis.[40]

The [appellants] argue that the district court misapplied the law of personal jurisdiction and New Jersey's conflict of laws rules. Because these issues involve the selection, interpretation, and application of legal precepts, review is plenary.[41]

§ 6.15 Summary

From my twenty years of experience as an adjunct professor at the University of Pittsburgh School of Law, I learned that the average law student leaves law school with virtually no formal study or understanding of the standards of review. Added to this is my very long experience with those lawyers who rarely appear before appellate courts. Like almost all members of the lay world, the neophyte appellate counsel believes that on the appellate level, the court is endowed with total freedom to substitute their views in a *de novo* review in every case, without an understanding of the more limited standards of review, such as clearly erroneous and the intricacies of discretion.

This chapter has emphasized how important it is to recognize that not all judicial review is plenary, that the scope of review is extremely narrow when it comes to fact finding, that the review of the exercise of discretion is somewhat broader but still severely circumscribed and that the broadest review is employed to determine *de novo* error in the choice, interpretation or application of a legal precept.

I am convinced that if reviewing courts required appellate briefs to contain proper statements of trial and appellate court jurisdiction and to set forth the precise scope of review for each point asserted on appeal, not only briefs, but also oral argument would be more effective, producing, in turn, better judicial decisions. More precise in content, stripped of surplusage, opposing briefs could hit the issues head on instead of glancing off. Presented with more accurate and efficient arguments, the courts would upgrade the product of their work while judge-made laws would contribute to a life wholly spirited, ever-improving and basically unimpaired.

---

40. Pullman-Standard v. Swint, 456 U.S. 273, 287 (1982).
41. Dent v. Cunningham, 786 F.2d 173, 175 (3d Cir. 1986).

EXORDIUM

EXCUSE ME, BUT WHAT THE HECK IS AN EXORDIUM?

AN EXORDIUM IS WHAT THE ANCIENTS CALLED AN OPENING STATEMENT THAT TELLS THE WHO, WHAT, WHERE AND HOW OF AN ARGUMENT.

CHAPTER SEVEN

ORIENTATION PARAGRAPH

§ 7.1 Overview

The opening paragraph is the first thing you write when drafting an opinion and the last thing you rewrite. In it, you must let the reader know the scope, theme, content and outcome of the opinion, all within the confines of one or two paragraphs. Crafting the opening or orientation paragraph takes skill and concentration. Skilled writers are highly professional, trained to describe an issue as comprehensively as possible using minimal wordage.

§ 7.2 Drafting the Opening Paragraph

A judge is a professional writer. Whether the judge writes well or poorly, he or she writes for publication. By force of circumstance, everything he or she does in the conduct of his or her office must be expressed in words, preferably—but alas, not always—with a high degree of clarity and precision. Other writers may have the assistance of elegant typography and graphic illustration. The judge is armed only with the figurative pen.

Users of judicial opinions—lawyers, judges, researchers and law students—tend to be very busy. As a result, they have highly selective reading habits. They need and expect to know what a given case is about, and the opening of an opinion should tell them immediately. Detective mysteries and narratives with O. Henry surprise endings have their place—in fiction. Apply these techniques to the writing of opinions and you risk losing your audience. Instead, the opinion writer must give an early signal to his potential reader. That signal is the *exordium*, the opening or orientation paragraph.

Professor Stevenson observes that, as readers, we crave an immediate sense of overview. At the beginning of an opinion we are not interested in hearing all the details of the case. We want to know whether we should continue reading, we want to know what kind of case this is, what issues it addresses, and what the judge has concluded. We do not want to be forced to read a detailed history of the case until we know that the case is relevant to our interests.[1]

These views are shared by many experienced, literate judges. For example, George Rose Smith, a veteran Arkansas Supreme Court justice, gave this valuable advice:

> The importance of the first paragraph cannot be overemphasized. Remember the advice to the cub reporter: Let the opening paragraph of a news story answer broadly such questions as Who? Where? When? What? Why? For judicial cubs there is similar advice. The readability of an opinion is nearly always improved if the opening paragraph (occasionally it takes two) answers three questions. First, what kind of case is this: Divorce, foreclosure, workmen's compensation, and so on? Second, what roles, plaintiff or defendant, did the appellant and the appellee have in the trial court? Third, what was the trial court's decision? A fourth question, [w]hat are the issues on appeal?, should also be answered unless the contentions are too numerous to be easily summarized.
>
> Such an opening paragraph leads the reader into the opinion with enough information for him to understand it as he proceeds. By contrast, an opinion that begins with a two or three page narrative of the litigation, in chronological sequence, with a multitude of dates and other details, fails to tell the reader what to look for. More often than not some rereading becomes necessary when the opinion writer finally lets the cat out of the bag by revealing the secret of what the case is all about.[2]

The late Judge Frederick G. Hamley, who sat on the Ninth Circuit after serving as Washington State's chief justice, and was an acknowledged pioneer in continuing education programs for judges, observed:

> The purpose of this part of the opinion is to set the stage for the discussion to follow. It tells the reader at once whether he should begin thinking about contract law, tort law, criminal law, or some other area in the vast field of jurisprudence. Such a statement also establishes at the outset the roles of the plaintiff and defendant as appellant or appellee. It may also supply other essential information. For example, it

---

1. Dwight W. Stevenson, *Writing Effective Opinions*, 59 JUDICATURE 134, 136–37 (1975).

2. George Rose Smith, *A Primer of Opinion Writing, For Four New Judges*, 21 ARK. L. REV. 197, 204–05 (1967).

can inform a reader as to whether there was a jury trial and, if so, whether the judgment follows the verdict.[3]

Cardozo noted that "[o]ften clarity is gained by a brief and almost sententious statement at the outset of the problem to be attacked. Then may come a fuller statement of the facts, rigidly pared down, however, in almost every case, to those that are truly essential as opposed to those that are decorative and adventitious. If these are presented with due proportion and selection, our conclusion ought to follow so naturally and inevitably as almost to prove itself."[4]

§ 7.3 The Bottom Line: Five Questions

Writing the opening should discipline you to focus on the central issues of the case and to verify the procedural history of the case.

In your opening, you should answer these questions:

Who: Who is taking the appeal? Who won in the trial court?

What: What is the specific nature of the main issues and the area of law implicated in the appeal?

When: When was the alleged error committed? Is the appeal from an adverse verdict because of insufficiency of evidence? Is it alleged that error was committed during the pleading stage, at pretrial, trial or post-trial?

Where: Where does the appeal come from? A trial court? An administrative agency?

How: How did the final judgment arise? Was the judgment entered as a result of summary judgment, a directed verdict, a jury verdict or a nonjury award?

Whether the holding of the case should be included at the beginning as well as the end of an opinion is a matter of style about which reasonable judges may differ. I will not attempt to improve upon the excellent analysis offered by B.E. Witkin:

---

3. FREDERICK G. HAMLEY, INTERNAL OPERATING PROCEDURES OF APPELLATE COURTS 29–37 (1961), *reprinted in* ROBERT A. LEFLAR, APPELLATE JUDICIAL OPINIONS 172 (1974).

4. Benjamin N. Cardozo, *Law and Literature*, 14 YALE L.J. 705 (1925), *reprinted in* SELECTED WRITINGS OF BENJAMIN NATHAN CARDOZO 339, 352–53 (Margaret E. Hall, ed. 1967); *see also* FRANK M. COFFIN, THE WAYS OF A JUDGE 159 (1980) (explaining how the first words of an opinion slowly emerge on the blank sheet of paper).

§7.4 Preview of the Opinion[5]

By B.E. Witkin

The *preview* type of orientation statement … may cover all the conventional items (action, parties, and issues) or omit some, but it always adds one significant element: the conclusion the opinion will reach after principles and authorities have been discussed. In doing so it follows the best traditions of journalistic reporting.

Some writers prefer to proceed objectively, weighing alternative principles and precedents, and stating the conclusion only when it has been justified by the discussion. It is a familiar literary practice to allow the fact story to unfold, and the issues to emerge, without disclosing the conclusion. It has even been suggested that opinions giving a preview of the holding lend support to the dark suspicion that judges sometimes reach a conclusion by intuition or snap judgment and then look for reasons.

These considerations cannot be ignored, but they only emphasize the point that there is no single approved method of introducing an opinion. The advantages of a preview of the holding are, in most cases, significant:

First, its usefulness to third persons—associates on the bench, other courts, lawyers, and law writers—is obvious. Most readers today are busy readers. In magazines, the essayist or editor frequently presents just this kind of statement to announce what the text is about. In a judicial opinion, why should a reader have to wait until the fourth or fourteenth page to discover how the point was decided? With this information divulged at the outset, a reading of the facts, proceedings below, contentions on appeal, and authorities and reasoning is more informed and fruitful.

Second, the preview introductory statement also helps the opinion writer. The first draft may set forth the facts and systematically examine the contentions, large and small. If, after drafting the conclusion, the author simply duplicates it at the beginning, and then reads through the opinion, he may note, as many a reader would, that some of the issues and factual details are tangential or irrelevant to the point on which the case was finally decided and are not worth keeping in the final draft.

---

5. B.E. Witkin, Manual on Appellate Court Opinions §57, at 92–94 (1977).

Needless to say, the preview statement is only a guide to intelligent reading of the opinion. It is not intended to be a perfect and complete repetition of the conclusion or summary of the holding, and it should not be assigned to that purpose. This is particularly true if the opinion deals with multiple issues and if it is inconvenient to set out each in detail. The orientation statement may note generally that many points have been raised and considered in reaching the conclusion. However, there is nothing wrong with a preview that states each issue and the conclusion reached on each.

Since the preview merely repeats the conclusion reached in the normal process at the end of the discussion, it should be the last part of the opinion to be written. The author can then fill in the blank left at the beginning, writing with finality and not by guesswork. To state the expected conclusion before the writing is completed makes the task of impartial discussion more difficult. Opinion writers, like other law writers, often discover, in Justice Traynor's words that "tentative views will not jell in the writing."[6] And there is the horrendous picture conjured up by Lasky: "Like Procrustes and his iron bed, the opinion lops off some of the facts or some of the law if they are too much for the desired conclusion or stretches them if they fall somewhat short."[7]

§ 7.5 Previews: A Personal Preference

I try to use a preview statement at the beginning of my signed opinions. From an author's standpoint, I think this helps me to write tighter opinions by forcing me to determine what the central issues are and what can be ignored. It helps separate the important from the merely interesting. I hope it helps me to resist the human tendency to ramble. From the standpoint of the opinion reader—the litigants, the trial court, the lawyers and the commentators—the preview is extremely useful because it provides them both the question posed in the opinion and the answer.

The simplest form of preview statement sets forth the legal issue and the answer to it in the most concise form possible. Examine the following opening paragraph; this is a classic:

---

6. Roger J. Traynor, *Some Open Questions on the Work of State Appellate Courts*, 24 U. Chi. L. Rev. 211, 218 (1957).

7. Moses Lasky, *Observing Appellate Opinions from Below the Bench*, 49 Cal. L. Rev. 831, 839 (1961).

We are called upon to determine whether "attempted assault" is a crime in the state of California. We conclude that it is not.[8]

§ 7.6 Excerpts from Court Opinions

§ 7.6.1 Effective Opening Paragraphs

This litigation arises out of an installment contract for the sale of quantities of battery lead by a Canadian seller to a Pennsylvania buyer. The seller sued for the price of a carload of lead delivered but not paid for. The buyer counterclaimed for damages caused by the seller's failure to deliver the remaining installments covered by the contract. The district court sitting without a jury allowed recovery on both claim and counterclaim. This is an appeal by the seller from the judgment against him on the counterclaim. The ultimate question is whether the buyer had committed such a breach of contract as constituted a repudiation justifying rescission by the seller.[9]

The issue on this appeal is whether the district court or the court of appeals has jurisdiction to review certain regulations promulgated by the Administrator of the Environmental Protection Agency under the Federal Water Pollution Control Act Amendments of 1972 (the Act). 33 U.S.C. §§ 1251–1376. The district court held that jurisdiction lay exclusively in the court of appeals and sustained a motion to dismiss. We affirm.[10]

The question in these consolidated cases is whether a state prosecutor may seek to impeach a defendant's exculpatory story, told for the first time at trial, by cross-examining the defendant about his failure to have told the story after receiving *Miranda* warnings at the time of his arrest. We conclude that use of the defendant's post-arrest silence

---

8. *In re* James M., 510 P.2d 33, 34 (Cal. 1973).
9. Plotnick v. Penn. Smelting & Refining Co., 194 F.2d 859, 861 (3d Cir. 1952).
10. Am. Petrol. Inst. v. Train, 526 F.2d 1343, 1344 (10th Cir. 1975).

in this manner violates due process, and therefore reverse the convictions of both petitioners.[11]

_____

Qualified lawyers admitted to practice in other States may be admitted to the Virginia bar "on motion," that is, without taking the bar examination which Virginia otherwise requires. The State conditions such admission on a showing, among other matters, that the applicant is a permanent resident of Virginia. The question for decision is whether this residency requirement violates the Privileges and Immunities Clause of the United States Constitution, Art. IV, § 2. We hold that it does.[12]

_____

The issue raised on this appeal is whether the method devised by appellant, Bruce Howes, which makes possible the faithful transfer of color art work to fabric by means of treated heat transfer paper is a process which is patentable under 35 U.S.C. § 101. We believe that it is and reverse the order of the district court which determined as a matter of law that it was not.[13]

_____

Three principal issues are presented in this appeal from sentences imposed on a guilty verdict in a criminal anti-trust prosecution: whether the proof at trial varied from the indictment charging a single, continuing conspiracy; whether the government introduced sufficient evidence to prove the interstate commerce element of the Sherman Act violation; and whether this court should set aside or modify, on appeal, the one million dollar fine levied against defendant Fischbach & Moore. Appellants assert several less-significant arguments, including the admission of an allegedly prejudicial government exhibit; prosecutorial misconduct during closing argument; errors in jury instructions; and the denial of a continuance to defendant Arbogast. Because we find no reversible error, we affirm the judgment of the district court.[14]

_____

11. Doyle v. Ohio, 426 U.S. 610, 611 (1976).
12. Supreme Court of Va. v. Friedman, 487 U.S. 59, 61 (1988).
13. Howes v. Great Lakes Press Corp., 679 F.2d 1023, 1024 (2d Cir. 1982).
14. United States v. Fischbach & Moore, Inc., 750 F.2d 1183, 1187–88 (3d Cir. 1984).

§ 7.6.2 Less Effective Openings

Gary Lee Roberson is presently serving a term of imprisonment of not less than ten nor more than twenty years based upon convictions obtained in a jury trial conducted in March of 1976 before the Honorable Lawrence Prattis. Roberson's convictions included robbery and rape. A direct appeal to our court resulted in an affirmance of the judgment of sentence.[15]

We have consolidated the tax appeals of Affiliated F.M. Insurance Company and Providence Washington Insurance Company from decisions of the Board of Finance and Revenue sustaining the settlements by the Department of Revenue of the gross premium tax of each for the years ending respectively December 31, 1977, and December 31, 1976.

The facts in both cases have been stipulated of record. We adopt these as our findings of fact. The stipulations are identical except with respect to the numerical details concerning the refunds and settlement of each petitioner. In the course of our discussion we shall refer to such of the stipulated facts as we deem essential to disposition of the appeal.[16]

George and Sarah Lehan (appellees) own real estate on which their residence is situated in Butler Township, Luzerne County, abutting the south side of Legislative Route 653. Near the western boundary of appellees' property, the Pennsylvania Department of Transportation (appellant) maintains an earthen ditch running in a north-south direction designed to carry runoff water away from the state highway. Originally, the runoff is collected in a drain on the north side of said highway and flows under the roadway through a pipe which empties into the ditch on appellees' property.

For a number of years, appellees' neighbors, whose properties lie on the north side of Legislative Route 653, have been discharging sewage and other waste materials into appellant's drain which by grav-

---

15. Commonwealth v. Roberson, 473 A.2d 147, 147–48 (Pa. Super. Ct. 1984)

16. Providence Wash. Ins. Co. v. Commonwealth, Dep't of Revenue, 463 A.2d 68, 69 (Pa. Commw. Ct. 1983).

ity flows onto appellees' property through the aforementioned drainage system. As a result, appellees' well has been polluted and other distasteful conditions have been created on their land.[17]

Author's Note: *The question for decision was whether the Department of Transportation had effected a de facto taking of landowner's property by permitting the discharge of sewage into the highway drainage system, thereby entitling the landowner to damages under the Eminent Domain Code.*

§ 7.6.3 Mystery Stories

It was a tragic end to a pleasant day. Patricia Oja, with her mother and aunt, Sally and Suoma Oja, had left home in Ilwaco that morning of October 16, 1965, to go shopping in Longview. The three, with Patricia driving, were returning on Highway No. 401 in a 1964 Chevrolet in the early evening. It was dark, raining, and slightly foggy on the highway when, near the town limits of Naselle, the Oja car, moving in a southerly direction around a broad sweeping curve to the left, was struck head on by the car driven by defendant George H. Eike. In the terrific impact, Sally and Suoma Oja were killed, but Patricia lived to describe the accident in court.[18]

On June 10, 1971, H. O. Hirt, President and Manager of the Erie Insurance Exchange, discharged Sanford Dunson, a black man, from his employment with the Exchange. On June 14, 1971, Dunson filed a formal complaint with the Erie Human Relations Commission alleging unlawful racial discrimination in his discharge. Subsequently, on March 6, 1972, after two informal investigatory hearings revealed that probable cause did exist for crediting Dunson's allegations, a formal public hearing on the charge was held. On April 14, 1972, the Commission determined that the Exchange was guilty of unlawful racial discrimination in the discharge of Dunson. The Commission ordered the Exchange to reinstate Dunson to the position he had formerly held and to recompense Dunson for back pay from the date of his discharge. The Exchange received notice of this adjudication on April

---

17. Lehan v. Commonwealth, Dep't of Transp. 349 A.2d 492, 493 (Pa. Commw. Ct. 1975).

18. State v. Eike, 435 P.2d 680, 681 (Wash. 1967).

15, 1972. However, it failed to comply with the Commission's directives; nor did it appeal the Commission's findings.

Failing to obtain compliance with its order the Commission, on October 16, 1972, filed a complaint in equity with the Court of Common Pleas of Erie County seeking a mandatory injunction to compel compliance with its prior order. Annexed to the complaint was a copy of the Commission's findings and order. The Exchange then filed preliminary objections in the nature of a demurrer on the grounds that the Commission, in its complaint, had failed to sufficiently allege unlawful racial discrimination and had failed to adequately identify the reason for Dunson's discharge. The court, after a review of the record, sustained the Exchange's preliminary objections and dismissed the complaint. The court found that the Commission had improperly concluded there was unlawful racial discrimination in Dunson's discharge.[19]

Author's Note: *The next two openings were written by the same judge, released on the same day, and treated kindred issues.*

The question here is whether the Due Process Clause of the Fourteenth Amendment entitles a state prisoner to a hearing when he is transferred to a prison the conditions of which are substantially less favorable to the prisoner, absent a state law or practice conditioning such transfers on proof of serious misconduct or the occurrence of other events. We hold that it does not.[20]

On June 7, 1972, respondent Haymes was removed from his assignment as inmate clerk in the law library at the Attica Correctional Facility in the State of New York. That afternoon Haymes was observed circulating among other inmates a document prepared by him and at the time signed by 82 other prisoners. Among other things, each signatory complained that he had been deprived of legal assistance as the result of the removal of Haymes and another inmate from the prison law library. The document, which was addressed to a federal judge but

------

19. Erie Human Relations Comm'n *ex rel.* Dunson v. Erie Ins. Exch., 348 A.2d 742, 743 (Pa. Super. Ct. 1975).

20. Meachum v. Fano, 427 U.S. 215, 216 (1976).

sought no relief, was seized and held by prison authorities. On June 8, Haymes was advised that he would be transferred to Clinton Correctional Facility, which, like Attica, was a maximum-security institution. The transfer was effected the next day. No loss of good time, segregated confinement, loss of privileges, or any other disciplinary measures accompanied the transfer. On August 3, Haymes filed a petition with the United States District Court which was construed by the judge to be an application under 42 U.S.C. §1983 and 28 U.S.C. §1343 seeking relief against petitioner Montanye, the then Superintendent at Attica. The petition complained that the seizure and retention of the document, despite requests for its return, not only violated Administrative Bulletin No. 20, which allegedly made any communication to a court privileged and confidential, but also infringed Haymes' federally guaranteed right to petition the court for redress of grievances. It further asserted that Haymes' removal to Clinton was to prevent him from pursuing his remedies and also was in reprisal for his having rendered legal assistance to various prisoners as well as having, along with others, sought to petition the court for redress.[21]

---

21. Montayne v. Haymes, 427 U.S. 236, 237–38 (1976).

CHAPTER EIGHT

SUMMARY OF ISSUES

§ 8.1 What Issues Do We Address?

The next task for the opinion writer is to present a summary of issues for review. Here, too, is a threshold question: Must we write on every issue presented in the appellant's or petitioner's brief? The answer: It depends.

§ 8.2 Appeal as of Right or by Writ of Certiorari

What issues must be addressed depends, in the first instance, on what court you are in. If yours is a certiorari court, you probably accept only certain questions for review. This is true in the U.S. Supreme Court, which requires "[t]he questions presented for review, expressed concisely in relation to the circumstances of the case, without unnecessary detail."[1] If yours is a court with mandatory jurisdiction over a case, as in an appeal of right, you may generally address more issues than a court with discretionary jurisdiction, as in an appeal by writ of certiorari. Most appeals to the U.S. Courts of Appeals are as of right.

Most states have a three-tiered judicial system with two tiers of appellate relief. Only 10 states and the District of Columbia still have only one appellate court.[2] Many states with intermediate appellate courts do not allow appeals as of right to the state's highest court.[3] Therefore, litigants desiring further review are relegated to certiorari procedures.

---

1. SUP. CT. R. 14(a) ("The questions should be short and should not be argumentative or repetitive.... [A]ny question presented is deemed to comprise every subsidiary question fairly included therein. Only the questions set out in the petition, or fairly included therein, will be considered by the Court.").

2. COURT STATISTICS PROJECT, STATE COURT CASELOAD STATISTICS (National Center for State Courts 2009).

3. DAVID R. ROTTMAN & SHAUNA M. STRICKLAND, STATE COURT ORGANIZATION 2004 (U.S. Department of Justice, Bureau of Justice Statistics 2006).

In some states, court rules provide that writs of certiorari may only be issued in certain types of cases.[4] In a majority of state courts, whether a writ issues is purely a matter of discretion.

Even if your state does not have a rule limiting review, review should be limited to the issues presented and preserved in the petition for certiorari. The same considerations that prompted the adoption of Supreme Court Rule 14— limited resources, jurisdictional limits and institutional integrity—counsel all third-tier courts to address only the issue for which certiorari was granted. Most state courts have adopted a similar rule.[5]

§ 8.3 Courts of General Jurisdiction

If yours is an appellate court of general jurisdiction, it decides what points raised in the briefs and preserved for appeal deserve discussion in the opinion. Preferably reached at the multi-judge decision conference, this determination depends upon whether the issue (a) is one of novel, precedential or institutional value or is totally foreclosed by a line of cases establishing a rockbound precedent (more about this species later), (b) is relevant to the controlling issue, or (c) is a portion of an interdependent argument that need not be reached because preliminary issues totally foreclose further discussion.

At least one direction is in order: The judge is not required to discuss every issue presented in the briefs. Judges, not lawyers, control the opinion.

When I see an opinion heavily overwritten, it is a signal to me that it is the product not of a judge, but of a law clerk, a person who is generally not sophisticated or perhaps confident enough to separate that which is important from that which is merely interesting. I see a confounding prolixity in many opinions issued by those of my colleagues who are too timid to wield a firm and uncompromising blue pencil. More than 100 years ago, in his *Treatise on Evidence*, Dean John H. Wigmore made this point very clear as he reacted to the many thousands of judicial opinions he had studied in the course of preparing his treatise. Some of the criticisms he set down then are, unfortunately, still appropriate today:

> Overconsideration of every point of law raised on the briefs. This shows faithfulness and industry, for which we should be and are grate-

---

4. Marlin O. Osthus, State Intermediate Appellate Courts 10 (1980).
5. Robert L. Stern, Appellate Practice in the United States 142–43 (1981).

ful. But it tends to remove the decision from the really vital issues of each case and to transform the opinion into a list of rulings on academic legal assertions. The opinion is as related to the meat of the case as a library catalogue is to the contents of the books. This is far from exercising the true and high function of an appellate court.[6]

Thus, you need not address the merits if the decision is based on lack of jurisdiction, or if you find that the complaining party lacked standing. If you agree to a judgment notwithstanding the verdict, the considerations relating to a new trial become moot, unnecessary for discussion.

If a new trial is granted on the basis of an error in the admission of evidence, it is usually unnecessary to determine whether a proper objection to the judge's jury instructions was made. Yet there are times when an opinion that grants a new trial on one issue — for example, the introduction of evidence — requires discussion of other issues. The reviewing court may need guidance to avoid matters raised on appeal that will be repeated at the second trial. In performing this function, the appellate court gives directions to the trial court.

§ 8.4 Clean-Up Phrases

In a civil case where the court decides not to discuss all the issues presented in the briefs, a clean-up phrase may suffice:

We have considered the other contentions presented by the appellant, or
We have considered the other issues presented by the appellant and conclude that no further discussion is necessary, or
Because we have reversed the judgment (or granted a new trial) on the basis of statutory law, it is not necessary to meet the constitutional law contention.

In a criminal law case, on the other hand — whether on direct appeal or collateral review — the better practice is to list the issues that have been rejected by the court without having been discussed. This is important in order for a record to be kept of what the court has considered, no matter how frivolous the contention. If an evidentiary ruling was presented or rejected in the direct appeal, without discussion, a notation in the opinion will alert courts in a subsequent post-conviction collateral attack that the issue has been raised

---

6. 1 John Henry Wigmore, Evidence in Trials at Common Law § 8a, at 617 (1983).

and a ruling made. When and if the unsuccessful state prisoner files a federal habeas corpus petition under 28 U.S.C. §2254, a record of what was presented to the state court system will then be available to the federal court to help determine whether the petitioner has exhausted state remedies on every issue of constitutional law presented in the federal habeas petition, thus satisfying the concerns of federalism and comity.

§8.5 Excerpts from Court Opinions

We have considered the appellants' contentions 1) that the district court erred in refusing their lawyer's request to leave the courtroom to confer with the appellants after the voir dire examination of the jurors; 2) that the court improperly restricted the scope of the appellants' voir dire examination of prospective jurors; 3) that the court erred in admitting certain items of evidence allegedly prejudicial to appellants; 4) that the court committed reversible error in referring to "statutes" (in the plural) allegedly violated by the appellants, and in condoning similar reference by the Government, though in fact the appellants were charged with violating only a single provision of Mississippi law; 5) that the evidence was insufficient to sustain a verdict of conviction and the denial of a motion for acquittal; 6) that the court erred in permitting FBI agent Files to testify as to an allegedly inculpatory statement made by Peter J. Martino shortly after his arrest in the presence of counsel and after he had been advised of his rights; 7) that the district court made prejudicial remarks concerning the appellants in the presence of the jury; 8) that the court erred in overruling the appellants' motion to dismiss the indictment because it charged the appellants with bookmaking, allegedly not a violation of Mississippi law; 9) that the court erred in denying the appellants' motion for a bill of particulars; 10) that the court erroneously failed to instruct the jury as to the elements of the Mississippi law which the appellants were charged with violating. None of these contentions has sufficient merit to warrant further discussion. Affirmed.[7]

We have considered the remaining contentions raised by appellant and do not believe that the district court's treatment of them amounted

---

7. United States v. Martino, 459 F.2d 1032, 1033 (5th Cir. 1972) (per curiam).

to reversible error, viz., that appellant alleged facts sufficient to establish a conspiracy among the police officers, that the district court abused its discretion in denying a request to amend the complaint, and that it erred in applying the teachings of *Imbler v. Pachtman*, 424 U.S. 409 (1976), to the actions of prosecutor Hepting, and in determining that the conduct of the police officers did not constitute the proximate cause of Williams' injury.[8]

§ 8.6 Judicial Reaction to Advocacy

We judges react differently to the stimuli of advocacy. I recognize that our initial impressions vary, of course, but I must confess to an idiosyncrasy. When faced with a brief that raises only three points, I breathe a sigh of satisfaction and conclude that the brief writer really has something to say.

I probably react in the same manner, or perhaps to a slightly lesser degree, when four or five points are presented. Beyond this point, I must confess, a small beast bearing the name of intolerance begins to nibble at my habitually disinterested judgment. With over 40 years of federal appellate court experience behind me, I can say that even when we reverse a trial court, it is rare that a brief successfully demonstrates that the trial court committed more than one or two reversible errors. I have said in open court that when I read an appellant's brief containing seven points or more, a presumption arises that there is no merit to *any* of them. I do not say that this is an irrebuttable presumption, but it is a presumption nevertheless that reduces the effectiveness of the writer's brief. As James Russell Lowell wrote, "In general those who have nothing to say/Contrive to spend the longest time in doing it."[9] Appellate advocacy is measured by effectiveness, not loquaciousness.

Many of my friends in the bar have a sort of Pavlovian reaction when they encounter my distaste for shotgun briefs. "We don't know what may attract the attention of the given court at any time," they say, "so we have to file briefs that touch all bases; we *have* to use the shotgun approach." Many lawyers sum up their reasons for producing briefs that don't clearly indicate what the court should consider by saying: "I don't know what the court will consider to be important." I respond, simply, with my own three-word riposte: "You *should* know!" With the widespread availability of Westlaw and Lexis, any reasonably competent researcher should be able to determine which aspects of a given

---

8. Williams v. Hepting, 844 F.2d 138, 145 (3d Cir. 1988).
9. 9 JAMES RUSSELL LOWELL, THE WRITINGS OF JAMES RUSSELL LOWELL 142 (1890).

case have merit or don't have merit, and, therefore, will or will not command the interest of a given court.

But I have digressed. You will recall that even before you wrote the introductory paragraphs, you listed the issue or issues to be discussed in the opinion. In a multi-issue case, the statement of issues may be expressed as a summary paragraph of all issues to be presented. This summary may repeat the major issue identified in the opening and a statement of its subordinate points.

§ 8.7 Summary of Issues

Some judges do not present an introductory summary of issues. Instead, they state each issue separately as a topic sentence that introduces discussion of one particular segment. As a general rule, you should set forth the statement of all the issues very early in the opinion. The reason is obvious: You are giving the reader a preview of what the opinion will discuss. There are times, though, when you do not want to give the same dignity to each and every issue.

The summary of issues is prepared after preliminary research has been completed and the decision has been made as to what points the opinion will cover. Hours of opinion writing and opinion circulating may be saved if there can be a collegial agreement at the decision conference as to what issues the opinion should discuss.

Where in the opinion do we place the statement of issues? I believe the statement usually should precede the narration of the facts. This is a kind of self-imposed safeguard because it tends to restrict the necessary facts to only the material adjudicative facts, to the facts necessary to the treatment of the issues that have been set forth. This does not mean that the statement of issues must *always* precede the statement of facts in the final draft of the opinion. That may depend on style. In any event, the reader who knows the issues before reading the facts will find the facts much more meaningful. The effect is like reading a review of a movie before seeing it, so that one knows what to look for in the theater.

The phrasing of the issue must be as fair and as neutral as possible. This is critical for several reasons. The litigants must get the impression that the court was fair and not one-sided. If you incline away from absolute neutrality, at least bend over backwards to express the question most favorably to the party you rule against. Recall Justice Frankfurter's statement: "In law also the right answer usually depends on putting the right question."[10] Judge Abraham Freed-

---

10. Estate of Rogers v. Commissioner, 320 U.S. 410, 413 (1943).

man, my colleague of happy memory, used to say, "How you come out here depends on how you come in." Unfortunately, we do at times encounter skewed statements of issues. An example of a slanted and unfair statement comes to mind. It emanated from Justice Fortas, writing for the Court in *United States v. Yazell*: "Specifically, the question presented is whether, in the circumstances of this case, the Federal Government, in its zealous pursuit of the balance due on a disaster loan made by the Small Business Administration, may obtain judgment against Ethel Mae Yazell of Lampasas, Texas."[11]

With the "question" so framed, could there be any doubt about the "answer"?

§ 8.8 Excerpts from Court Opinions

Justice Fortas was not alone in this practice. Consider the "neutrality" in the two following examples:

§ 8.8.1 Statements of Issues

The crucial question we face here is whether a citizen may properly be subjected to the peering of the policeman who, without a search warrant, walks over ground to which the public has not been invited, but which has been reserved for private enjoyment, stands by a window on the side of a house and peeks through a two-inch gap between the drawn window shade and the sill, and thus manages to observe the conduct of those within the residence. We conclude that the questioned police procedure too closely resembles the process of the police state, too dangerously intrudes upon the individual's reasonable expectancy of privacy, and thus too clearly transgresses constitutional principle; the prosecution cannot introduce into evidence, and the courts cannot be tainted with, that which the intrusion yields.[12]

We must adjudicate another case involving ambiguous provisions in a certificate of insurance pursuant to a group insurance policy. On countless occasions we have inveighed against the careless draftsmanship of documents of insurance and have decried the evil social consequences that flow from lack of clarity. [Citations omitted.] We

---

11. United States v. Yazell, 382 U.S. 341, 342–43 (1966).
12. Lorenzana v. Superior Court, 511 P.2d 33, 35 (Cal. 1973).

have emphasized that the uncertain clause leaves in its murky wake not only the disillusioned insured and the protesting insurer but also the anguished court.[13]

§ 8.8.2 Phrasing the Issue

If you are not careful in phrasing the issue, a dissenter may complain and dilute the efficacy of your opinion. Consider the following example:

> Justice Frankfurter would teach us that "[i]n law ... the right an-swer usually depends upon putting the right question." If the ques-tion is, as [the majority] states in [the] opening sentence, "whether the acts of the defendant come within the privilege to interfere with the contractual relations of a competitor," much leeway is provided to frame the answer. If, as stated nine paragraphs later, "[t]he question on this appeal is whether the plaintiff adduced sufficient evidence to support the jury's finding of an absence of privilege," the parameters for furnishing the answer are severely circumscribed. I am in com-plete agreement with the latter statement of the issue before us. Thus, the function of this reviewing court is simply to evaluate the quan-tum of evidence.[14]

Implicated here is more than the consideration of convincing the litigant and the reader that the court has been objective. The subsequent value of the opinion as a forceful precedent may depend upon the neutrality manifested in the statement of issues. What Justice Walter V. Shaefer of Illinois once stated in another context is relevant here: "[I]t remains true that an opinion which does not within its own confines exhibit an awareness of relevant considera-tions, whose premises are concealed, or whose logic is faulty is not likely to enjoy either a long life or the capacity to generate offspring."[15]

§ 8.8.3 Neutral Issue Summaries

> Initially, for the sake of clarity, we shall set forth what is not dis-puted. First, there is no question that the counts in negligence and strict liability under 402A are barred by the two-year statute. Second,

---

13. Bareno v. Empl'rs Life Ins. Co. of Wausau, 500 P.2d 889, 890 (Cal. 1972).

14. Kademenos v. Equitable Life Assur. Soc'y of U.S., 513 F.2d 1073, 1078 (3d Cir. 1975) (Aldisert, J., dissenting).

15. Walter V. Schaefer, *Precedent and Policy*, 34 U. Chi. L. Rev. 3, 11 (1966).

a prerequisite to an action for breach of warranty is that there must be a sale. Clearly, the only "sale" in the instant case was the transaction involving the ladder. As to West Penn Power Company, the Bahr Brothers and the Slovenian Hall Association of Broughton, there was no "sale" and therefore no viable breach of warranty claim. Third, *Salvador II* unequivocally disposes of Mr. Williams' suit. He is, as an employee of B & M, a third party to the sale of the ladder and, therefore, his breach of warranty action is barred by the two-year statute of limitations. [Citation omitted.] Fourth, Mr. Banks is a direct purchaser only from Commercial Services Company; he is a third party to the sale of the ladder from Reimann and Georger, Inc. to Commercial Services Company. Thus, under *Salvador II*, Mr. Banks' action is likewise barred by the two-year statute of limitations. In sum, what remains is Mr. and Mrs. Banks' breach of warranty claim against Commercial Services Company. It is to this aspect of the lawsuit that we must determine whether the Code's four-year statute or the two-year personal injury statute applies. Specifically, does the rationale enunciated in *Salvador II* logically extend to the instant situation where the direct purchaser is the injured party?[16]

The issues pertinent to our resolution of this matter are:

A. Do members of the SPCA who are receiving or eligible to receive pensions have a vested contractual right such that the renders them creditors to the SPCA thus entitled to priority treatment over the other members upon dissolution?

B. Should the assets of the SPCA which remain after the satisfaction of creditors and other obligations be distributed to the membership on a pro rata basis?

C. Should those members of the SPCA who ceased paying dues pursuant to the 1974 moratorium on the payment thereof, be liable for interest on their dues balance?

These issues were raised by all the parties, with the exception of the issue of payment of interest on dues owed to the SPCA which was raised only by the RSPAP, and we will address them seriatim.[17]

---

16. Williams v. W. Penn. Power Co., 460 A.2d 278, 281 (Pa. Super. Ct. 1983).

17. *In re* Petition of Bd. of Directors of State Police Civic Ass'n, 472 A.2d 731, 735 (Pa. Commw. Ct. 1984).

While four separate appeals have been filed, we are presented with only two issues. First, the Kozubs, the Wykes and the Estate of Trzyna claim that the trial court erred in refusing to allow the admission of the proffered evidence against DOT, which necessarily culminated in verdicts in DOT's favor. Second, the Estate of Trzyna claims that the trial court erred in directing verdicts against the Estate when it ruled that Robert Elliot had not been negligent as a matter of law.[18]

On appeal, Papercraft presses three basic contentions. First, it argues that the district court erred in assessing penalties under the FTC Act, which has a maximum daily fine of $10,000, rather than under the Clayton Act, which has a maximum daily fine of $5,000. Second, Papercraft urges that the district court erred in using December 16, 1973 as the date from which to calculate the penalty. Third, Papercraft argues that the district court erred in applying the relevant criteria to fix the daily penalty at $7,500. Specifically, the company contends that the court erred in its considerations of the "public interest" and of "good faith", and that it "relied upon clearly erroneous findings, reasoning and conclusions as to Papercraft's 'profits' and their relevance." Appellant's Brief at 16–17.

We will treat these arguments seriatim.[19]

§ 8.8.4 Issues Summarized in Opening Paragraphs

This is an appeal from judgment of sentence dated September 24, 1981. Appellant, Charles Frisbie, raises two issues for our consideration. The first issue is whether the trial judge erred in ruling that the evidence presented at appellant's trial was not sufficient to put appellant's sanity in issue. The second issue is whether the trial judge erred in sentencing appellant to one year probation on each of nine counts of recklessly endangering another person when these charges arose out of an automobile accident resulting from one unlawful act. Of these two issues, we find only the second to be meritorious. We there-

---

18. Wyke v. Ward, 474 A.2d 375, 397 (Pa. Commw. Ct. 1984).
19. United States v. Papercraft Corp., 540 F.2d 131, 135 (3d Cir. 1976).

fore vacate the sentences imposed below on all counts of recklessly endangering another person and remand for resentencing.[20]

Appellant was convicted in a nonjury trial of retail theft, third offense and sentenced to 3 1/2 to 7 years imprisonment. Two issues are raised on this direct appeal: (1) whether the trial court erred in denying appellant's petition to dismiss the complaint pursuant to Pa. R. Crim. P. 1100 and (2) whether the trial court erred in accepting into evidence appellant's prior, uncounseled summary retail theft convictions to raise the grade of the instant charges to a felony. Finding merit in appellant's first argument, we vacate judgment of sentence and discharge appellant.[21]

After a jury had by verdict determined that appellant was guilty of robbery and trial counsel had filed post-verdict motions, the trial court, upon the *pro se* petition of appellant, appointed new counsel who filed amended motions for a new trial and in arrest of judgment which included allegations of ineffectiveness of trial counsel. Following the denial of these motions, appellant was sentenced to a term of imprisonment of from four and one-half years to nine years. This direct appeal followed. We affirm.

Appellant contends that (1) the evidence was insufficient to sustain the conviction; (2) the trial court erred in refusing to charge the jury that they could find appellant guilty of theft only; and (3) the trial court erred in ruling that a prior conviction could be used to impeach his credibility. Appellant also contends that trial counsel was ineffective for (1) failing to file pre-trial motions to suppress identification evidence; (2) failing to request a pre-trial lineup; and (3) failing to object when an expert witness allegedly testified beyond the scope of his expertise. The distinguished Judge John F. Rauhauser, Jr., in his opinion denying the post-trial motions, has so ably discussed these claims of error that we only address the contention that the trial court erred in ruling that the prior conviction of appellant in 1976 was admissible to impeach his credibility.[22]

---

20. Commonwealth v. Frisbie, 464 A.2d 1283, 1284–85 (Pa. Super. Ct. 1983).
21. Commonwealth v. Lomax, 472 A.2d 217, 217 (Pa. Super. Ct. 1984).
22. Commonwealth v. Kearse, 473 A.2d 577, 578 (Pa. Super. Ct. 1984).

Following trial by jury, Edward Newman was acquitted on a charge of riot but convicted of recklessly endangering another person and disorderly conduct. Post-trial motions were denied, and Newman was sentenced to pay total fines of $2,000.00 and to serve consecutive periods of probation totaling three years. On direct appeal, Newman's principal argument is that videotape evidence established incontrovertible physical facts and that, therefore, the trial court erred (1) when it denied a defense request for a directed verdict and (2) when it refused to instruct the jury that videotape evidence constituted proof of incontrovertible physical facts. He also contends that the trial court erred in refusing a requested instruction pertaining to his right of assembly. There is no merit in these contentions. For sentencing purposes, however, the conviction for disorderly conduct merged into the conviction for recklessly endangering another person. Therefore, we must remand for resentencing.[23]

This appeal is from judgment on the verdict in a civil case concerning a motorcycle accident. Plaintiff/appellee was the owner/rider of the vehicle and appellants are its manufacturer and seller. Appellants raise, collectively, 14 different issues for our review. Seven of these are addressed substantively in the following opinion and in seven we rely upon the opinion of the court below. On all issues we hold in appellee's favor. Judgment is, accordingly, affirmed.[24]

Claimant David H. Greenwood appeals an order of the Department of Military Affairs denying state benefits for a substantial back injury sustained in the line of duty while on annual two-week encampment with the Pennsylvania Army National Guard in 1975. At that time, state military benefits were governed by section 844 of The Military Code of 1949. The basis for the department's order is that the claimant was exclusively engaged in federal service and that the federal government has compensated him.

---

23. Commonwealth v. Newman, 470 A.2d 976, 978 (Pa. Super. Ct. 1984).

24. Matsko v. Harley Davidson Motor Co., Inc., 473 A.2d 155, 156 (Pa. Super. Ct. 1984), *abrogated by* Duchess v. Langston Corp., 564 Pa. 529 (2001).

The questions are: (1) Does participation in federally funded and mandated training mean that a Pennsylvania National Guardsman is in federal service exclusively, thereby precluding any state compensation for injuries sustained during the training? (2) Does receipt of federal incapacitation benefits render the guardsman ineligible for state compensation?[25]

There are other questions, but the principal issue presented for decision is whether a private cause of action for damages against corporate directors is to be implied in favor of a corporate stockholder under 18 U.S.C. §610, a criminal statute prohibiting corporations from making "a contribution or expenditure in connection with any election at which Presidential and Vice Presidential electors ... are to be voted for." We conclude that implication of such a federal cause of action is not suggested by the legislative context of §610 or required to accomplish Congress' purposes in enacting the statute. We therefore have no occasion to address the questions whether §610, properly construed, proscribes the expenditures alleged in this case, or whether the statute is unconstitutional as violative of the First Amendment or of the equal protection component of the Due Process Clause of the Fifth Amendment.[26]

---

25. Greenwood v. Commonwealth, Dep't of Military Affairs, 468 A.2d 866, 868 (Pa. Commw. Ct. 1983), *rev'd by* 508 A.2d 292 (Pa. 1986).
26. Cort v. Ash, 422 U.S. 66, 68–69 (1975).

CHAPTER NINE

STATEMENT OF FACTS

§9.1 The Importance of the Statement of Facts

In addition to ruling in favor of a party in a dispute, judicial opinions have a by-product which the common law tradition elevates to the status of a legal precept. This generally takes the form of a legal rule which we have previously described as a detailed legal consequence attached to a detailed set of facts. Thus, the facts set forth in an opinion are more than merely informative. This being so, it is necessary to use care in selecting what facts you set forth. For this reason, I offer two suggestions:

- Never write the facts first; do not begin writing the facts until you have decided what issues you will address.
- Write tersely; tailor the statement of the facts to fit only the issues raised.

The facts should be stated as tightly as possible and confined to those material to the issues that will be discussed. One who thought otherwise was my dear friend, the late Robert Braucher, former justice of the Massachusetts Supreme Judicial Court and former professor of law at Harvard. He believed that an extensive factual narrative should be presented so that the reader "could catch a true flavor of the case."

§9.2 What Facts Should Be Set Forth?

I suppose I come off as an unreconstructed common law lawyer, one of those simple souls who believe that *stare decisis* is a combination of antecedent facts and a consequential statement of a legal precept attached to those facts. *Stare decisis* means "keep to the decisions," and a decision is a mix of the material facts and the legal consequences flowing therefrom. Readers of an opinion should be able to prophesy and to evaluate the effectiveness and relevance of the case, so long as the only facts stated are those material to the adjudication.

I perceive a distinction between facts that are merely interesting and those that are important. For example, in deciding a murder case, the fact that a window on the fiftieth floor was installed in 1968 and contained stained glass may be interesting; the fact that the victim was thrown out of the window is important. For the opinion to possess legitimate institutional or precedential value, the common law tradition requires that the opinion reader be given signals as to what facts are adjudicative, i.e., what facts are material to the decision.

Thus, how the facts are stated may be more than a question of writing style. Those facts may constitute an extremely important ingredient in evaluating the opinion's precedential or institutional value. Recall what has been suggested by the giants of the common law tradition:

> Oliver Wendell Holmes, Jr.: "The prophecies of what the courts will do in fact, and nothing more pretentious, are what I mean by the law."[1]
>
> Roscoe Pound: Rules of law are "precepts attaching a definite detailed legal consequence to a definite, detailed state of facts."[2]
>
> Edward H. Levi: "[T]he scope of a rule of law, and therefore its meaning, depends upon a determination of what facts will be considered similar to those present when the rule was first announced. The finding of similarity or difference is the key step in the legal process."[3]
>
> Jerome Frank: "[P]art of the judge's function is to pick out the relevant facts.... [T]his means that in writing his opinion he stresses ... those facts which are relevant to his conclusion.... [H]e unconsciously selects those facts which, in combination of the rules of law which he considers to be pertinent, will make 'logical' his decision."[4]

Catherine Drinker Bowen kept a sign posted above her desk to discipline herself as she wrote her books: "Will the reader turn the page?" What Barbara Tuchman described in *Practicing History* as the responsibility of the historian is equally applicable to the judge writing the opinion:

---

1. Oliver Wendell Holmes, Jr., *The Path of the Law*, 10 Harv. L. Rev. 457, 461 (1897).

2. Roscoe Pound, *Hierarchy of Sources and Forms in Different Systems of Law*, 7 Tul. L. Rev. 475, 482 (1933).

3. Edward H. Levi, *An Introduction to Legal Reasoning*, 15 U. Chi. L. Rev. 501, 502 (1948).

4. Jerome Frank, Law and the Modern Mind 134–35 (1930).

The writer of history, I believe, has a number of duties *vis-à-vis* the reader, if he wants to keep him reading. The first is to distill. He must do the preliminary work for the reader, assemble the information, make sense of it, select the essential, discard the irrelevant—above all, discard the irrelevant—and put the rest together so that it forms a developing dramatic narrative. Narrative, it has been said, is the lifeblood of history. To offer a mass of undigested facts, of names not identified and places not located, is of no use to the reader and is simple laziness on the part of the author, or pedantry to show how much he has read. To discard the unnecessary requires courage and also extra work, as exemplified by Pascal's effort to explain an idea to a friend in a letter which rambled on for pages and ended, "I am sorry to have wearied you with so long a letter but I did not have time to write you a short one."[5]

§ 9.3 Where Do You Place the Facts?

The facts should appear *after* the statement of issues but *before* the discussion of the issues. In an unusually complex case it may be well to segment the factual narration and introduce related issues with a separate narration. When a case requires discussion of a series of unrelated issues, it may be more effective to omit facts in the initial summary and set them forth preceding the relevant analysis.

In any event, I repeat, the facts should appear after the statement of issues. This is important because it enables the reader to relate the facts to the issues to be discussed.

§ 9.4 The Polestar Is Accuracy

The principal directive in narrating the facts is accuracy. Be honest. Don't steal the facts. A report of the American Bar Association warned that "[e]xtreme care must always be taken to assure a fair and impartial statement. This is particularly true with respect to the facts favorable to the side which is going to lose on the appeal. It has been said that a lawyer may forgive a judge for mistaking the law. But, not so if his facts are taken away from him."[6]

---

5. Barbara Tuchman, Practicing History 17–18 (1981).

6. ABA, Section of Judicial Administration, Committee Report: Internal Operating Procedures of Appellate Courts 31 (1961), *reprinted in* B.E. Witkin, Manual on Appellate Court Opinions 102 (1977).

San Francisco lawyer Moses Lasky, obviously burned in a case, sadly observed:

> An opinion writer is entitled to the greatest leeway in his law as in his reasoning, for they are his. But honesty allows no leeway in his statement of the facts, for they are not his. There is no substitute whatever for adherence to the exact and precise record in the case. No "result-orientation" can justify omission of a single relevant fact or the inclusion of a single factual statement that is false. This should go without saying. Unfortunately it needs saying.[7]

Always prepare the facts as if a member of the court will be writing a concurrence or dissent. Remember that in post-trial motions and appellate review, what the fact finder finds must be construed in the light most favorable to the winner of the verdict. Where the evidence has been controverted, it is helpful to indicate, in the narration of facts, a record page number to verify the finding. The opinion writer cooks the books when he or she drafts an opinion that appears to be logically sound but is grounded on unfairly edited facts.

Judge Frank Coffin, former Chief Judge of the U.S. Court of Appeals for the First Circuit, taught that we should immerse ourselves in the facts of a case "until there develops a feel for the terrain":

> [T]here are many, many appeals in which there are facts overlooked by the parties, under- or overplayed, or taken out of context. A judge treads in such a domain with confidence only if he has made himself privy to all that the record contains. If there is anything that we can instill in our young law clerks, who seldom need instruction in legal analysis, it is a healthy respect for a factual record.[8]

§9.5 Narration Should Be Limited to Material Facts

Only material, adjudicative facts should be set forth in the opinion. The reasons are enshrouded in the formation of the common law tradition. We treat like cases alike. But what makes a "like case"? A like case is one where the material facts are identical with or substantially similar to those in the putative precedent. If facts in the case at hand do not run on all fours with those in the previous one, resort must be made to the process of analogy. This in-

---

7. Moses Lasky, *A Return to the Observatory Below the Bench*, 19 Sw. L.J. 679, 689 (1965).
8. FRANK COFFIN, THE WAYS OF A JUDGE 167 (1980).

volves an analysis of the facts of the several compared cases. It also requires an identification of resemblances, which we may call positive analogies, and differences, which we may call negative analogies.

Some considerations should help to determine the positive analogies and negative analogies we should consider in applying a putative precedent to a given case. Whether the stated facts serve to provide a true resemblance or a difference depends upon whether a court deems those facts to be material. To one judge, the added or subtracted circumstances may be immaterial, so that the new case is simply a new fact scenario governed by a prior case; to another judge, they may appear so entirely new as to constitute a material difference, thus persuading him or her that the new case does not fall within the holding of the putative precedent.

The analytical process comes down to this: first, establish the holding of the case claimed to be a precedent in order to learn the legal consequence attached to that specific statement of facts and to exclude any dictum (suggested legal consequences to hypothetical facts not found in the record). Next, determine whether that holding is a binding precedent for a succeeding case in which the facts are *prima facie* similar. This involves a double analysis. We must first determine the material facts in the putative precedent and then attempt to find those that are material in the compared case. If they are identical, or substantially similar, then the first case is a binding precedent for the second, and the court should reach the same conclusion it reached in the first. If the first case lacks any fact deemed material in the second case, or contains any material fact not found in the second, then it may not be a direct precedent, but only an argument—albeit sometimes very persuasive argument.

This aspect of the judicial process is not new. About 80 years ago, the prominent English jurisprudent, Arthur L. Goodhart, commented:

> The judge founds his conclusions upon a group of facts selected by him as material from among a larger mass of facts, some of which might seem significant to a layman, but which, to a lawyer, are irrelevant. The judge, therefore, reaches a conclusion upon the facts as he sees them. It is on these facts that he bases his judgment, and not on any others. It follows that our task in analyzing a case is not to state the facts and the conclusion, but to state the material facts as seen by the judge and his conclusion based on them. It is by his choice of the material facts that the judge creates law.[9]

9. Arthur L. Goodhart, *Determining the Ratio Decidendi of a Case*, 40 YALE L.J. 161, 169 (1930).

§ 9.6 Guidelines to Determine Material Facts

Here are some guidelines to help determine, in the process of analogy, which facts are material and which are immaterial. The U.S. Supreme Court gives guidance here: "As to materiality, the substantive law will identify what facts are material. Only disputes over *facts that might affect the outcome of the suit* under the governing law will properly preclude the entry of summary judgment."[10]

In 2006, and in the context of a defendant's claim under *Brady v. Maryland*, the Supreme Court reiterated that "[s]uch evidence is material if there is a reasonable probability that, had the evidence been disclosed to the defense, *the result of the proceeding would have been different.*"[11]

I add some suggestions, condensed from Professor Goodhart's writing, with trepidation and advance them not as truths, not even as probabilities, but only—to use the most weaselly of terms—as possible possibilities:

- All facts that the court specifically stated to be material must be considered material.
- All facts that the court specifically stated to be immaterial must be considered immaterial.
- All facts that the court *implicitly* treats as immaterial must be considered immaterial.
- All facts of person, time, place, kind and amount are immaterial unless said to be material.
- A conclusion based on facts not in the record or based on hypothetical facts is considered dictum.[12]

In the case of the judge, then, the law is reduced to the art of drawing distinctions; in the case of the lawyer, it is reduced to the art of anticipating the distinctions the judge is likely to draw.[13] To be sure, "[i]n a system bound by precedent such distinctions may often be in the nature of hair-splitting, this being

---

10. Anderson v. Liberty Lobby, Inc., 477 U.S. 242, 248 (1986) (emphasis added).

11. Youngblood v. West Virginia, 547 U.S. 867, 870 (2006) (quoting Strickler v. Greene, 527 U.S. 263, 280 (1999), and United States v. Bagley, 473 U.S. 667, 676 (1985)) (emphasis supplied).

12. Arthur L. Goodhart, *Determining the Ratio Decidendi of a Case*, 40 Yale L.J. 161, 173–83 (1930).

13. *See* Dennis Lloyd, *Reason and Logic in the Common Law*, 64 L.Q. Rev. 468, 482 (1948).

the only instrument to hand for avoiding the consequences of an earlier decision which the court considers unreasonable, or as laying down a principle which is 'not to be extended.' "[14]

§ 9.7 Materiality: One Man's Meat

Involved here is an interrelationship between two terms that sound alike, but whose meanings diverge in the decisional process: "reasonable" and "reasoning." A judge's decision on the choice, interpretation and application of a legal precept may involve a value judgment justifiable in his or her mind because the decision is "reasonable," in the sense that it is fair, just, sound and sensible. One judge may believe that it is "reasonable" to maintain the law in harmony with existing circumstances and precedents, and may accede to the magnetic appeal of consistency; another may assert that the issue should be considered pragmatically, and will respond only to its practical consequences.

What is "reasonable" in given circumstances gives rise to endless differences of opinion. This is as it should be. The inevitable variance of views found in multi-judge courts is one of the most vitalizing traditions in the growth of the common law. So is the balance between respect for and ongoing re-examination of precedents. We are all influenced by the traditional Holmes-Pound-Cardozo philosophy, which tells us that the great aim of the law is to improve the welfare of society. We seek to achieve this aim by reaching decisions that are "reasonable."

Therefore, determining what consequences a previous case has on the current case requires determination of what facts are material. If A has been found to be liable in set of circumstances B, we have to decide, often without an exact precedent to guide us, whether A is liable also if B obtains plus or minus circumstance C. To do this, we must determine which facts are material. That is, we must decide whether the addition or deletion of circumstance C is material or immaterial.

Two famous cases dramatically illustrate this. In *Rylands v. Fletcher*,[15] the defendant employed an independent contractor to make a reservoir on his land. Because of the contractor's negligence in failing to fill up some unused mine shafts, water escaped and flooded the plaintiff's mine. The case could

---

14. *Id.*
15. L.R. 3 H.L. 330 (1868).

have been decided solely on the basis of the contractor's negligence, but the court chose to decide it on the basis of strict liability; it determined that the negligence of the contractor was immaterial. Compare the actual facts of the case with the facts deemed material by the court:

Actual Facts

- D had a reservoir built on his land.
- Through the negligence of the contractor (our plus circumstance C), water escaped and injured P.
- Conclusion: D is liable to P.

Material Facts as Seen by the Court

- D had a reservoir built on his land.
- Water escaped and injured P.
- Conclusion: D is liable to P.

Thus, by the determination that circumstance C was immaterial, the doctrine of absolute liability was established in 1868. It is still alive and kicking today.

In *Brown v. Board of Education*,[16] the Court addressed circumstance B, this issue of segregated schools. It decided that under the doctrine of "separate but equal," no segregated schools could be considered "equal." In *Mayor of Baltimore v. Dawson*[17] the Court again confronted a segregation issue — this time, minus circumstance C (i.e., minus the context of schools). The Court affirmed the Fourth Circuit's ruling that the *Brown* decision would nevertheless apply to end segregation in public beaches and bathhouses. Segregation minus circumstance C led to the same result in *Holmes v. Atlanta*[18] (municipal golf course) and *Gayle v. Browder*[19] (buses). When *Browder* came down, it was recognized that, as a matter of law, the entire doctrine of separate but equal was overruled without being limited to the reasons stated in *Brown*: the special and particular problems of segregated education. Changing social and judicial perspectives had rendered that circumstance immaterial.[20]

* * *

---

16. 347 U.S. 483 (1954).

17. 350 U.S. 877 (1955).

18. 350 U.S. 879 (1955).

19. 352 U.S. 903 (1956).

20. For a more detailed discussion on material facts see Ruggero J. Aldisert, Logic for Lawyers: A Guide to Clear Legal Thinking 230–33 (3d ed. 1997).

Because the facts of an individual case contribute to a judge's larger role in developing legal precepts, the statement of facts is a crucial part of any judicial opinion. It is for this reason that judges should carefully consider, and then reconsider, what facts to set forth.

OPINION WRITING

I KNOW THE "WHAT," BUT I DON'T KNOW
THE "HOW" AND THE "WHY."

CHAPTER TEN

WRITING THE REASONS
FOR THE DECISION

§ 10.1 Overview

We come now to the core of our subject—to the opinion's sinew, muscle and fiber—as we describe the process of stating reasons for the decision. This is the *ratio decidendi,* the *how* and *why* we have reached the decision. It is said that the judicial process is divided into two separate parts. The first is the process of discovery-reaching the decision. The second is the process of justification—writing a public explanation that logically justifies the decision we have made. It is here that the major criticisms are directed against our opinions. It is here that all of us must buckle down to demonstrate superior writing and explanatory skills.

Many lawyers, in their briefs, and judges, in their opinions, seem, like the poor little lambs in Yale's Whiffenpoof song, to have lost their way. Many of those briefs and those opinions are no longer instruments of persuasion or explanation. Rather, they emerge from word processors as instruments of commentary, looking more like wide-blade axes of the glossators than decision-making tools.

In many judicial opinions we see a mishmash of citation in text and footnotes. We who sit on the appellate benches of the land suffer chronic cases of literary hiccups. We insert citations as often as possible, three or four in a simple declaratory sentence—irrespective of how they interfere with the flow of the prose, the rhythm of the presentations or the logical order of the argument. A promiscuous uttering of citations has replaced the crisply stated, clean lines of legal reasoning. Somehow we seem not to care that such static impedes easy comprehension of a statement of reasons. It is not too unkind to suggest that often what poses as a work of scholarship is actually a work of journalism. Rodell said, "a pennyworth of content is most frequently concealed beneath a pound of so-called style."[1]

---

1. Fred Rodell, *Goodbye to Law Reviews,* 23 VA. L. REV. 38, 38 (1936).

The late best-selling historian, Barbara W. Tuchman, sounded a call for "clear, easy-reading prose" from the writing community. She asked all writers to avoid "the Latinized language of academics with their endless succession of polysyllables, their deaf ear for sentence structure, and unconcern for clarity."[2]

I say all this not to suggest that effective legal writing should be graded purely for literary style. Rather, I emphasize this problem because the purpose of all legal writing is persuasion. Without clear writing, communication is lessened. To the extent that we diminish communication, we dilute our powers of persuasion. Certainly the purpose of a brief is persuasion, as a lawyer must convince the judicial reader of the rightness of his or her cause. Similarly, the purpose of a judicial opinion is to convince any reader that sound logic supports the court's decision.

A friend who has for the past four decades made a respectable living with his figurative pen once sent me a letter in which he said: "The first job for any piece of writing is to entice the reader into reading it, start to finish. That accomplished, the words must convey clearly what the writer wants them to convey. Finally, the text must perform the missionary act of persuasion, reinforcing the support of those who agree with the author and changing the minds of those who do not."

In substance, then, to write effectively is to sell effectively. That is why I can comfortably think of judges and lawyers as salesmen, a function they do not always recognize and one that many of them would probably deny. There comes to mind the rebuke flung into the face of Willy Loman in the play, *Death of a Salesman*: "The only thing you got in this world is what you can sell. And the funny thing is that you're a salesman, and you don't know that."[3] Excessive citation, excessive footnoting and excessive pedantry, bloated and awkward, are three mighty horsemen running against your sole purpose: to sell your argument to your readers.

Unfortunately, the paradigm for stilted writing is found in the highest court of our land. Let me pause to assure the reader that as a judge and a lawyer, I admire and respect the Court and its nine justices above any government institution, in this land or abroad. My dear friend, the late Professor Bernard J. Ward of the University of Texas, once similarly described his unabashed affection for the court. To have known Bernie was to have recognized that the following statement was not hyperbole but a statement of strongly felt conviction:

---

2. Barbara W. Tuchman, *An Author's Mail*, 54 Am. Scholar 313, 322 (1985).
3. Arthur Miller, Death of a Salesman 97 (1949).

There are with me but two articles of faith: neither the Roman Pon-
tiff nor the Supreme Court of the United States can be guilty of error.
Unhappily, both are upon occasion the recipients of miserable advice. More unhappily still, the miserable advice sometimes finds its
way into their judgments. But the judgments are not upon that account to be deemed erroneous. It would be an affront to their dignity to suppose that they intended us to confuse miserable advice
with their solemn judgments. And so we must read their judgments
shorn of the miserable advice. But the objection is put that that process
may lead us to nothing at all. *Nego.* It is a reaffirmation of our un-
deviating loyalty: they can neither err nor be victimized by miserable advice.[4]

Like Bernie, I say nothing in derogation of the Justices' solutions to difficult decisions and their discharge of profound responsibilities.

As a student of the judicial process, however, I am constrained to say that
they have been "victimized by miserable [opinion-writing] advice." Because
their case loads are swollen by frivolous petitions for certiorari, the Justices
must turn to brilliant but inexperienced law clerks and to fuddled offerings
of professional commentators for advice. What results is text that unnecessarily emphasizes minor or trifling points of learning, shows a questionable
sense of propriety (or proportion), and fails to recognize the difference between what is necessary as a statement and what is pseudo-academic show-
and-tell.

§ 10.2 The Rationale Must Offer Clarity

As I will later develop in detail, every opinion should ideally begin with a
clear statement of the flash point of controversy between the litigants. We must
identify precisely where the litigants differ and tell the reader whether their
clash concerns the choice of the controlling legal precept or the interpretation
of an agreed-upon precept or, if there is no dispute over either, a statement
that the controversy concerns the application of settled law to settled facts.
Having identified these contours, we should then proceed to resolve the diffi-

---

4. Letter from Professor Bernard Ward to United States Circuit Judge James Braxton
Craven, Jr. (1971), *reprinted in* Charles Alan Wright, *The Wit and Wisdom of Bernie Ward*,
61 Tex. L. Rev. 13 (1982).

culty and explain why one choice, or one interpretation or given application, is preferred over the other.

The *ratio decidendi* must offer the reader clarity. There must be exposition of analysis and more selective use of legitimate case law support. Lawyers and judges both have an obligation to evaluate the effect of previous cases and to decide which they will authenticate and which they will consider simple duplicates; which of them are necessary to the argument and which only validate obvious statements of reason.

The brute fact is that not all precedent represents currency of equal value. An authoritative gradation of legal precepts does exist. Some precedents are much more important than others. Recognition that a hierarchy of value exists is essential if judges are to find the proper grounds of decision; if lawyers are to find the basis for prediction on the course of decision; and if members of society are to find reasonable guidance toward conducting themselves in accordance with the demands of legal order. Even more important—*much* more important—is the necessity to bring greater order to the design of law by identifying clearly, and at the earliest opportunity, the fundamental family of law implicated in the case.

The time has come for judges to simplify, rather than to complicate, current legal issues. The time has come to identify clearly the controversy in each case, and always identify the branch of the law governing that controversy. The first step must be to concentrate on the tree's trunk and its main branches, rather than to fuss over the buds and blossoms, which continually sprout and grow, but will be gone in the autumn.

This arboreal metaphor reminds me of something Dean John H. Wigmore observed more than 50 years ago:

> Another shortcoming [of opinions] is overemphasis on the technique of legal rules in detail, with corresponding underemphasis on policies, reasons, and principles. This is a difficult thing to describe to those who do not sense it without description, but it is very marked. It is the kind of thing that is like the dead bark on the outside of a tree, in contrast to the living, growing inner core. Too much of our law is dead bark, at least in the judicial opinions.[5]

We must emphasize basic legal precepts because at the starting point of every judicial decision must be a recognition of controlling dogma, doctrine and fundamental principles. Only this recognition will permit our decisions

---

5. 1 JOHN HENRY WIGMORE, EVIDENCE IN TRIALS AT COMMON LAW §8a, at 616 (1983).

to be both consistent and coherent. The call for more simplicity and more order in briefs and opinions will cause us not to regress, but to progress. It will create better communication between lawyer and judge and between judge and community. It will seek to remove from judicial decisions everything that is idiosyncratic, and in its place will attempt to establish predictability and reckonability.

I do not offer a panacea, but I do suggest that certain criteria point the way to answer the call.

§ 10.2.1 Let the Reader Recognize an Outline

A lengthy discussion of a multifaceted single issue or of multiple issues should be segmented. Each segment should be preceded by a Roman numeral or a letter. In this way, the reader has a visual outline to aid in understanding the opinion.

Unless it is a very short opinion, I adopt the U.S. Supreme Court style of segmenting each identifiable segment of the opinion, using Roman numerals. Not all judges agree. Some prefer the opinion to be uninterrupted; they like it to flow like a legal essay. Others prefer subheadings to introduce the issues, in law review style. Still others follow the styles of legal memoranda by compartmentalizing with subheads titled "Facts," "Discussion" and "Conclusion."

No one style fits all judges. For appellate court opinions, I prefer the Roman-numeral system, because it allows the writer to proceed with each segment as a self-contained unit. This encourages coherent, concise, issue-centered writing. It separates the issue, facts and rationale into easily identifiable segments. It eliminates the need for stodgy, artificial transitional phrases because the numeral serves to indicate the transition to a new subject.

If the writing is clear, it is not necessary to label one section "Facts." The reader will know. Such a label is necessary in the trial court where the judicial officer makes findings of fact. With the exception of the Louisiana Intermediate Court of Appeals, American appellate courts do not "find" facts, and in Louisiana, they do so only in civil cases.

Certain considerations militate against the use of a subhead to introduce each issue. First, there is the common law tradition. Through the years, the great courts—state and federal, here and in England—have eschewed subheads in judicial opinions. Second, the subhead is usually a restatement of the topic sentence. You don't need to tell us what you are going to say; then say it; then tell the reader what you said. That exercise is tautological. Furthermore, in the modern era, West and Lexis provide numbered headnotes to immediately direct you to the location of each issue. I prefer the following outlines:

§ 10.2.1.1 Simple Opinion Outline

Orientation paragraph
Statement of Jurisdiction
Summary of Issues
Statement of Standards of Review
    I.
    Facts and Procedural History
    II.
    First Issue
    III.
    Second Issue
    IV.
    Conclusion and Disposition

§ 10.2.1.2 More Sophisticated Opinion Outline

Orientation paragraph(s)
Statement of Jurisdiction
    I.
    Summary of Issues
    Statement of Standards of Review
    II.
    General Statement of Facts and Procedural History
    III.
    First Issue
    Statement of Relevant Facts
    IV.
    Second Issue
    V.
    Third Issue
    VI.
    Summary of Conclusions
    VII.
    Disposition

In many cases the most important reason for the use of segments indicated by Roman numerals is that it shortens and clarifies the separate concurring or dissenting opinions written by judges on the same panel. A judge wishing to join in an opinion except a portion of the discussion on damages can say:

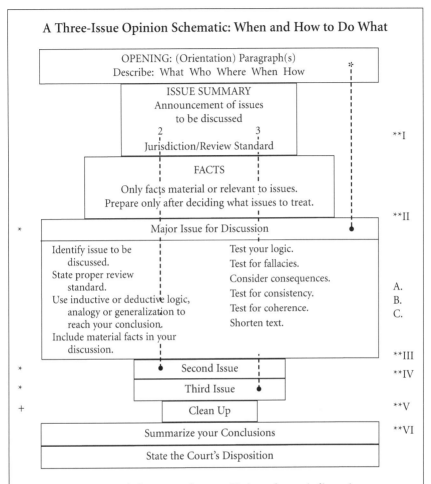

A Three-Issue Opinion Schematic: When and How to Do What

Legend: Writing proceeds from top to bottom. Horizontal space indicates importance. Vertical space indicates quantity of writing. Dotted lines tie announcement with the development of issue.

* Reposition for final draft to suit style.

+ Recognize other issues considered without much, if any, discussion.

** Roman numerals and caps introduce separate parts of opinion.

"Judge Alpha concurs in the opinion of the majority and dissents only to Part III of the opinion."

The net effect of this is that the reader can quickly understand where there is unanimity in the court and, if there is disagreement, precisely where it exists. Having said all this, however, I recognize that many good writers of appellate opinions prefer to use subheadings. It is a matter of personal style. There is no specific convention giving the seal of approval to one over the other.

Unless the opinion is very short, however, either a Roman numeral (sometimes followed by letters) or a subheading should be used to assist the reader in segmenting discrete parts of the opinion.

§ 10.2.2 Identify the Precise Jurisprudential Conflict

For each point in your opinion, you must identify the precise conflict between the parties. There are three potential conflicts:

(a) Where the law and its application alike are plain or, to put it another way, where the rule of law is clear and its application to the facts found by the fact finder is equally clear.

(b) Where the rule of law is clear and the sole question is its application to the facts. In Cardozo's formulation: "[T]he rule of law is certain, and the application alone doubtful."[6]

(c) Where neither the rule nor, *a fortiori*, its application, are clear.

The opinion writer should not waste effort or unduly pad the opinion if the point falls within category (a); one or two sentences with relevant citation should suffice. If the point fits into category (b), do not waste effort on justifying the controlling rule. Concentrate only on the conflict, the application of the rule to the facts. If the point comes within category (c), it is necessary first to identify the flash point of the conflict. Here, too, I suggest there are three subcategories:

(1) *Choosing the law.* Here, you must choose among competing legal precepts to determine which should control. Finding the law is another process. From a study of cases each announcing a specific rule of law attached to a detailed set of facts you may be able to "find" or create a broader legal precept attached to a broad set of facts. Both these processes require the deepest development because once you "choose" or "find," you must interpret that precept.

(2) *Interpreting the law.* Here there is no dispute about which competing precept controls, but only the question of interpreting what has been chosen or found. This arises most frequently in statutory construction. If the conflict falls within this category, do not discuss choice of other precepts; discuss only interpretation of the law (category 2), and application to the facts (category 3).

---

6. Benjamin Cardozo, The Nature of the Judicial Process 164 (1921).

(3) *Application of the law to the facts.* Here, you need only discuss the application of the precept—as chosen and interpreted—to the facts as found by the fact finder.

§ 10.2.2.1 Excerpts from Court Opinions

a. Finding or Choosing the Law

This appeal requires us to decide if a sufficient quantum of admissible evidence was presented at trial to establish a prima facie case of negligence. We determine that plaintiff-appellee Aloe Coal Company did not present sufficient evidence of causation to submit its negligence claim to the jury.

We also visit again the issue that was before us in *Pennsylvania Glass Sand Corp. v. Caterpillar Tractor Co.*, 652 F.2d 1165 (3d Cir. 1981): whether Pennsylvania courts would permit a purchaser of industrial equipment to bring a tort action against the manufacturer for damages to the product caused by a sudden fire.[7]

....

In the context of admiralty law, the Supreme Court in *East River S.S. Corp. v Transamerica Delaval, Inc.*, 476 U.S. 858 (1986), specifically rejected our *Pennsylvania Glass Sand* position. We now predict that Pennsylvania courts, although not bound to do so, would nevertheless adopt as state law the Supreme Court's reasoning in *East River*.[8]

The Commonwealth of Pennsylvania finds itself between a rock and a hard place. A consent decree entered in August 1978 by the federal court commands it to implement a vehicle emission inspection and maintenance program. At the same time, its own state court system by an order dated January 9, 1984, enjoins it from carrying out the federal decree. The January Pennsylvania court order implemented a decision by that state's supreme court determining that the parties to the federal consent decree lacked the authority to consent to establishing and implementing an auto emissions inspection program and ordered that "an injunction should issue enjoining [the state]

---

7. Aloe Coal Co. v. Clark Equip. Co., 816 F.2d 110, 111 (3d Cir. 1987).
8. *Id.*

from performing the terms and conditions of the consent decree." *Scanlon v. Commonwealth*, 467 A.2d 1108, 1115 (Pa. 1983).[9]

The question for decision is whether the captain of a merchant ship violated applicable maritime law when he buried at sea a seaman who died of a heart attack on the return trip of the vessel eight days from its next port-of-call. After seaman James Floyd died, the captain conducted a burial-at-sea ritual. Maria Floyd, the seaman's daughter, for herself, as executrix of her father's estate, and for the next-of-kin, sued the vessel's owner for improperly disposing of her father's body. The district court granted summary judgment in favor of Lykes Bros. Steamship Company. Maria Floyd has appealed. We will affirm....

On appeal, Floyd contends that state tort law has established that the spouse or next-of-kin is entitled to possession of a body for the purpose of arranging for final disposition of the remains, *see, e.g., Blanchard v. Brawley*, 75 So.2d 891, 893 (La.Ct.App.1954), and that violation of the right of possession and burial is an actionable tort. *See, e.g., Papieves v. Lawrence*, 437 Pa. 373, 263 A.2d 118, 120 (1970). She argues that this state law tort precept should be incorporated into general maritime law. She says that currently recognized maritime authority deems burial at sea anachronistic and improper when the next-of-kin are not notified in advance.

Lykes responds that this case is not governed by state tort concepts, but by federal maritime law. Relying on *Brambir v. Cunard White Star, Ltd.*, 37 F. Supp. 906 (S.D.N.Y. 1940), *aff'd mem.*, 119 F.2d 419 (2d Cir. 1941), Lykes argues that maritime law does not provide a cause of action for burial at sea.[10]

b. Interpreting the Law

In this appeal by two coal producing companies from summary judgment in favor of the government, we must decide what is meant by the expression "coal produced by surface mining" under the Surface Mining Control and Reclamation Act (SMCRA or the Act), 30 U.S.C. §§ 1201–1328. This is not mere semantic exercise, because upon

---

9. Del. Valley Citizens' Council for Clean Air v. Pennsylvania, 755 F.2d 38, 39 (3d Cir. 1985).

10. Floyd v. Lykes Bros. S.S. Co., 844 F.2d 1044, 1044–46 (3d Cir. 1988).

our decision depends the extent of tonnage upon which a reclamation fee of 35 cents per ton may be levied by the Secretary of the Interior. The government argues, and the district court found, that tonnage of "coal produced" includes the weight of rock, clay, dirt and other debris mined with the "coal" that was delivered by the companies to a coal washing and sizing plant. The companies seem to borrow from Gertrude Stein's "a rose is a rose is a rose" and argue that coal is coal and it means a mineral that is combustible. We conclude that we have jurisdiction to hear this appeal, and that the district court erred in determining that all the material mined by appellants was subject to the reclamation fee. Accordingly, we reverse the judgment of the district court.[11]

———————————

The major question for decision is one of first impression in the United States Courts of Appeals. We must decide whether a claim deemed filed in a Chapter 11 (reorganization) proceeding remains effective when the debtor converts the Chapter 11 case into one under Chapter 7 (liquidation). The issue requires that we construe relevant statutes and the rules of practice and procedure in bankruptcy. The bankruptcy judge, 43 B.R. 937, and, after appeal, the district court, 52 B.R. 960, held that listing the claim on the debtor's schedule, which was filed under Chapter 11, did not preserve the claim under Chapter 7. We disagree and reverse.[12]

———————————

There are other questions, but the principal issue presented for decision is whether a private cause of action for damages against corporate directors is to be implied in favor of a corporate stockholder under 18 U.S.C. §610, a criminal statute prohibiting corporations from making "a contribution or expenditure in connection with any election at which Presidential and Vice Presidential electors ... are to be voted for." We conclude that implication of such a federal cause of action is not suggested by the legislative context of §610 or required to accomplish Congress' purposes in enacting the statute. We therefore have no occasion to address the questions whether §610, properly

———————————

11. United States v. Brook Contracting Corp., 759 F.2d 320, 321 (3d Cir. 1985).
12. *In re* Crouthamel Potato Chip Co., 786 F.2d 141, 142 (3d Cir. 1986).

construed, proscribes the expenditures alleged in this case, or whether the statute is unconstitutional as violative of the First Amendment or of the equal protection component of the Due Process Clause of the Fifth Amendment.[13]

In this appeal we are required to construe Section 25(a) of the Act of July 9, 1976, P.L. 586, No. 142, effective June 27, 1978, and determine whether it was intended to reduce the two year limitation established by the Judicial Code, 42 Pa.C.S.A. § 5524, for the commencement of an action for trespass to real estate. The trial court held that the statute of limitations had been so reduced and granted a motion for summary judgment which dismissed an action for blasting damages which had occurred less than 23 months prior to commencement of the action. We reverse.[14]

c. Applying the Law to the Facts

Although the contents of a document may not be privileged under the fifth amendment, the act of producing or authenticating the document may be privileged. This terse summary of the law originated with *Fisher v. United States*, 425 U.S. 391, 410 (1976), and was confirmed in *United States v. Doe*, 465 U.S. 605 (1984). Application of this precept may produce profound consequences when an individual is the target of an Internal Revenue Service (IRS) investigation and the IRS directs a summons to a corporation solely owned by the individual. We have been asked to address such consequences in this case.[15]

The major question for decision raised by these two appeals from a judgment in favor of plaintiff in a diversity action brought under Pennsylvania law is the extent to which delay damages may be awarded under Rule 238, Pa. R. Civ. P. Here, defendant obtained a directed verdict at the close of the first trial, but, after a retrial was ordered by

---

13. Cort v. Ash, 422 U.S. 66, 68–69 (1975).
14. Wilson v. Cent. Pa. Indus., 452 A.2d 257, 258 (Pa. Super. Ct. 1982).
15. Rogers Transp., Inc. v. Stern, 763 F.2d 165, 166 (3d Cir. 1985).

this court, ultimately lost on the merits. Because defendant lost and because he never made a settlement offer, plaintiff was awarded Rule 238 delay damages totaling $247,500. This award included damages for the time the case was on appeal from the directed verdict, but, because of plaintiff's mathematical miscalculation, did not include damages for the 17 days immediately preceding the final verdict. For these reasons, the defendant, at No. 82-5711, argues that the delay damages award was excessive and the plaintiff, at No. 82-5836, contends that it was insufficient.[16]

This appeal requires us to decide whether Blue Shield's prepaid dental service program in Pennsylvania violates the antitrust laws. Several Pennsylvania dental associations and individual dentists appeal from a summary judgment dismissing their antitrust and state law claims brought against the Medical Service Association of Pennsylvania, doing business as Pennsylvania Blue Shield. Appellants argue that Blue Shield engaged in a price-fixing conspiracy and a group boycott in violation of the Sherman Act, 15 U.S.C. § 1, attempted to monopolize and monopolized in violation of § 2 of the Act, and that the district court abused its discretion in refusing to certify a subclass of cooperating dentists for treble damages purposes. We conclude that appellants' contentions are without merit, and therefore affirm the judgment of the district court.[17]

The question for decision is whether appellant would be placed in double jeopardy in violation of the fifth amendment were he to be prosecuted in the Western District of Pennsylvania on a charge of conspiracy to distribute and possess marijuana following a plea of guilty and subsequent sentence in the Northern District of Florida on a similar charge. Appellant argues that the Florida and Pennsylvania activities were part of the same conspiracy; the government argues otherwise. The district court agreed with the government and denied appellant's double jeopardy motion to dismiss the indictment. 592 F. Supp. 172. This appeal followed. Although the question is close, we are persuaded

---

16. Barris v. Bob's Drag Chutes & Safety Equip. Inc., 717 F.2d 52, 53–54 (3d Cir. 1983).
17. Pa. Dental Ass'n v. Med. Servs. Ass'n of Pa., 745 F.2d 248, 251 (3d Cir. 1984).

that the government failed to meet its burden of proving the existence of two distinct conspiracies.[18]

At this point, the opinion writer must rely on the rules of formal logic to solve the conflict. Having already set forth in detail elsewhere the discussions of inductive and deductive logic, I am content only to summarize here.[19]

§ 10.3 The Required Logical Structure of Each Issue: Overview

It is the discussion of issues that formally constitutes your argument, and here the word "argument" is that used by the logicians—a group of propositions in which one is claimed to follow from the others, the others being treated as furnishing support for the truth of the original. An argument is not a random collection of propositions, but rather a formally structured grouping.

The purpose of an opinion is to publicly state reasons justifying a conclusion. A rule of law promulgated by a court as a by-product of a judicial conflict is valid only to the extent that sound reasoning supports it.

We all know "the why" of logic in the law. As stated before in Chapter 1, Justice Felix Frankfurter said it best on his retirement after 23 years on the Supreme Court: "Fragile as reason is and limited as law is as the expression of the institutionalized medium of reason, that's all we have standing between us and the tyranny of mere will and the cruelty of unbridled, unprincipled, undisciplined feeling."[20]

We also know the test for a good legal argument or brief. It comes from what I call the Harry Jones/Roscoe Pound test for a good opinion: "[H]ow thoughtfully and disinterestedly the Court weighed the conflicting social interests involved in the case and how fair and durable its adjustment of the interest-conflicts promised to be."[21] You cannot advocate or pronounce a position that is "fair and durable" unless formal rules of logic go into the process. We cannot have decisions by judicial fiat alone.

Because reason must always support the conclusion presented for acceptance, we turn to some basic concepts of legal reasoning to assist the opinion writer.

---

18. United States v. Felton, 753 F.2d 276, 277 (3d Cir. 1985).

19. *See* Ruggero J. Aldisert, Logic for Lawyers: A Guide to Clear Legal Thinking (3d ed. 1997); Ruggero J. Aldisert, Winning on Appeal: Better Briefs and Oral Argument 257–79 (2d ed. 2003).

20. As quoted in Time, Sept. 7, 1962, at 15.

21. Harry W. Jones, *An Invitation to Jurisprudence*, 74 Colum. L. Rev. 1023, 1029 (1974).

§ 10.3.1 Introduction to Deductive and Inductive Reasoning

The logic of the law is neither all deductive nor all inductive. Where the law is clear and the application of the facts to the law equally plain, the argument often sounds solely in deductive reasoning. Where the law is clear and the sole question is application of facts to the law, both inductive and deductive reasoning are used. And where the law is not clear, in Cardozo's phrase, where the courts "work for the future," both types of reasoning are very much involved.

Any development of the law becomes a recursive process. First, as cases are compared and their resemblances and differences noted, a judicial decision is made and a legal precept is created. Next there is a period when that newly minted precept becomes more or less fixed. A further stage takes place when the "new" precept becomes "old" and breaks down, or evolves, as new cases are decided. Inductive reasoning usually dominates the first stage — the creation of the precept. Deductive reasoning is used in refining the created precept and in applying it to the facts before the court. Inductive reasoning appears again at a later stage when efforts are made in subsequent cases to break down the precept.

This being so, what form of reasoning do we discuss first? Here we have a chicken-or-the-egg question. As we have explained, the common law develops from specific narrow rules to broader precepts, a classic process of inductive reasoning. Yet, to understand induction, it is best to first learn deduction. Hence we put the deductive cart before the inductive horse with some introductory observations on deductive reasoning.

§ 10.3.2 Deductive Reasoning

Deductive reasoning is a mental operation that a judge must employ every working day. Formal deductive logic is an act of the mind in which, from the relation of two propositions to each other, we infer, that is, we understand and affirm, a third proposition. In deductive reasoning, the two propositions which imply the third proposition, the *conclusion*, are called *premises*. The broad proposition that forms the starting point of deduction is called the *major premise*; the second proposition is called the *minor premise*, and in law, this states the facts found by the fact finder. They have these titles because the subject of the major premise, known as the *middle term*, represents the *all*; the minor premise represents something or someone included in the all.

Logical argument is a means of determining the truth or falsity of a purported conclusion. We do this by following well established canons of logical order in a deliberate and intentional fashion. In law, we must think and reason logically. We must follow a thinking process that emancipates us from impulsively jumping to conclusions, and frees us from argument supported only by strongly felt emotions or superstitions. That which John Dewey said of school teachers in generations past is still vital and important today: Reflective thought "converts action that is merely appetitive, blind, and impulsive into intelligent action."[22]

The classic means of deductive reasoning is the *syllogism*. Aristotle, who first formulated its theory, offered this definition: "A syllogism is discourse in which, certain things being stated, something other than what is stated follows of necessity from their being so."[23] He continued: "I mean by the last phrase that they produce the consequence, and by this, that no further term

EVERY ISSUE MUST FOLLOW THIS FORMAT.
WITHOUT IT, YOU ARE MERELY WRITING A
LITERARY ESSAY AND NOT A JUDICIAL OPINION.

---

22. John Dewey, How We Think 17 (1933).

23. L. Susan Stebbing, A Modern Introduction to Logic 81 (6th ed. 1948) (quoting *Anal. Priora* 24b, 18).

is required from without to make the consequence necessary."[24] From this definition we can say that a syllogism is a form of implication in which two propositions jointly imply a third.[25]

In his book, U.S. Supreme Court Justice Antonin Scalia has an entire chapter titled "Legal Reasoning," that begins with the following advice:

Think syllogistically.

Leaving aside emotional appeals, persuasion is possible only because all human beings are born with a capacity for logical thought. It is something we all have in common. The most rigorous form of logic, and hence the most persuasive, is the syllogism. If you have never studied logic, you may be surprised to learn—like the man who was astounded to discover that he had been speaking prose all his life—that you have been using syllogistic reasoning all along. Argument naturally falls into this mode, whether or not you set out to make it do so. But the clearer the syllogistic progression, the better.[26]

Special rules of the syllogism serve to inform exactly under what circumstances one proposition can be inferred from two other propositions. Consider the classic syllogism:

All men are mortal.
Socrates is a man.
Therefore, Socrates is mortal.

This is a *deductive categorical syllogism*, an argument having three propositions: two premises and a conclusion.

A categorical syllogism contains exactly three terms or class names, each of which occurs in two of the three constituent propositions. A "term" is defined as a word or group of words contained in a premise or conclusion. Understand this completely, because logicians use this expression to identify certain fallacies of form, or formal fallacies. Learn to identify the three terms of a categorical syllogism:

Major Term: Usually the predicate of the major premise and also of the conclusion.

---

24. *Id.*
25. *Id.*
26. ANTONIN SCALIA & BRYAN A. GARNER, MAKING YOUR CASE 41 (2008).

Minor Term:	The subject of the minor premise and also of the conclusion. It is called minor because it is less inclusive than the middle term, which is the predicate of the minor premise. It is usually part of the class represented by the middle term. In most arguments, the minor term is the fact found or to be found by the fact finder.
Middle Term:	Appears in the two premises, but not in the conclusion. It is the medium of comparison between the major and minor term. In the categorical syllogism, it appears as the subject of the major premise and the predicate of the minor premise.

In the standard form categorical syllogism, as used in the law, the major premise is stated first, the minor premise second, and finally the conclusion. Returning to our classic example, let us parse this syllogism identifying its parts:

Major Premise:	"All men" (middle term) are "mortal" (major term).
Minor Premise:	"Socrates" (minor term) is a "man" (middle term).
Conclusion:	Therefore, "Socrates" (minor term) is "mortal" (the major term).

Some helpful hints derive from the foregoing rules: The middle term ("All men") may always be known by the fact that it does not occur in the conclusion. In law, the major term ("mortal") often is the predicate of the conclusion. The minor term ("Socrates") is always the subject of the conclusion.

§ 10.3.3 The Deductive Categorical Syllogism Must Appear in Every Issue You Discuss

The major premise of the issue usually takes the form of a rule of law or a broader precept enunciated in a previous case, or found in a clause of a constitution or statute, that forms the topic sentence of the discussion of each issue. This is represented as a legal precept on which all members of the court will agree as to its legitimacy. (If the parties do not agree with the major premise, logical structure is not the principal issue.).

If the major premise is not true, your entire argument fails. All is lost. All the facts you set forth, all the citations that follow, will not help you.

The bottom line: be absolutely certain that you accurately state your *major premise*. This anchors your entire deductive argument as the beginning point of your logical argument. A legal argument generally has three sources of major premises: *text* (constitution, statute, regulation, ordinance or contract), *precedent* (caselaw, etc.), and *policy* (i.e., consequences of the decision). Often the major premise is self-evident and acknowledged by both sides.[27]

The *minor premise* is easy to describe. The subject of this proposition, the *minor term,* must (a) be part of the *middle term* (the subject of the major premise) and (b) must be a fact found by the fact finder. The minor premise is derived from the facts of the case. There is much to be said for the proposition that "legal reasoning revolves mainly around the establishment of the minor premise."[28]

§ 10.3.4 Deductive Reasoning in the Discussion of an Issue

I now turn to the precise formula that undergirds the deductive categorical syllogism. You all know it by the familiar form:

Major Premise:	All men are mortal.
Minor Premise:	Socrates is a man.
Conclusion:	Therefore, Socrates is a mortal.

Apply this inference from two other propositions to the opinion of Judge Cardozo in *MacPherson v. Buick Motor Car Co.*:[29]

Major Premise:	Any manufacturer who negligently constructs an article that may be inherently dangerous to life and limb when so constructed is liable in damages for the injuries resulting.
Minor Premise:	A manufacturer who constructs an automobile in which the spokes on a wheel are defective creates an article that is inherently dangerous to life and limb.
Conclusion:	Therefore, a manufacturer who constructs an automobile in which the spokes on a wheel are defective is liable in damages for the injuries resulting.

---

27. *Id.* at 41–42 (quoting O.C. Jensen, The Nature of Legal Argument 20 (1957)).
28. *Id.*
29. 11 N.E. 1050 (N.Y. 1960).

Again referring to Justice Scalia's book: "If the major premise (the controlling rule) and the minor premise (the facts invoking that rule) are true (you must establish that they're true), the conclusion follows inevitably."[30]

§ 10.3.5 Inductive Reasoning

Deductive reasoning and adherence to the Socrates-is-a-man type of syllogism is only one of the major components of the common law tradition. Inductive reasoning is equally important. In legal logic, it is very often used to form either the major or the minor premise of the deductive syllogism.

Inductive logic may take two forms in the law—*inductive generalization* and *analogy*. In legal analysis, a statute or specific constitutional provision qualifies as the controlling major premise. It is the law of the case, with which the facts (appearing in the minor premise) will be compared, so as to reach a decision (conclusion). Where no clear rule of law is present, however, in Lord Diplock's phrase, it is necessary to draw upon "the cumulative experience of the judiciary" and then fashion a proper major premise from existing legal rules—the specific holdings of other cases. This is done by the form of inductive reasoning known as *inductive generalization*. It is reasoning from many particulars to a generalization. In the minor premise, we often reason from one particular to another particular; it is a form of inductive reasoning known as *analogy*.

As we now proceed to explain the difference between deductive and inductive reasoning, we do so with a pronounced caveat. This is a discussion of *legal* reasoning, not *general* reasoning. Our formulations of definitions are guided by Max Radin's comment that the test of a definition is whether it is useful. We therefore acknowledge that our explanations may be considered by some logicians to be simplistic, if not precisely accurate when viewed against the universal cosmos of logic.

But the law is made up of particulars. In litigation, the particular facts found by the fact finder are the objective of any trial. In a commercial or business transaction, it is the particulars of the conduct, deal, arrangement, agreement, bargain or understanding that create the conflict between the parties. Tight particulars are controlling in the law. And although, in a series of syllogisms (polysyllogisms), we may reason deductively from the universal to a less broad universal before reaching the conclusion of the last of a series of syllogisms, the ultimate conclusion sought in deductive reasoning in the law is a particular.

---

30. ANTONIN SCALIA & BRYAN A. GARNER, MAKING YOUR CASE 41–42 (2008) (quoting O.C. JENSEN, THE NATURE OF LEGAL ARGUMENT 20 (1957)).

Thus, for our purposes, we can say that deductive reasoning moves by inference from the general ultimately to the particular; inductive reasoning, in the form of inductive generalization, moves from particulars to the general, or from the particular to the particular in the form of analogy.

To summarize, in law logic, as in general logic, there are fundamental differences between the two types of reasoning:

- In deduction, the connection between a given piece of information and another piece of information concluded from it is a *necessary* connection. A deductive argument is one whose conclusion is claimed to follow from its premises with absolute necessity. In a valid deductive argument, if the premises are true, the conclusion *must* be true.
- In induction, the connection between given pieces of information and another piece inferred from them is *not* a logically necessary connection. Its premises do not provide *conclusive* support for the conclusion; they provide only *some* support for it. Inductive arguments may be evaluated, for better or for worse, by the degree of likelihood or probability which their premises confer upon the conclusion.

Thus, the core of the difference between deductive and inductive reasoning lies in the strength of the claim that is made about the premises and their conclusion. In the deductive argument, the claim is that if the premises are true and valid, then the conclusion is true and valid. In the inductive argument, the claim is merely that if the premises are true, the conclusion is more probably true than not.

Finally, in the law, *deductive* reasoning moves from the general (universal) to the particular, whereas *inductive* reasoning moves from the particular to the general (induced generalization by enumeration of instances), or from the particular to the particular (analogy).

§ 10.3.6 Testing the Conclusion of Each Issue

Your conclusion can be true only when (1) the other propositions (premises) are true, and (2) these propositions imply the conclusion. The conclusion is always inferred from the other propositions.

Not all means of persuasion are based on reflective thinking or formal logic. For example, rhetoric is a means of persuasion. Seekers of public office, columnists, television commentators, editorial writers, advertising experts—and trial lawyers—are all masters of persuasion. They often appeal to emotions rather than to reason. Their aim is to induce belief, not to demonstrate a conclusion by pure logical means. These presentations may be works of art, but they do not always demonstrate the logic that distinguishes legal argument from impassioned summations to a jury.

This is not to say that all good reasoning must be stated in the order of formal correctness. Often, the conclusion is stated first: "Socrates is a mortal because all men are mortal and Socrates is a man"; or, in a Supreme Court case, "It could hardly be denied that a tax laid specifically on the exercise of those freedoms would be unconstitutional. Yet the license tax imposed by this ordinance is, in substance, just that."[31]

At times, the argument can skillfully be compressed to a single sentence. Thus, in *Roe v. Wade*, Justice Blackmun wrote:

> This right of privacy, whether it be founded in the Fourteenth Amendment's concept of personal liberty and restrictions upon state action, as we feel it is, or, as the District Court determined, in the Ninth Amendment's reservation of rights to the people, is broad enough to encompass a woman's decision whether or not to terminate her pregnancy.[32]

Implicit in this statement was the following syllogism:

Major Premise:	The right of privacy is guaranteed by the Fourteenth (or Ninth) Amendment.
Minor Premise:	A woman's decision to terminate her pregnancy is protected by a right of privacy.
Conclusion:	Therefore, a woman's decision to terminate her pregnancy is protected by the Fourteenth (or Ninth) Amendment.

§ 10.3.7 Determine Whether Your Premises Are Free from Material Fallacies

Material, or factual, fallacies do not result from violations of formal logic rules. They are called "material" because they exist not in the form of an argument, but in its factual content or matter, hence the description "material" or "factual" fallacies.[33] It is difficult to condense into a single definition every-

---

31. Murdock v. Pennsylvania, 319 U.S. 105, 108 (1943).

32. 410 U.S. 116, 163 (1973).

33. Material fallacies include distraction (appeals to pity or prestige or personal ridicule or to the masses or *ad terrorem*), accident, hasty generalization, false cause (*post hoc ergo propter hoc*), *non sequitur* or the most insidious fallacy that creeps up on all of us—begging the question. For definitions and examples, see RUGGERO J. ALDISERT, LOGIC FOR LAWYERS: A GUIDE TO CLEAR LEGAL THINKING (3d ed. 1997).

thing encompassed by material fallacies, yet two basic tenets of logic provide keys to their understanding:

- Logical reasoning presupposes that the terms shall be clearly and unambiguously defined and, as used in the premises and the conclusion, signify a uniform, fixed and definite meaning throughout.
- The discipline of logic demands that the conclusion be derived from the premises rather than assumed.

§ 10.4 Consider the Consequences of Your Analysis

Legal and logical analyses do not act in a vacuum, no matter whether you choose among rival precepts, interpret a precept or decide to apply a chosen and interpreted precept to the facts found by the fact finder. It may have been the practice to follow a legal precept to a dryly logical extreme in the nineteenth century, but we entered a new jurisprudential era in the twentieth. Today's judge must consider the consequences of every decision. The pressures of his docket leave little time to emulate Samuel Butler's "expert," who "was in logic a great critic,/Profoundly skill'd in analytic;/He could distinguish and divide/A hair 'twixt south and south-west side."[34]

Part of this has to do with the common law tradition that a decision in any one case may serve as ruling case law for another. There must be more than justice *in personam*, a consideration for the peculiar rights of the parties before their court; there must also be justice *in rem*, fidelity to what has been decided in the past as a guide to setting the course for the future. Professor Kent Greenawalt has written:

> Judges must decide all the issues in a case on the basis of general principles that have legal relevance; the principles must be ones the judges would be willing to apply to the other situations that they reach; and the opinion justifying the decision should contain a full statement of those principles.[35]

---

34. Samuel Butler, *Hudibras Part I, in* ENGLISH POETRY (1170–1892) 193, 193 (John Matthews Manly ed., 1907).

35. Kent Greenawalt, *The Enduring Significance of Neutral Principles*, 78 COLUM. L. REV. 982, 990 (1978).

This, I suggest, is the jurisprudential equivalent of Kant's categorical imperative: "Act as if the maxim of your action were to become through your will a universal law."[36]

Modern adjudication, however, demands more than strict adherence to the common law tradition. Because of the precise nature of today's litigation, judges must now cautiously and carefully consider—especially in the dynamic fields of criminal law, tort law and constitutional law—exactly what social, economic or political consequences will follow from their decision. Consider, for example, the current emphasis on drinking and driving or the new concepts by which pecuniary loss is allocated. In the allocation of pecuniary loss, the pendulum now swings in favor of individual rights and away from the rights of society. These subjects, light years away from "lawyer's law" of another era, require judges to consider consequential concerns in varying degrees when discussing an issue. Professor Neil MacCormick has offered excellent advice here: "To consider the consequences we face the question: what, if any, limits can govern the judicial choice of rulings to test, and how, in any event, can judges begin to frame any ruling appropriate to fit the concrete case when so vast a range of possibilities is open?"[37]

§ 10.4.1 Guidelines in Considering Consequences

What are the guidelines? We must first admit that the logical process is intrinsically evaluative. We inquire about the acceptability or unacceptability of consequences. There is, however, no reason to assume that this involves evaluation in terms of a single scale, e.g., as the Benthamite scale of supposedly measurable aggregates of pleasure and pain. Rather, when judges weigh the case for and against given rulings, they characteristically refer to certain criteria as "justice," "common sense," "public policy," "convenience" or "expediency." I suggest that decisions should never be justified by such buzzwords without the support of reasoned elaboration. At best, an opinion that relies on these labels for its rationale begs the question; at worst, it resorts to an *ad hominem*.

A decision influenced by consequential factors responds not to the rules of inductive or deductive logic, but to what we call "value judgment." Max Weber, an important European social theorist, suggested that the term refers "to 'prac-

---

36. IMMANUEL KANT, GROUNDWORK OF THE METAPHYSICS OF MORALS 89 (Paton trans. 1964) (1785).

37. NEIL MACCORMICK, LEGAL REASONING AND LEGAL THEORY 119 (1978).

tical' evaluations of a phenomenon ... as worthy of either condemnation or approval."[38] He distinguished between "logically demonstrable or empirically observable facts" and the "value-judgments which are derived from practical standards, ethical standards or world views."[39] I concede there are decisions that necessitate the use of value judgments. What I criticize is the reliance on value judgments to the exclusion of reasoned analysis. Set forth your rationale and explain your value-based choice, dwelling not in the murky waters of subjectively defined buzzwords. Remember Humpty Dumpty, who proclaimed that any word he used "means just what I choose it to mean—neither more nor less." We all know what happened to that hubristic egghead.

We judges who evaluate consequences of rival possible rulings give different weight to different criteria. Not surprisingly, we do not agree as to what degree of either perceived injustice or predicted inconvenience will arise from the adoption or rejection of a given ruling. Sometimes we differ sharply, and even passionately, as to the acceptability of a ruling under scrutiny. At this level there can simply be irresoluble differences of opinion. Hence, a multi-judge court, as a reviewing tribunal, must use thorough ratiocination in its elaboration of the statement of reasons.

§ 10.4.2 The Requirement of Consistency in Considering Consequences

What institutional device do we have to keep the brakes on freewheeling concepts of what are and are not desirable consequences? Fortunately, the system does provide such a device: *stare decisis*. Just as fortunately, this goes to the heart of the common law tradition. Our decisions at all times must be congruent with and not antagonistic to some valid and binding rule of the system. We must respect at all times the notion of consistency.

We are no longer at 1215 A.D., the year when the barons forced King John to issue the Magna Carta at Runnymede, marking the start of the common law tradition in England. Our own country has a tradition that goes back more than two centuries, originating in an era when we had already absorbed further centuries of the English common law experience with cases, recorded at least since the days of Sir Edward Coke and, later, Sir William Blackstone. Our nation's oldest appellate tribunal, the Pennsylvania Supreme Court, has been

---

38. Max Weber, *Value-judgments in Social Science, in* Weber Selections in Translation 69 (W.G. Runciman ed., 1978).

39. *Id.*

handing down recorded decisions since 1686. We have, therefore, a long history of judicial experience to ensure consistency.

Justice William O. Douglas noted the reservoir of conceptual grounds for decisions in hard cases: "There are usually plenty of precedents to go around; and with the accumulation of decisions, it is no great problem for the lawyer to find legal authority for most propositions."[40] The tradition of *stare decisis* places the judge under an obligation to follow prior judicial decisions unless exceptional circumstances are present.[41] (Here, of course, I may be begging the question because any judicial decision that departs from precedent already implies that the circumstances are exceptional.)

Adherence to the tenet of consistency keeps the march of the law at a measured cadence. The point riders can go just so far; the outriders must keep close to the flanks; and the drags must not fall too far behind.

§ 10.4.3 The Tenet of Coherence in Considering Consequences

Finally, we will discuss coherence, a concept closely related to, but in a sense somewhat different from consistency. An action may be consistent without being coherent. It may be consistent in the sense of establishing a set of norms that do not contradict one another. At the same time, the action may pursue no intelligible value or policy. The child who constantly lies to his parents is certainly consistent.

Two sets of statutes come to mind, that are internally consistent, but rather incoherent. In 1977, when the Social Security system began to hurt for funds, some bright-eyed, bushy-tailed counters of beans in the Social Security Administration came up with an idea that they blushingly pronounced a work of genius. They had found a way to save, they said, some money for the funds they had sworn to protect. They decided that those of us born between 1917 and 1921 (and I am one) should receive a lower replacement rate to calculate our preretirement income than those born before or after this limited period, and that accordingly, those of us born between these years should receive lower benefits. We became known as "notch babies." (The same "babies," as it happened, made up the bulk of those who served in World War II). Consistent? Yes. Coherent? Of course not.

---

40. William O. Douglas, *Stare Decisis*, 49 Colum. L. Rev. 735, 736 (1949).

41. In a small percentage of cases, no legal principles exist for guidance. These cases require the court to examine some justificatory principle of morality, justice and social policy. *See* Ruggero J. Aldisert, The Judicial Process: Readings, Materials and Cases (1976).

The other statute was enacted by the Italian parliament. A majority could not get together on a uniform speed limit for the *autostrade*, the nation's highway system. The objective of the legislation was automotive safety. Before that time, the *autostrade* resembled the Indianapolis 500, with speed limited only by the vehicle's power and the driver's inclination. At some curves, drivers had to slow down sharply—to 130 kilometers (almost 80 miles) per hour. The solution was to set one limit for small Fiats, another for midsized cars, and still another for luxury sedans and sports cars. Moreover, each automobile owner had to purchase and post on the rear a decal to identify the vehicle's proper speed limit. Consistent? Yes. Coherent? Well, you guess. Did it work? Absolutely not. No one put decals on cars. And the Italian road police made no effort to enforce it. So goes it in *il bel paese*.

§ 10.5 Cut Down on Citations

I would like to share with you some case histories of acute, if not chronic, "citationitis." In a school prayer case, the Supreme Court had to use 135 citations to state what it concluded to be the obvious;[42] in a civil RICO case, 114 citations;[43] in a copyright case, 164 citations.[44] What makes this problem serious is that the disease is contagious. Too many opinion writers—state and federal—and too many lawyers—administrative, trial and appellate—mimic the law review writing style. Thus, in my own Third Circuit court, in a case involving an award of attorneys' fees, there were 199 citations;[45] in another case handed down the same month, the majority required 188 citations to discuss appropriate sanctions for an attorney's misconduct.[46]

George Gopen, professor of the Practice of Rhetoric at Duke University and possessor of a Harvard doctorate in English literature as well as a law degree, tells of a 17th-century judge "who was so outraged at the length of a brief that he cut a hole in the middle and hung it around the neck of the lawyer who wrote it."

The common law tradition demands no more than a clear statement of reasons. The judicial process expects no more. The brief reader and the opinion reader deserve no less.

---

42. Wallace v. Jaffree, 472 U.S. 38 (1985).
43. Sedima, S.P.R.L. v. Imrex Co., 473 U.S. 479 (1985).
44. Harper & Row Publishers, Inc. v. Nation Enter., 471 U.S. 539 (1985).
45. Institutionalized Juveniles v. Sec'y of Pub. Welfare, 758 F.2d 897 (3d Cir. 1985).
46. Eash v. Riggins Trucking, Inc., 757 F.2d 557 (3d Cir. 1985).

What is needed first is to terminate the boring and interminable use of citations in text. Take a second look at those awful "but see" footnotes that weaken the authority in the text or that confess, upon close analysis, to the extreme fragility of the argument's main structure. Francis Bacon hit the nail on the head almost four centuries ago when he criticized legal writers who wrote as philosophers: "They make imaginary laws for imaginary commonwealths; and their discourses are as the stars, which give little light because they are so high."[47]

§ 10.5.1 How to Cut Down on Citations

There is a cure for the malady. It doesn't take too long to take the cure.

Why do you cite a case in your opinion? Think about it. Think about this question every time you are inclined to use a citation. It's something like when you reach for a cigarette and you're trying to shake the habit. Just stop what you're doing and ask yourself: "Just why in the heck am I doing this?" Usually, there are three separate reasons why you cite a case:

> For the facts.
> For the reasons.
> For the rule of the case.

Decide why you are citing the case. What you say in your opinion depends on why you are citing it.

First, you may be citing the case for the purpose of analogy, for the purpose of comparing the *material facts* in the case before you with those of the compared case.

Second, you may be citing the case only for the *reasons* stated in the compared case. You cite the case because you like the reasons. You like the reasons because they support your theory.

Third, you may be interested only in the *rule of law* emanating from the case, and are citing it only to support the legal consequence attached to a set of facts.

The length of your discussion of any case you cite is determined by why you have cited it—for the facts, for the reasons or for the conclusion, or for any combination of the three.

The question is always the same: Why have I cited the case? The answer to this depends upon the overarching question: Where does this case fit into the

---

47. Francis Bacon, The Advancement of Learning, Book II (1605), *quoted in* 3 The Works of Francis Bacon 475 (J. Spedding ed., 1876).

theme or focus of the opinion? When you answer this question, you recognize that a case should not be cited, in Loyola Marymount President and former Law Dean David W. Burcham's words, "in the nude"—that is, without any explanation for it.

§ 10.5.2 Use a Parenthetical if You Can

In recent years, the parenthetical has become very popular, and I strongly recommend its use. You've cited the case. No life history is necessary.

If a case is cited to show *resemblances or differences in the facts*, a parenthetical disclosing the material facts of the cited case will be very effective: *Francisco v. Angeles*, 845 F.4th 666, 678 (9th Cir. 2025) (holding that the reuse of burial caskets differs from the reuse of funereal urns under the statute).

The parenthetical can also be used to state the *reasons* that supported the conclusion of the cited case: *Upton Sinclair Muckraking Indus. v. Jimmy Dean Co.*, 619 F.4th 697, 722 (5th Cir. 2025) ("Where the parties agreed to sell and purchase a specific number of dressed hogs and live hogs and the seller failed to deliver the live hogs as promised, there was not substantial performance of the contract, and the purchaser is entitled to damages for the missing degree of performance.").

The parenthetical also may be used to state the *legal rule* that constitutes the holding: *Gandolfini v. HBO, Inc.*, 543 F.4th 123, 126 (2d Cir. 2025) ("Where a party has not performed to a substantial extent of the contract, the other party is entitled to damages for the missing degree of performance.").

Accompanying a citation with a parenthetical serves three important purposes: (1) it tells the opinion reader why you are citing the case, (2) it shows where the case fits into the theme or focus of your opinion, and (3) it achieves the objective of concise opinion writing.

§ 10.6 Issue Discussion: A Recapitulation

We have discussed at great length the writing of the *ratio decidendi* because it is the most important part of the opinion, as it provides justification for the decision. In addition, the quality of the discussion may determine the opinion's vitality or longevity as a precedent. Justice Jackson addressed this very point:

> The first essential of a lasting precedent is that the court or the majority that promulgates it be fully committed to its principle. That means such individual study of its background and antecedents, its draftsmanship and effects that at least when it is announced it represents not

a mere acquiescence but a conviction of those who support it. When that thoroughness and conviction are lacking, a new case presenting a different aspect or throwing new light, results in overruling or in some other escape from it that is equally unsettling to the law.[48]

Justice Walter V. Schaefer of the Illinois Supreme Court also observed:

> The intrinsic quality of the precedent relied upon is significant in determining its fate. Judges in the act of overruling a prior decision have often reconciled their action with the general requirements of *stare decisis* by stating that there is no duty to follow decisions which are absurd or manifestly in error ... Yet it remains true that an opinion which does not within its own confines exhibit an awareness of relevant considerations, whose premises are concealed, or whose logic is faulty is not likely to enjoy either a long life or the capacity to generate offspring.[49]

We may not apply precedents blindly. The putative precedent must be analyzed carefully to determine whether material facts and issues in the compared cases are similar. It must be studied to determine whether the precept deduced therefrom is the holding of the case or merely dictum. Almost 90 years ago, Benjamin Cardozo warned that:

> [P]recedents [should not be] ultimate sources of the law, supplying the sole equipment that is needed for the legal armory, the sole tools, to borrow Maitland's phrase, "in the legal smithy." Back of precedents are the basic juridical concepts that are the postulants of judicial reasoning, and farther back are the habits of life, the institutions of society, in which those conceptions had their origin, and which, by process of interaction, they have modified in turn.[50]

Cardozo also condemned the process of search, comparison and little more, which he called the color matching process, stating:

> Some judges seldom get beyond that process in any case. Their notion of their duty is to match the colors of the case at hand against he colors of many sample cases spread out upon their desk. The sample nearest in shade supplies the applicable rule. But, of course, no system of living law can be evolved by such a process, and no judge of a

---

48. Robert H. Jackson, *Decisional Law and Stare Decisis*, 30 A.B.A.J. 334, 335 (1944), *reprinted in* Walter V. Schaefer, *Precedent and Policy*, 34 U. Chi. L. Rev. 3, 10 (1965).

49. Walter V. Schaefer, *Precedent and Policy*, 34 U. Chi. L. Rev. 3, 10–11 (1965).

50. Benjamin Cardozo, The Nature of the Judicial Process 19 (1921).

high court, worthy of his office, views the function of his place so narrowly. If that were all there was to our calling, there would be little of intellectual interest about it. The man who had the best card index of the cases would also be the wisest judge.[51]

We ask ourselves questions: Has the precept emerging from the prior case originated in a thorough, well-reasoned opinion that was itself based upon clear and binding precedents? Is the precept seriously weakened by a trenchant dissent, or by a concurring opinion that casts doubt upon the wisdom of the majority opinion? Is the precept found in a single case, or has it been restated and applied in several cases that have reaffirmed its value and social desirability?

The answers to these questions tell us that the value of precedents varies widely. They are not all currency of equal value. At one extreme are those that are rock-bound, those that I call precedents *fortissimo*; at the other extreme are those that may be subject to question, precedents *pianissimo*.

If you apply the foregoing tenets in the preparation of your opinion, the finished product, more likely than not, will demonstrate substance, acceptability and continuity. This is so because your product will display an awareness of broad relevant considerations and will be faithful to the canons of logic. Such an effort does not come about automatically. It results from the judge's participation in the scholarly life, succinctly described by Gilbert Highet:

> It is a curious life we lead, the life of scholarship.... Consider first the life of learning. It is based on certain principles which people outside the academic field seldom fully understand or appreciate.
>
> The first of these is *devotion*: devotion and diligence. The Germans pithily call it *Sitzfleisch*, "flesh to sit on" because they admire the will power that keeps a man at his desk or laboratory table hour after hour, while he penetrates inch by inch to the heart of a problem. But many of us now find that *Sitzfleisch* is not so important as what newspaper men call "leg work."
>
> The second principle of scholarships ... which is *humility*....
>
> The third principle of scholarship is far easier to apply now than it has ever been throughout history. This is *organization*. Closely allied to this intellectual ideal is a fourth principle of scholarship ... [C]*ollaboration*.[52]

---

51. *Id.* at 20–21.
52. GILBERT HIGHET, THE IMMORTAL PROFESSION: THE JOYS OF TEACHING AND LEARNING 59 (1976).

§ 10.7 The Disposition

The appellate opinion writer has an obligation to the trial court and to the litigants to articulate clearly the action taken by the reviewing court. When the judgment or order is affirmed, this task is simple. An even greater necessity to clarify exists, however, when the judgment is reversed, vacated and remanded, or modified in some manner. The task in this instance is much more complicated.

Often it is enough to say, "The judgment of the trial court will be vacated and the cause remanded for further proceedings in accordance with the foregoing." This is appropriate only when there has been a clear-cut ruling on a discrete issue—most often the issue is evidentiary, procedural or pertaining to jury instructions.

Where the judgment is "vacated and the cause remanded for further proceedings," the trial tribunal is obligated to undertake further consideration of the case. The opinion writer should clearly and systematically set forth exactly what consideration is expected. If additional consideration of a legal issue is expected because the reviewing court is satisfied that the trial court should have passed on an issue in the first instance, the appellate court should be very clear in its directions:

> The judgment of the trial court is vacated and the cause remanded with a direction that the district court reconsider its decision in light of the intervening U.S. Supreme Court Case of *Alpha v. Bravo*, 949 U.S. 111 (2099).

———

> The judgment of the trial court is vacated and the case remanded for further determination of whether the interest rate was 6% or 8%.

———

> The summary judgment of the district court in favor of the defendant will be vacated and the cause remanded with a direction to dismiss the complaint.

———

> The judgment of the district court will be affirmed to the extent that it directed a verdict in favor of the defendant on the plaintiff's two counts alleging an antitrust violation, but will be reversed to the extent that it granted judgment n.o.v. on the remaining count of securities fraud. The cause will be remanded with a direction to enter judgment on the verdict in favor of the plaintiff in the securities count.

CHAPTER ELEVEN

Concurring and Dissenting Opinions

§ 11.1 Overview

Largely through the efforts of Chief Justice John Marshall, the United States declined to adopt the English practice in which each appellate judge writes a separate opinion. Rather, our practice has always called only upon one judge to write the "Opinion of the Court." The presumption is that the writer speaks for the entire court unless another judge writes a concurring or dissenting opinion or is noted as not having participated in the case.

Separate opinions may or may not provide a positive contribution to jurisprudence. Whether they do depends upon the degree of collegiality in the court or the degree of receptiveness to suggestions from colleagues. A good practice for judges who do not agree with the original draft is to make suggestions for incorporation in the majority opinion. For the sake of the law's predictability and stability, I suggest that no separate opinion should ever be written unless there has been a collegial effort toward consensus.

- The judge who is inclined to write a separate opinion should be required first to offer his or her view to the majority opinion writer. If the suggested view is rejected, it is then fair game for the disagreeing judge to write a concurrence.
- Whether the disagreeing judge writes a separate opinion depends upon that judge's view of the court as an institution: Some judges believe that a court should present its decision in a clear and workable manner, and thus the decision should be reached and presented in a uniform voice; others feel that it is better that individual views be set forth as vigorously and as often as possible, irrespective of the dictates of clarity and the desirability that there be predictability and stability in the law.

R. Dean Moorhead has also discussed the proper functions of the separate opinion:

a. To assure counsel and the public that the case has received careful consideration.

b. To help attain the objective of the law: a just result through careful formulation and application of a system of legal principle.

c. To appeal to the intelligence of a future day, when a change in the law may be forthcoming.

d. To warn that a holding laid down must not be pressed too far; *i.e.,* that it is dangerous if given a wider application.

e. By its threat, to improve craftsmanship in an opinion by causing the writer to scrutinize it carefully for defects before submitting it.[1]

§ 11.2 Concurring Opinions

§ 11.2.1 Proper Concurring Opinions

A concurring opinion is a separate opinion by a judge who agrees with the ultimate result reached by the majority—affirm or reverse—but arrives there by different routes that have dissimilar jurisprudential overtones.

One type expresses total agreement with the judgment of the majority opinion and joins in both the reasoning and breadth of the decision. The other type agrees with the judgment reached by the majority, but does not join in its reasoning and may or may not agree with the breadth of its decision.

These types may operate as jural winds that blow alternately hot and cold. Although the first type certainly bolsters the majority, the second type may be even more helpful. We are all familiar with the majority-goes-too-far and the majority-does-not-go-far-enough types. In such a case, a judge may expressly join the majority's result and write a concurrence to explicate a rationale that differs from that of the majority but still achieves the same conclusions. By offering a different theory to support the same result, a concurrence strengthens the holding.

Justice Harry Blackmun took this type of concurrence to the extreme when he wrote a concurring opinion to his *own opinion* of the court. There, he wrote:

> It cannot be suggested that in cases where the author [in writing by assignment] is the mere instrument of the Court he must forego expression of his own convictions. *Wheeling Steel Corp. v. Glander,* 337 U.S. 562, 576 (1949) (separate opinion); *see also Abbate v. United*

---

1. Moorhead, *Concurring and Dissenting Opinions*, 38 A.B.A.J. 821 (1952).

States, 359 U.S. 187, 196 (1959) (separate opinion); *Helvering v. Davis*, 301 U.S. 619, 639–640 (1937).[2]

§ 11.2.2 Whether to Respond to a Dissenting Opinion

Whether to respond to a dissenting opinion is a judgment call usually made by the majority opinion author. Sometimes a judge who joins the majority feels strong about the dissent and prefers to write a concurring opinion expressing his or her views. This is what Justice Kennedy did in the very controversial flag burning case of *Texas v. Johnson*.

> I write not to qualify the words Justice Brennan chooses so well, for he says with power all that is necessary to explain our ruling. I join his opinion without reservation, but with a keen sense that this case, like others before us from time to time, exacts its personal toll. This prompts me to add to our pages these few remarks.
>
> The case before us illustrates better than most that the judicial power is often difficult to exercise. We cannot here ask another branch to share responsibility, as when the argument is made that a statute is flawed or incomplete. For we are presented with a clear and simple statute to be judged against a pure command of the Constitution. The outcome can be laid at no door but ours.
>
> The hard fact is that sometimes we must make decisions we do not like. We make them because they are right, right in the sense that the law and the Constitution as we see them, compel the result. And so great is our commitment to the process that, except in rare case, we do not pause to express distaste for the result, perhaps for fear of undermining a valued principle that dictates the decision. This is one of those rare cases.
>
> Our colleagues in dissent advance powerful arguments as to why respondent may be convicted for his expression, reminding us that among those who will be dismayed by our holding will be some who have had the singular honor of carrying the flag in battle. And I agree that the flag holds a lonely place of honor in an age when absolutes are distrusted and simple truths are burdened by unneeded apologetics.
>
> With all respect to those views, I do not believe the Constitution gives us the right to rule as the dissenting members of the Court urge, how-

---

2. Logan v. Zimmerman Brush Co., 455 U.S. 422, 438 n.1 (1982) (Blackmun, J., concurring).

ever painful this judgment is to announce. Though symbols often are what we ourselves make of them, the flag is constant in expressing beliefs Americans share, beliefs in law and peace and that freedom which sustains the human spirit. The case here today forces recognition of the costs to which those beliefs commit us. It is poignant but fundamental that the flag protects those who hold it in contempt.

For all the record shows, this respondent was not a philosopher and perhaps did not even possess the ability to comprehend how repellent his statements must be to the Republic itself. But whether or not he could appreciate the enormity of the offense he gave, the fact remains that his acts were speech, in both the technical and the fundamental meaning of the Constitution. So I agree with the Court that he must go free.[3]

§ 11.2.3 Improper Concurring Opinions

Two types of concurrence are totally improper. One is the get-into-the-act type, which, unfortunately, is all too common. This is the practice in which the concurring judge restates the reasons of the main opinion, writing in his or her own style a version that simply duplicates what was said by the majority. Here is a real question of judicial propriety, because such a practice leaves the reader puzzled as to what to make of the separate declarations of a supposedly unanimous decision, and as to how the opinions differ substantively. It also may lessen the precedential value of a decision. This practice is sometimes uncharitably known as "running for the U.S. Supreme Court."

In this connection, we might consider the time-honored notion that dissent is a judge's prerogative and a part of judicial independence, abused or not. Concurrence, however, is also a legitimate function in the opinion-writing world. Generally speaking, it is fair to say that a separate concurring opinion is justified only when the majority is unwilling to accept the suggestion for incorporation in the main opinion.

The second type of improper concurrence is the naked statement, "I concur in the result." This is the kind of thing that prompts the young to scoff, "Big deal!" I scoff at the "concurrence in the result" practice as an abomination. What is being served? Very little, except, perhaps — to use the vernacular again — an ego trip.

---

3. 491 U.S. 397, 420–421 (1989) (Kennedy, J., concurring).

B.E. Witkin has observed:

> The cryptic statement, "I concur in the judgment," has bothered many readers.
>
> (a) It produces all the evils of a concurring opinion with none of its values; i.e., it casts doubt on the principles declared in the main opinion without indicating why they are wrong or questionable.
>
> (b) It is equivocal: it could mean that the concurring justice does not agree with the principles; or that he agrees with the principles, or some of them, but not with the manner of their statement or the reasoning of authorities set forth in support of them; or that he neither agrees nor disagrees, but wishes to stay aloof and keep himself intellectually free to examine the question anew at some later date (perhaps as the author of an opinion); or that he objects to something in the opinion—a quotation, reliance on an authority that is anathema to him, humor or satire, or castigation of a litigant or counsel—and withholds his signature because the author would not take it out.
>
> This uninformative statement should be used sparingly. If the disagreement is not substantial, the main opinion ought to be signed; if the disagreement is substantial, the reason should be stated.[4]

"Concurrence under compulsion" is a species that may or may not be legitimate, depending upon the passage of time from the original opinion. This type is written by a judge who did not join the old majority in the precedent that now forms the centerpiece of the present opinion of the court: "I dissented in *Alpha v. Bravo* three years ago and I am now constrained to join in the judgment of the Court." We all know judges who continue to dissent, as much as 15 years after their court went the other way, but this raises a serious question: How many years should such behavior go on? Is it proper for judges to continue to do this as a means of keeping their jurisprudential reputations clean at the expense of unanimity in declaration of precedents? I believe that the better practice is to write a grudging concurrence to situations in which a judges envisages possible changes in the law. At the same time, it bades fealty to the jurisprudence of the court as expressed by majority opinions. Examine, for example, what Justice Stevens has done here:

---

4. B.E. Witkin, Manual on Appellate Court Opinions 223 (1977).

Although I remain convinced that the Court misconstrued Title VII in *American Tobacco Co. v. Patterson*, 456 U.S. 63 (1982), *see id.*, at 86–90 (dissenting opinion), and in *Delaware State College v. Ricks*, 449 U.S. 250 (1980), *see id.*, at 265–267 (dissenting opinion), the Court has correctly applied those decisions to the case at hand. It is the Court's construction of the statute—rather than the views of an individual Justice— that becomes a part of the law. *See Johnson v. Transportation Agency*, 480 U.S. 616, 644 (1987) (Stevens, J., concurring); *Dougherty County Board of Education v. White*, 439 U.S. 32, 47 (1978) (Stevens, J., concurring). Accordingly, I join the Court's opinion.[5]

§ 11.2.4 Concurring Opinions: In Sum

A concurring opinion serves a valid purpose other than that of the majority opinion's precedential value. Precedent is the holding of a case; it is the definite legal consequence attached to a detailed state of facts. A concurring opinion, however, often presents an additional rationale to support the holding. By offering a different theory to support the conclusion, a concurrence may strengthen the holding. At the same time a concurring opinion that has rejected the majority's reasons may serve as a clarion call for a new development of the law. The classic example was the concurring opinion of the great California Supreme Court Justice Roger Traynor in *Escola v. Coca Cola* in 1944. His opening statement is a classic orientation paragraph:

> I concur in the judgment, but I believe the manufacturer's negligence should no longer be singled out as the basis of a plaintiff's right to recover in a case such as the present one. In my opinion it should now be recognized that a manufacturer includes an absolute liability when an article he has placed on the market, knowing that it is to be used without inspection, proves to have a defect that causes injury to human beings.[6]

Yet Justice Traynor had to wait 18 years before his view would command a majority of the Court.[7]

---

5. Lorance v. AT&T Techs., Inc., 460 U.S. 900, 913 (1989).
6. 150 P.2d 436, 440 (Cal. 1944) (Traynor, J., concurring).
7. *See* Greenman v. Yuba Power Prods., Inc. 377 P.2d 897 (Cal. 1962).

§ 11.3 Dissenting Opinions

By definition, a dissent is the minority of the court and is an opinion of one or more judges expressing disagreement with the judgment of majority opinion. A dissenting opinion cannot create binding precedent because its holding is not that of the court. It is an utterance, but not "a performative utterance." However, dissenting opinions are sometimes cited as persuasive authority when arguing that the majority's decision should be limited or overturned. In some cases, a dissent in an earlier case is used to spur a change in the law, and a later case will contain a majority opinion pronouncing the same rule of law urged by the dissent in the earlier case.

Unlike a concurring opinion, no dissent agrees with the judgment of the majority and would have ruled precisely contrary to the majority's view. A dissent in part is a dissenting opinion which disagrees only with some specific part of the majority decision. In decisions that require multi-part holdings because they involve multiple legal claims or consolidated cases, judges may write an opinion "concurring in part and dissenting in part."

A dissenting opinion has more institutional legitimacy than a concurring opinion because it is a statement of reasons calling for a result *different* from that of the majority. Care should be taken, however, for the sake of collegiality. Specifically, a dissent should attack arguments of the parties, not the discussion of the majority, unless the majority judges are off on an intellectual frolic of their own. A dissent should be impassive in tone rather than angry. It should not exaggerate the holding of the majority and then simply attack the straw person it has itself constructed. Taking my cue from Ecclesiasticus — "Let thy speech be brief, comprehending much in few words"[8] — I believe that the most effective dissents are short. They are easier to write and to read because they provide the opportunity to use the informal first-person style.

Must one always write a dissent when one disagrees? I think not. Oliver Wendell Holmes, "The Great Dissenter," wrote a dissent only when he "got the blood of controversy in [his] ... neck"[9] and when the majority "opinion came and stirred [his] fighting blood."[10] Although they do not have the same weight as majority opinions, care should be taken in writing and reasoning through a dissenting opinion. Justice Brandeis recorded that his preparation of a dis-

---

8. *Ecclesiasticus* 32:8 (King James).
9. 1 HOLMES-LASKI LETTERS 266 (Howe ed. 1953).
10. *Id.* at 560.

senting opinion was sometimes foregone because the demands of other items of work prevented an adequate treatment.

§ 11.3.1 Some Open Questions on the Work of State Appellate Courts[11]

By Roger J. Traynor

There are some who regard the dissenting opinion as the *enfant terrible* of appellate practice, though they differ as to whether it is dreadful or merely provoking. Others, conceding its antic possibilities, stoutly defend it, though they differ as to whether it is an expansive expression of internal disagreement or an indispensable part of diagnosis.... [H]ere is a problem that is not to be solved by martinet rules. If a judge merely deems his own view preferable, and the establishment of some rule counts more than the rule itself, he should at most record his dissent in two words or preferably keep his silence. If he is convinced that the majority has so misapplied settled law or so erroneously devised a new rule as to foster a malignant growth of the law, he should at least record his dissent. Should he decide to set forth his reasons, he should do so with painstaking care. Above all, he should keep his opinion impersonal. No conscientious judge will undertake a dissent without first asking himself the searching question whether it is likely to serve the law by extracting from the shadows the problems left unstated and the theories that should eventually control. Reference to the majority opinion should be kept at a minimum, unless it serves as a time-saving device to indicate the relevant defects and gaps that compel the rationale of the dissent.

Paradoxically the well-reasoned dissent, aimed at winning the day in the future, enhances the present certainty of the majority opinion, now imbedded in the concrete of resistance to the published arguments that beat against it. For that very reason the thoughtful dissident does not find it easy to set forth in his dissent.

Once he has done so he has had his day. He should yield to the obligation that is upon him to live with the law as it has been stated. He may thereafter properly note that he is concurring under compulsion,

---

11. Roger J. Traynor, *Some Open Questions on the Work of State Appellate Courts*, 24 U. Chi. L. Rev. 211, 218–19 (1957) (footnotes omitted). Reprinted with permission by the University of Chicago Law Review.

abiding the time when he may win over the majority, but he should regard dearly enough the stability of the law that governs all the courts in the state not to renew the rataplan of his dissent. When the trial court properly follows the declared law and is duly affirmed by the intermediate court, he should not vote for a hearing on the basis of his dissent. Conversely, should the trial court be reversed on the basis of his dissent, he should vote for a hearing. When the court has granted a hearing in a case with multiple issues, including the ancient one, and there is a nucleus of dissenters on other issues, he should not cast his vote on the basis solely of his ancient dissent to achieve a reversal or affirmance that would not otherwise have materialized. To do so would only work mischief. The judge's responsibility to keep the law straight is not less when he is a dissenter.

That is easier said than done. A dissenter is usually in dead earnest, resilient against the odds. Like many another judge, I have had to learn to give up dissenting while holding fast to a conviction. Thus I still believe, though still against the odds, in a dissent of several years ago against the California rule that presumptions are evidence and as such can be weighed. I no longer believe that it serves any useful purpose to reiterate that dissent. It rests with the professors and practicing lawyers to revive it in commentary if they see fit, or hasten its oblivion by criticism, or to let it wither away if they choose in the stillness of indifference.

§ 11.4 Final Thoughts

A question as to precedential value is always present where there are numerous concurrences and dissents. Society must then inquire whether the majority opinion can survive. If only a plurality opinion is left, label it "Opinion Announcing the Judgment of the Court" and not "Opinion of the Court." You owe this to your reader.

Does the majority respond to the concurrence or dissent? Some majority opinion authors always rush to respond to every point raised in the dissent. This is often done with flaccid footnotes, but just as often in the text. In most cases, however, a response is not necessary. Although I have at times made responses, I prefer what my colleagues describe as "Aldisert's disrespectful silence."

A writer has much greater literary freedom in preparing a concurring or dissenting opinion than does the majority opinion writer. Here the writing style does not require the approval of other members of the court. Consider these examples:

§ 11.5 Excerpts from Dissenting Opinions

"Basta!"

This is an Italian exclamation that, translated, means "Enough!" I now say "Basta!" on the question of special verdicts in criminal cases. I believe that the issue has sufficiently percolated in our cases for a court to exercise its supervisory power and prohibit special verdicts or special interrogatories in all criminal cases except where specifically requested by the defendant for cause shown.

To support my position, I add nothing to the majority's thorough and dispassionate discussion. My disagreement goes only to the bottom line. The majority are content to remind the trial courts again of our continued displeasure with the use of special verdicts in criminal cases and again to state the reasons for our position. As fairly set forth in the majority opinion, it is a displeasure we forcefully expressed in 1979 and 1980, but its genesis was not recent: Thirty-six years ago, Judge Maris observed that special verdicts in criminal cases have become "virtually unknown in federal criminal practice" and that "[n]o provision for them is made in the Federal Rules of Criminal Procedure." *United States v. Noble*, 155 F.2d 315, 317 n.4 (3d Cir. 1946). It is bottomed on the concept that, in our tradition, a jury may assume power it has no right to exercise, that although its verdicts may be the result of compromise or mistake, they "cannot be upset by speculation or inquiry into such matters."....

What separates the majority and me is that I am less patient than they. They seem to be saying to the district courts, "We will give you more time to heed the repeated warnings of this court." For me, the time is now.[12]

Frequently an issue of this sort will come before the Court clad, so to speak, in sheep's clothing: the potential of the asserted principle to effect important change in the equilibrium of power is not immediately evident, and must be discerned by a careful and perceptive analysis. But this wolf comes as a wolf.[13]

---

12. United States v. Desmond, 670 F.2d 414, 420–21 (3d Cir. 1982) (Aldisert, J., dissenting).

13. Morrison v. Olson, 487 U.S. 654, 699 (1988) (Scalia, J., dissenting).

In the grand scheme of things it makes no difference whether the majority's conclusion or mine prevails in this case. Under either formulation, District Council 47, American Federation of State, County and Municipal Employees AFL-CIO and the two class representatives would have their day in court at some time.

The majority, however, excuse the atrocious pleadings drafted by District Council 47's lawyers in this important case. I would not. This is not a *pro se* matter; plaintiffs here were represented by experienced lawyers, a Philadelphia-based firm and the prestigious Washington, D.C.-based Lawyers' Committee for Civil Rights Under Law. The majority also excuse the failure of plaintiffs' counsel to make any effort to amend the complaint. I would not. I would require plaintiffs' counsel (at their expense and not that of their clients) to file a new complaint naming the proper defendants and explaining what particular constitutional deprivations have been suffered by the plaintiffs and how the named defendants are responsible. I see no reason to torture and twist controlling case law to accommodate plaintiffs' counsel. I would not reward slipshod lawyering by making [the trial judge] the patsy for counsel's derelictions and by branding the judge's action as reversible error. Because my disagreement with the majority is fundamental, I set forth my views at length.[14]

As the Court's opinion acknowledges, this case is "another in a series." More specifically, it is an attempt to clarify, for the fourth time since 2007, what distinguishes "violent felonies" under the residual clause of the Armed Career Criminal Act (ACCA), 18 U.S.C. §924(e)(2)(B)(ii), from other crimes. *See James v. United States*, 550 U.S. 192 (2007); *Begay v. United States*, 553 U.S. 137 (2008); *Chambers v. United States*, 555 U.S. 122 (2009). We try to include an ACCA residual-clause case in about every second or third volume of the United States Reports.

As was perhaps predictable, instead of producing a clarification of the Delphic residual clause, today's opinion produces a fourth ad hoc judgment that will sow further confusion. Insanity, it has been said,

---

14. Dist. Council 47 v. Bradley, 795 F.2d 310, 316–317 (3d Cir. 1986) (Aldisert, C.J., dissenting).

is doing the same thing over and over again, but expecting different results. Four times is enough. We should admit that ACCA's residual provision is a drafting failure and declare it void for vagueness. *See Kolender v. Lawson*, 461 U. S. 352, 357 (1983).[15]

The question presented is not whether it is desirable for a railroad to spend its money wisely. It clearly is. The question is not whether Congress could authorize the Interstate Commerce Commission to regulate a railroad's expenditure of funds for capital improvements, deferred maintenance, or costs of material. It clearly could. The question is simply whether or to what extent Congress did grant the Commission such authority.[16]

What divides this panel is a philosophical difference in two separate, but in this case related, broad concepts: the extent to which an EEOC administrative subpoena may cast an immense discovery net that comprises privacy expectations of innocent third parties without the EEOC being put to the most meager burden of asserting a factual justificatory predicate for its actions; and the extent, if any, to which an employment discrimination claim based on professional tenure denial in a four-person Department of French in a small liberal arts college differs from a discrimination claim against a multinational corporation such as Shell Oil Company.

The majority believe that there is absolutely no difference between what may be obtained by an EEOC administrative subpoena when a claim for lifetime tenure and position is implicated in the context of a small liberal arts college or when the claim is made in the context of a typical commercial employer. Notwithstanding the wealth of materials already furnished to the EEOC by the college relating to Montbertrand's application for tenure, the majority would not place any burden whatsoever on the EEOC to show that it could not intelligently evaluate the claim until it was in possession of case histories of every tenured position, implicating confidential communications of innocent third parties. I reject both approaches because I abhor dogmatic application of

---

15. Sykes v. United States, 131 S. Ct. 2267, 2284 (2011) (Scalia, J., dissenting).

16. United States v. Chesapeake & Ohio Ry., 426 U.S. 500, 521 (1976) (Stevens, J., dissenting).

the law. I reject slot machine justice, what Roscoe Pound called "Mechanical Jurisprudence," because it has been my experience that in many cases everybody may be a bit right, that nobody is completely right or completely wrong, and that each case has its own pathology. Thus, automatic and unbridled EEOC subpoena searches cannot be the law; and if they are, I must resort to Chamfort's aphorism: "It is easier to make certain things legal than to make them legitimate."[17]

––––––––––

The majority reaches a contrary decision by distinguishing between two methods of financing religion: A taxpayer has standing to challenge state subsidies to religion, the Court announces, when the mechanism used is an appropriation, but not when the mechanism is a targeted tax break, otherwise called a "tax expenditure." In the former case, but not in the latter, the Court declares, the taxpayer suffers cognizable injury.

But this distinction finds no support in case law, and just as little in reason. In the decades since *Flast v. Cohen*, 392 U.S. 83 (1968), no court—not one—has differentiated between appropriations and tax expenditures in deciding whether litigants have standing. Over and over again, courts (including this one) have faced Establishment Clause challenges to tax credits, deductions, and exemptions; over and over again, these courts have reached the merits of these claims. And that is for a simple reason: Taxpayers experience the same injury for standing purposes whether government subsidization of religion takes the form of a cash grant or a tax measure. The only rationale the majority offers for its newfound distinction—that grants, but not tax expenditures, somehow come from a complaining taxpayer's own wallet—cannot bear the weight the Court places on it. If *Flast* is still good law—and the majority today says nothing to the contrary—then the Plaintiffs should be able to pursue their claim on the merits....

Our taxpayer standing cases have declined to distinguish between appropriations and tax expenditures for a simple reason: Here, as in many contexts, the distinction is one in search of a difference. To begin to see why, consider an example far afield from *Flast* and, indeed, from religion. Imagine that the Federal Government decides it should

––––––––––

17. EEOC v. Franklin & Marshall Coll., 775 F.2d 110, 117 (3d Cir. 1985) (Aldisert, C.J., dissenting).

pay hundreds of billions of dollars to insolvent banks in the midst of a financial crisis. Suppose, too, that many millions of taxpayers oppose this bailout on the ground (whether right or wrong is immaterial) that it uses their hard-earned money to reward irresponsible business behavior. In the face of this hostility, some Members of Congress make the following proposal: Rather than give the money to banks via appropriations, the Government will allow banks to subtract the exact same amount from the tax bill they would otherwise have to pay to the U.S. Treasury. Would this proposal calm the furor? Or would most taxpayers respond by saying that a subsidy is a subsidy (or a bailout is a bailout), whether accomplished by the one means or by the other? Surely the latter; indeed, we would think the less of our countrymen if they failed to see through this cynical proposal.[18]

The Court creates constitutional law by surmising what is typical when a social guest encounters an entirely atypical situation. The rule the majority fashions does not implement the high office of the Fourth Amendment to protect privacy, but instead provides protection on a random and happenstance basis, protecting, for example, a co-occupant who happens to be at the front door when the other occupant consents to a search, but not one napping or watching television in the next room. And the cost of affording such random protection is great, as demonstrated by the recurring cases in which abused spouses seek to authorize police entry into a home they share with a nonconsenting abuser.[19]

Our profound national commitment to free and open debate is not a license for the vicious verbal assault that occurred in this case.

Petitioner Albert Snyder is not a public figure. He is simply a parent whose son, Marine Lance Corporal Matthew Snyder, was killed in Iraq. Mr. Snyder wanted what is surely the right of any parent who experiences such an incalculable loss: to bury his son in peace. But respondents, members of the Westboro Baptist Church, deprived him of that elementary right. They first issued a press release and thus

---

18. Ariz. Christian Sch. Tuition Org. v. Winn, 131 S. Ct. 1436, 1452, 1455–56 (2011) (Kagan, J., dissenting).

19. Georgia v. Randolph, 547 U.S. 103, 127 (2006) (Roberts, C.J., dissenting).

turned Matthew's funeral into a tumultuous media event. They then appeared at the church, approached as closely as they could without trespassing, and launched a malevolent verbal attack on Matthew and his family at a time of acute emotional vulnerability. As a result, Albert Snyder suffered severe and lasting emotional injury. The Court now holds that the First Amendment protected respondents' right to brutalize Mr. Snyder. I cannot agree.[20]

––––––––––

Saddam Hussein wants to keep advertisers from using his picture in unflattering contexts. Clint Eastwood doesn't want tabloids to write about him. Rudolf Valentino's heirs want to control his film biography. The Girl Scouts don't want their image soiled by association with certain activities. George Lucas wants to keep Strategic Defense Initiative fans from calling it "Star Wars." Pepsico doesn't want singers to use the word "Pepsi" in their songs. Guy Lombardo wants an exclusive property right to ads that show big bands playing on New Year's Eve. Uri Geller thinks he should be paid for ads showing psychics bending metal through telekinesis. Paul Prudhomme, that household name, thinks the same about ads featuring corpulent bearded chefs. And scads of copyright holders see purple when their creations are made fun of.

Something very dangerous is going on here. Private property, including intellectual property, is essential to our way of life. It provides an incentive for investment and innovation; it stimulates the flourishing of our culture; it protects the moral entitlements of people to the fruits of their labors. But … [o]verprotecting intellectual property is as harmful as underprotecting it. Creativity is impossible without a rich public domain. Nothing today, likely nothing since we tamed fire, is genuinely new: Culture, like science and technology, grows by accretion, each new creator building on the works of those who came before. Overprotection stifles the very creative forces it's supposed to nurture.

The panel's opinion is a classic case of overprotection. Concerned about what it sees as a wrong done to Vanna White, the panel majority erects a property right of remarkable and dangerous breadth: Under the majority's opinion, it's now a tort for advertisers to remind the

––––––––––

20. Snyder v. Phelps, 131 S. Ct. 1207, 1222 (2011) (Alito, J. dissenting).

public of a celebrity. Not to use a celebrity's name, voice, signature or likeness; not to imply the celebrity endorses a product; but simply to evoke the celebrity's image in the public's mind. This Orwellian notion withdraws far more from the public domain than prudence and common sense allow. It conflicts with the Copyright Act and the Copyright Clause. It raises serious First Amendment problems. It's bad law, and it deserves a long, hard second look.[21]

---

21. White v. Samsung Elecs. Am., Inc., 989 F.2d 1512, 1512–14 (9th Cir. 1993) (en banc) (Kozinski, J., dissenting).

CHAPTER TWELVE

THE IMPORTANT ROLE OF LAW CLERKS

Author's Note: This chapter consists of generous extractions from the LAW CLERK HANDBOOK: A HANDBOOK FOR LAW CLERKS TO FEDERAL JUDGES, FEDERAL JUDICIAL CENTER *(2007), and* The Law Clerk's Manual, *developed iteratively over the years by clerks in my chambers. The Manual's language emanates from the experience of generations of clerks and is designed as a* vade mecum *for brand new clerks. These are not instructions from a judge or judges, but from men and women who "have been there, and done that." They have walked the walk and talked the talk.*

§ 12.1 Overview

Law clerks must understand that this book is for them, too. If a law clerk does not have this book prior to starting in chambers, she should start reading this book on her very first day on the job. This is an exercise that will serve the law clerk well in the months that follow. A caveat, though, is necessary. What is said in this chapter reflects what takes place in my chambers. No two judges conduct their chambers in the same manner. Each of us judges has idiosyncratic methods of doing things. What follows in these pages is the product of 50 years of managing my chambers and my law clerks. When I first slipped on the robes of trial judge in 1961, in the Common Pleas Court of Allegheny County (Pittsburgh, Pennsylvania) I joined a court that was a pioneer in the use of law clerks on a state trial court level. There was a specific reason for creating this institution: an order of the Supreme Court of Pennsylvania that every Common Pleas court judge prepare an opinion in every case that was appealed to an appellate court. Thus, what these pages reflect is the sum total of my 50 years of experience.

§ 12.2 Writing Tasks:
General Considerations

Some judges do all of their own writing and rely on their law clerks only to prepare internal research memoranda. Others expect their law clerks to draft opinions and orders in final form, suitable for filing with the judge's approval. Some judges assume personal responsibility for writing final opinions in cases that have been tried, but require their law clerks to prepare drafts of opinions disposing of preliminary motions. Regardless of the drafting process, decision making remains exclusively the judge's responsibility.

§ 12.3 Suggestions for Good
Writing and Editing

Law clerks must write clearly, concisely, and logically. Below are some general rules of good writing and rewriting:

- *There is no such thing as good writing.* There is only good rewriting
- *Prepare an outline before starting.* The best way to organize your thoughts and ensure that everything pertinent is included is to prepare a topic sentence or topical outline before beginning to write. Such an outline is essential before writing a draft opinion or any long document.
- *Introduce the subject.* At the outset, let the reader know the subject of the document. When preparing a memorandum on a specific issue, do not include inconsequential facts that do not bear directly on the question to be decided.
- *Follow the proper format.* The judge may require a special organization and arrangement of intraoffice written materials and may have standardized formats for other written materials. Learn these standard formats and follow them. (Examples from past cases can be found in the judge's files.) The judge's secretary or judicial assistant can also advise you whether the judge has a prescribed format.
- *Be accurate and give appropriate references.* Be careful to quote accurately from a cited authority. Be certain that cited authority has not been overruled or qualified. Some judges require their law clerks to give citations to the sources of factual statements—for example, if a particular fact is established by Smith's deposition, its statement is followed with "(Smith dep. p. 10)." This reference allows the judge to locate the statement eas-

ily, read it in context, and verify its accuracy. Often, lawyers will support their statements of fact in a brief by citing a deposition, a transcript of trial, or an exhibit. You should verify those citations before incorporating them.

- *Write succinctly, clearly, and precisely.* Good legal writing is simple, brief, and clear. Unnecessarily abstract or complex words and phrases, flowery language, or literary devices may interfere with the reader's ability to understand the point. Unless the judge instructs otherwise, leave embellishment to the judge.

- *Subdivide.* In a lengthy opinion or order, the reader may find it easier to follow if the material is divided into subparts, each labeled with letters, numbers, or short subtitles. My own preference is Roman numeral → capital letter → Arabic numeral.

- *Final Editing.* After the clerk prepares a final draft of a writing, he or she must edit it carefully before presenting it to the judge. After the judge has approved the clerk's writing—opinion, order, memo—before you file it, or, on the appellate level, before you forward it to others judges for approval, a final editing procedure must take place. This is critical. The authoring clerk asks a co-clerk to participate in what my clerks describe as "reading rainbow," a procedure in which both clerks have a copy of the writing and the clerks take turn in reading aloud every word in the document. This guarantees that every word is spelled correctly, every citation takes the proper Bluebook form and every chambers practice is followed.

§ 12.4 Clerking Responsibilities[1]

§ 12.4.1 Preparing Bench Memoranda

A large part of the law clerks' work consists of preparing bench memoranda for each sitting of the court to which the judge is assigned. The purpose of the bench memorandum is to assist the judge in making his or her decision regarding the disposition of the case. The memo should set forth four

---

1. The following advice addresses issues common to all clerks, but, because of my station on the Court of Appeals, is stated in language that applies most directly to appellate clerks. Although the lessons within are applicable to all clerks, I address concerns specific to trial court clerks in § 12.6.

critical parts—the issues, the positions of the parties, the facts material to the issues and the relevant law to be applied. It should be as concise as possible. The judge is interested in the law clerk's analysis of the issues and the recommended disposition. Law clerks must be careful, however, not to get so involved in an issue that they lose sight of who is making the final decision. If clerks are having trouble deciding whether the trial court erred on a particular issue, it probably is because it is a close call. In such an instance, the law clerks should inform the judge regarding all the relevant facts and law and let him or her and the other panel members figure out what to do. Law clerks should not spend days trying to find the "right" answer. There probably isn't one.

In my chambers, I often refer to myself as the "Chief Law Clerk." This is because, unlike other chambers, in my chambers, the judge is the first person to read the briefs and prepare a memo. In a case which I describe as a "slam dunk," my memo is generally the only one prepared in the case. At the other extreme, in a case of precedential or institutional value, in which I will request oral argument, my memo serves as a starting point for my clerks, who then prepare a detailed memo on all of the issues presented.

Notwithstanding the time I expend in these cases, the law clerks are not bound by my reasons and conclusions in my initial memo. In my chambers, a sign instructs the clerks: "Do not simply defer to the judge's memo. He did not hire you to be a yes-person." I make my final decisions about a case after I read the formal memo of my law clerk and discuss the case with the writer.

With that said, there may be a time when a law clerk reaches a point beyond which their judge is unwilling to budge. At that point, the judge will say that a decision has been made and she does not look kindly upon further attempts to persuade her. At this point, a law clerk's job is to understand the judge's position and craft persuasive arguments on her behalf.

Keep in mind that the law clerk's bench memo often becomes the framework for an opinion. I like the language of a bench memo to be "opinion ready." If the case involves the interpretation of a statute or regulation, law clerks must include the exact language of the relevant provision in the bench memo. The judge will most likely begin his opinion with the statutory language to be interpreted, and expects to have this language in the bench memo so he can readily access it.

Bench memos are not law review articles. Memos should include: the applicable legal standards, the relevant facts, the lower court's decision, and the contentions of the parties. The writing needs to be concise, but not cursory (of course, this is easier said than done).

§ 12.4.2 Research

Only rarely do the briefs do all of the research. Often, the cases cited in the briefs are inapplicable (as when the attorneys unreasonably "stretch" a case's holding), and the law clerks must conduct significant research to understand the relevant law. Independent research is also required when the briefs are inadequate, which is a common problem. Even when relying on the parties' briefs, the law clerks must Shepardize the cited case law to ensure their vitality.

Aside from Supreme Court opinions, the cases of the court in which the judge is sitting will control (e.g., the Third Circuit). If that Court of Appeals has issued a viable decision on point, the research is probably at an end. Where no binding precedent exists, the judge often will look to the decisions of sister Courts of Appeals, particularly those cases which are strong factual analogs.

As a general rule, courts do not address issues that are not raised by the parties in their briefs, unless those issues affect the court's jurisdiction. That said, law clerks should speak with the judge if a potentially material issue not raised by the parties' briefs is identified. She will let you know whether she wants you to pursue it. Keep in mind, however, that a party's failure to raise an issue in the trial court generally precludes the appellate court from reviewing it on appeal.

§ 12.4.3 Ordering the Record or Supplemental Briefing

Sometimes there will not be enough information to prepare an adequate bench memo on a case; perhaps one or both of the parties have failed to address an issue, or perhaps key documents have been omitted from the appendix. Other times a supervening court decision—by either the Court of Appeals or the Supreme Court—changes the legal landscape long after the parties have submitted their briefs. In any of these cases, the judge may ask the court clerk to direct the parties to brief an issue further. Similarly, if the appendix does not include an important document from the record, the law clerks should request the document, or the entire record. It is important that the judge have all of the pertinent information to rule on a matter.

§ 12.4.4 Components of a Bench Memo

The following parts should be included in each bench memo:

(I) OVERVIEW—This section should give a brief description on the case, the main issues presented and the suggested disposition.

Example:

This is an appeal by the IRS from the Tax Court's determination that the IRS was not entitled to post-petition interest on certain fraud penalties because it had failed to issue a proper notice and demand to the debtor, Resyn Corporation. The issues are (1) whether the district court erred in failing to treat the IRS's proof of claim as a "constructive" notice and demand, and (2) if not, whether the IRS still is entitled to interest as of the date the bankruptcy court entered its judgment of fraud. This Court should affirm.

(II) JURISDICTION—Before an appellate court may address an appeal, it must satisfy itself that it has jurisdiction. This section should set forth the authority for jurisdiction in both the district court and the appellate court.

Example:

Jurisdiction was proper in the District Court based on 28 U.S.C. § 1331 (federal question). This Court has appellate jurisdiction under 28 U.S.C. § 1291. The appeal was timely filed under Rule 4(a), Federal Rules of Appellate Procedure.

(III) FACTS—This section should give a concise description of the facts *relevant* to the issues in dispute, with record citations where necessary.[2] **The facts should not be written until it is decided what issues will be discussed.** It should also give the procedural posture of the case, indicating what happened in the district court (jury verdict, summary judgment, etc.) and who is taking the appeal. In preparing a statement of facts, strive for accuracy and objectivity, and, if there are disputed factual issues, present the evidence supporting each position. You should neither allow a personal opinion to shade the statement of facts nor present a partisan view of the evidence. A narrative statement of the facts, arranged chronologically, is usually the easiest to understand. Depending on the status of the case, the judge may ask

---

2. In a trial court, the sources are the case file, trial exhibits, the law clerk's notes taken during hearings, and, when necessary, the court reporter's notes or transcripts.

you to express a view about how any conflicts in the evidence should be resolved.

(IV) ISSUES PRESENTED—This section should list the issues presented by the parties in interrogatory form and give a "Short Answer" to each query presented.

Example:

1. Did the District Court err in dismissing DeLucca's action under Rule 12(b)(6) on the ground that the two-year statute of limitations had expired?

No. DeLucca filed his federal cause of action on July 9, 2002, almost three years after his cause of action had accrued on August 27, 1999 (the date of his termination). Therefore, his action is time-barred.

(V) STANDARD OF REVIEW—This section is critical as it tells the judge what "lens" to use when examining the issues in the case. Here, law clerks should state whether the issue is a question of law requiring plenary review, a question of fact invoking the clearly erroneous standard, or an issue requiring review for abuse of discretion.[3] After stating the appropriate standard of review, law clerks should cite a recent case in the relevant Circuit (e.g. the Third Circuit) supporting that standard of review. Often the briefs will provide the appropriate standard with a citation.

Example:

The District Court based its decision not to compel arbitration on an interpretation of 47 C.F.R. §§ 76.1602 and 76.1603. We review the District Court's conclusions of law *de novo*. *See First Liberty Inv. Group v. Nicholsberg*, 145 F.3d 647, 649 (3d Cir. 1998).

(VI) DISCUSSION—This section is the heart of the bench memo. In this section, the law clerk should provide an in-depth discussion of each of the issues on appeal. The headings should parallel the issues as stated in the "Issues Presented on Appeal" section. After stating the issue, to the clerk must set forth the appropriate law and weave in the relevant facts for that issue. It is also important to set forth the language of relevant or governing statutes before beginning any analysis of the issue. An efficient way to organize the analysis

---

3. An effective description of standards of review can be found in Ruggero J. Aldisert, *The Appellate Bar: Professional Responsibility and Professional Competence—A View from the Jaundiced Eye of One Appellate Judge*, 11 Cap. U. L. Rev. 445 (1982).

follows: (1) identify the relevant law, (2) summarize what the lower court did, (3) identify the precise arguments of first the Appellant and then the Appellee, and then (4) provide a suggested resolution. At the end of the discussion of that issue, the law clerk should state whether the judgment should be affirmed or reversed on that point and why. It is important that the analysis and conclusion follow the principles of logic.[4]

(VII) CONCLUSION—Sums up the analysis with a one or two sentence recommendation.

Of course, an unusual case or issue may call for deviation from this format. For example, if there are a number of issues with different standards of review, it may be appropriate to place the standard of review in the discussion of each issue and make a note to that effect in the standard of review section.

§ 12.5 Writing an Opinion

My advice to a law clerk is to start with the first page of this text and read the entire book. But go one step further: do not wait to read the book until you start your clerkship. While still in law school, as soon as you have accepted a clerkship offer, that's the time to start reading because: (a) it may help you to better understand the opinions in casebooks; (b) it will assist you with your extracurricular activities on law review or moot court; and (c) it will increase your comfort level on your first day in chambers because you will not be a stranger to the concepts and ideas needed to construct a bench memo or opinion.

As I have stated elsewhere, if you take my preaching to heart and apply them faithfully, you will not only write better opinions but will merit the undying respect of your judge.

On your very first case, have photocopies on your desk for what I have described as "checklists" at the end of the text. Keep them handy on your desk or posted nearby. Although these are your cram course materials that will prepare you for that first opinion, they will also be extremely helpful when you prepare that first bench memo:

- Chapter 18 Appellate Opinion Writing Checklist
- Chapter 19 Appellate Opinion Testing Checklist
- Chapter 20 Shorten-Your-Appellate-Opinion Checklist

---

4. *See* RUGGERO J. ALDISERT, LOGIC FOR LAWYERS: A GUIDE TO CLEAR LEGAL THINKING (3d ed. 1997).

Rather than summarize what's contained in these chapters, my advice to all law clerks is to stop reading the text at this point, and turn to Chapters 19–20 and read them now!

§ 12.6 Special Instructions for Trial Court Clerks

Author's Note: *Most of the materials for trial judges are drawn from* Law Clerk Handbook: A Handbook for Law Clerks to Federal Judges, Federal Judicial Center *(2007). On your very first case, have photocopies on your desk for what I have described as "checklists" at the end of the text. The checklists applicable to clerks for trial court judges can be found in Chapter 21. Keep them handy on your desk or posted nearby.*

§ 12.6.1 Resolution of Motions in Trial Courts

The resolution of motions often constitutes a substantial part of the trial court's work on a case. Some motions may require an opinion equivalent in substance and length to a final opinion after trial. For most motions, the judge may write only a short opinion or order, dictate reasons into the record, or simply indicate disposition with a single word: "Granted" or "Denied." The law clerk is usually the member of the judge's staff charged with responsibility for knowing which motions are pending, what memoranda or other pleadings have been filed with respect to each motion, and the status of each motion. The judge will instruct the law clerk as to the type of memorandum or order indicated. Some judges want their law clerks to prepare a memorandum on every motion. Others require memoranda only on certain matters or for certain types of cases.

If you are required to prepare a memorandum, first examine the briefs or memoranda from both the moving party and the opposition. The legal standard or rule that applies is often fairly clear; the difficulty is in applying the rule to the facts. The facts are almost always incompletely presented, or at least slanted in the party's favor. You must examine and compare each party's version, and then check them against the exhibits, declarations, or other materials in the record.

Look for samples of predecessors' memos on motions and use them as guides. There is no one style or format for such memos, but certain features are common:

- Name and number of the case, perhaps the category of case (e.g., antitrust, diversity tort case), the date of the memo, and the writer's initials.
- Statement of the nature of the motion or motions now under consideration, identifying the moving party.
- Recommended disposition, summarized.
- Statement of facts and procedural posture. This should include a description of the parties and their relationships to one another, key events, and a notation of facts in dispute. The memo should indicate the source of the facts stated (particularly when they are controverted or perhaps intentionally vague), such as the paragraph of the complaint, the identification of the relevant affidavit and paragraph number, or the number of the exhibit from which the fact stated is derived.
- Discussion of the parties' chief arguments; the legal standard set by controlling statutes, rules, or precedent; and a succinct explanation of your reasons for recommending a particular result on each point.

Some judges may also wish to have a draft of a proposed order or judgment disposing of the matter along the lines recommended by the law clerk.

Law clerks should avoid two common errors: (1) failing to pay attention to the procedural status of the case, and (2) writing a law review style piece rather than a memorandum that meets the judge's needs.

§ 12.6.2 Findings of Fact and Conclusions of Law

A district judge who sits as the trier of fact in an evidentiary hearing or trial may prepare either (1) a conventional opinion or (2) findings of fact and conclusions of law. Findings of fact are statements set forth in separately numbered paragraph, with each paragraph containing a material fact that the judge concludes was proved. The conclusions of law follow the findings of fact, and state in separate paragraphs the legal precepts of law judge finds applicable to the facts.

Arranging findings of fact and conclusions of law in separately numbered paragraphs, each consisting of one or two relatively brief declarative statements, helps the parties understand the opinion and makes appellate review easier. The judge may direct the law clerk to prepare a draft of either the opinion or the findings of fact and conclusions of law.

In some cases, the judge requires plaintiff's counsel to prepare proposed findings of fact and conclusions of law and requires defense counsel to respond. Other judges may require each counsel to prepare a separate proposal.

The judge reviews the proposals and makes necessary revisions or additions before adopting any of them.

If proposed findings of fact are based on transcribed testimony—either of a deposition or of the trial—the court may insert citations to page numbers of the various transcripts at the end of each paragraph of findings. The judge may ask the law clerk to review those citations, and to review legal authorities cited by the parties in their trial briefs, to determine whether the proposed conclusions of law are correct.

§ 12.6.3 Federal Trial Court Orders

Author's Note: *The author has not included trial court orders in state courts because of the varying procedures in the states. It has been many decades since he served as a state court trial judge and is not familiar with the present practice.*

Unless the court orders otherwise, the Federal Rules of Civil Procedure require that the clerk of court promptly prepare, sign, and enter a judgment when the jury returns a general verdict, the court awards only costs or a sum certain, or the court denies all relief. If, however, the court grants other relief, or the jury returns a special verdict or a general verdict accompanied by answers to interrogatories, the clerk of court prepares a form of judgment and "the court must promptly approve the form of the judgment."

Routine orders are usually prepared in the office of the clerk of court. In some cases, however, it may be necessary for the court to prepare an order that states the relief to be granted. These orders are prepared in the judge's chambers and are sometimes drafted by the law clerk. In some courts, judges direct the prevailing party to prepare an order and submit it to opposing counsel for approval.

Most courts have a standardized format for orders, and the judicial assistant will be familiar with that format. This usually includes the name of the court, the docket number of the case, the caption of the case with the names of the parties, and a descriptive title indicating the nature of the order. The order should include a paragraph stating the date of the hearing (if any), appearances of counsel, and the nature of the matter decided by the order.

An order has two functional parts: (1) the factual or legal basis for the determination; and (2) a statement that tells the parties what action the court is taking and what they must do as a result of that action.

No specific language is required to make an order effective. Use simple and unambiguous language. The purpose of the order is to tell the person to whom the order is directed precisely what to do and to allow others to determine whether that person has done it correctly and completely.

The parties may submit a proposed order or judgment for the district judge's signature in the following circumstances: the judge ruled from the bench on a legal matter and asked the prevailing party to submit an appropriate order for the judge's signature; the judge decided a nonjury case, announced from the bench his or her findings or reasons and grounds, and asked the prevailing party to submit an appropriate judgment; or the parties stipulated to a result in a particular case, with or without the judge's prior involvement, and submitted a proposed order, accompanied by their stipulation, for the judge's approval and signature. In other cases, pursuant to Federal Rule of Civil Procedure 58, the clerk of court may submit a prepared form of judgment for court approval.

When these documents arrive at chambers, a law clerk is usually responsible for their detailed review and should take the following steps:

- If the order or judgment is submitted after the judge has made a determination in court with all parties present, check to be certain that the losing party agrees that the order or judgment conforms to the judge's decision. Such approval is usually indicated by the signatures of counsel for the losing party (e.g., "Approved as to form. Signed J. Attorney, Counsel for Defendant").
- If the parties agreed or stipulated to the decision, with or without the judge's prior involvement, confirm that the submitted order or judgment is accompanied by the stipulation, signed by the parties, and the order or judgment itself has been approved as to form and substance by all parties.
- Check the substance of the order or judgment to be certain that it complies with the judge's directions on the stipulation or agreement.

§ 12.6.4 Understanding Summary Judgment

The clerk for the trial judge is often, almost every week, called upon to consider a motion for summary judgment, one of the commonest methods for disposing of cases. Although originally discouraged by the Supreme Court, since 1986, when they announced a trilogy of cases—*Celotex*, *Anderson* and *Matsushita*—the justices and lower courts have been enthusiastic about the practice.

For those of us who have worn robes in the pre-summary-judgment era, the success of summary judgment, in sheer numbers as well as quality, has demonstrated that the frequency of gut-breaking conflicts of *material* facts is far less than originally predicted. A Federal Judicial Center study of summary judgments in fiscal year 2006 identified 62,938 motions and related orders in the 276,120 civil cases terminated. Of the total cases conducive to summary judgment—employment discrimination, contacts and torts—numbering 139,257 cases, or 50% of the cases terminated, 23,332 contained at least one motion for summary judgment, or 16.75%.

Because of this prevalence, a trial court law clerk should have at her fingertips a copy-and-paste-ready summary of the governing law, which should be rendered somewhat similarly to the following:

> Summary judgment is appropriate where the Court is satisfied that "there is no genuine issue as to any material fact and that the moving party is entitled to a judgment as a matter of law." Rule 56(c), Federal Rules of Civil Procedure; *Celotex Corp. v. Catrett*, 477 U.S. 317, 330 (1986). A genuine issue of material fact exists only if "the evidence is such that a reasonable jury could find for the nonmoving party." *Anderson v. Liberty Lobby, Inc.*, 477 U.S. 242, 248 (1986). When the Court weighs the evidence presented by the parties, "[t]he evidence of the nonmovant is to be believed, and all justifiable inferences are to be drawn in [her] favor." *Id.* at 255.
>
> The burden of establishing the nonexistence of a "genuine issue" is on the party moving for summary judgment. *In re Bressman*, 327 F.3d 229, 237 (3d Cir. 2003) (quoting *Celotex*, 477 U.S. at 331 (Brennan, J., dissenting)). The moving party may satisfy this burden by either (1) submitting affirmative evidence that negates an essential element of the nonmoving party's claim; or (2) demonstrating to the Court that the nonmoving party's evidence is insufficient to establish an essential element of the nonmoving party's case. *Id.* at 331.
>
> Once the moving party satisfies this initial burden, the nonmoving party "must set forth specific facts showing that there is a genuine issue for trial." Rule 56(e). To do so, the nonmoving party must "do more than simply show that there is some metaphysical doubt as to material facts." *Matsushita Elec. Indus. v. Zenith Radio Corp.*, 475 U.S. 574, 586 (1986). Rather, to survive summary judgment, the nonmoving party must "make a showing sufficient to establish the existence of [every] element essential to that party's case, and on which that party will bear the burden of proof at trial." *Celotex*, 477 U.S. at 322. Furthermore, "[w]hen opposing summary judgment, the non-movant

may not rest upon mere allegations, but rather must 'identify those facts of record which would contradict the facts identified by the movant.'" *Port Auth. of N.Y. and N.J. v. Affiliated FM Ins. Co.*, 311 F.3d 226, 233 (3d Cir. 2003).

In deciding the merits of a party's motion for summary judgment, the court's role is not to evaluate the evidence and decide the truth of the matter, but to determine whether there is a genuine issue for trial. *Anderson*, 477 U.S. at 249. Credibility determinations are the province of the factfinder, not the district court. *BMW, Inc. v. BMW of N. Am., Inc.*, 974 F.2d 1358, 1363 (3d Cir. 1992). Affidavits and declarations may be used to support a motion but summary judgment may be granted only "if the movant shows that there is no genuine dispute as to any material fact and the movant is entitled to judgment as a matter of law." Rule 54(a).

§ 12.6.5 Common Law Demurrer and Rule 12(b)(6)

Seeking judgment using common law demurrer—or its federal analogue, Rule 12(b)(6)—is much different from summary judgment, inasmuch as the motion occurs long before discovery occurs or evidence is collected. Demurrer is part of the pleadings, and is defined as "[a]n allegation, that, admitting the facts of the preceding pleading to be true as stated by the party making it, he has yet shown no cause why the party demurring should be compelled by the court to go further." Bouvier's Law Dictionary 8th Ed. (1914). Similarly, Rule 12(b)(6) of the Federal Rules of Civil Procedure provides: "Every defense to a claim for relief in any pleading must be asserted in the responsive pleading if one is required. But a party may assert the following defenses by motion: .... (6) failure to state a claim upon which relief may be granted."

Like summary judgment motions, Rule 12(b)(6) motions are ubiquitous in pretrial proceedings. A trial court clerk should likewise keep ready some paragraphs summarizing the applicable legal standard. One summation that would be common in district courts within the Third Circuit is as follows:

> In reviewing a dismissal under Rule 12(b)(6) of the Federal Rules of Civil Procedure, "we accept all factual allegations as true, construe the complaint in the light most favorable to the plaintiff." *Pinker v. Roche Holdings Ltd.*, 292 F.3d 361, 374 n.7 (3d Cir. 2002). Under Rule 12(b)(6), a motion to dismiss may be granted only if, accepting all well-pleaded allegations in the complaint as true and viewing them

in the light most favorable to the plaintiff, a court finds that plaintiff's claims lack facial plausibility. *Bell Atl. Corp. v. Twombly*, 550 U.S. 544, 555–556 (2007). This requires a plaintiff to plead "sufficient factual matter to show that the claim is facially plausible," thus enabling "the court to draw the reasonable inference that the defendant is liable for misconduct alleged." *Fowler v. UPMC Shadyside*, 578 F.3d 203, 210 (3d Cir. 2009) (internal quotation marks and citation omitted). After *Twombly* and *Ashcroft v. Iqbal*, 129 S. Ct. 1937 (2009), "conclusory or bare-bones allegations will no longer survive a motion to dismiss: threadbare recitals of the elements of a cause of action, supported by mere conclusory statements, do not suffice." *Fowler*, 578 F.3d at 210 (internal quotation marks and citation omitted). While the complaint "does not need detailed factual allegations ... a formulaic recitation of the elements of a cause of action will not do." *Twombly*, 550 U.S. at 555.

§ 12.7 Denouement

Whether clerking for a trial or appellate judge, state or federal, what a law clerk learns depends on what they want to learn in that year or two in chambers. To be sure, no two judges supervise their clerks the same. At one end of the spectrum, the appellate clerk does not have immediate access to the judge. Here, the clerk gets the writing assignment either from a senior or career clerk, and does not discuss the writing until the final product is placed on the judge's desk. At the other extreme—as is the tradition in my chambers—the clerk is free at any time to discuss any matter with the judge, who makes himself immediately available unless he, himself, is in the middle of writing.

In my chambers, I also make myself available to the law clerks during my lunch hour, eating with them three days a week. Our lunches are like Lewis Carroll's discussion of the walrus and the carpenter:

> "The time has come," the Walrus said,
> "To talk of many things:
> Of shoes—and ships—and sealing wax—
> Of cabbages—and kings—
> And why the sea is boiling hot—
> And whether pigs have wings."[5]

---

5. Lewis Carroll, Through the Looking-Glass, and What Alice Found There 75–76 (1897).

To be sure, the conversation eventually turns to talk of law and the cases we are wrestling with, but not before we touch upon politics, or the book I am currently working on, or how we spent our weekends, or the books we are reading, or my most recent golf score. I am proud of my law clerks. Two have gone

LUNCH IN JUDGE
ALDISERT'S CHAMBERS

on to clerk on the U.S. Supreme Court, one has become a university president, three have served as law school deans, one as a state and federal judge, several as law school professors—one of whom serves on the law faculty at Oxford—many have embarked on careers with the Department of Justice, and, by far, the majority have become senior partners in leading metropolitan law firms.

In my 50 years on the bench, I have come to believe that for judges to treat their clerks as family is to ensure their success in the years to come.

A TRIAL JUDGE AND HIS LAW CLERKS

CHAPTER THIRTEEN

OPINIONS OF TRIAL COURTS

§ 13.1 Overview

The emphasis of this book is on appellate court opinions, but much of it applies also to opinions of trial judges, arbitrators, administrative law judges and agency review boards. Because tribunals of the first instance have certain unique characteristics and emphases, this chapter will discuss both (a) the unique responsibilities of trial judges, which includes presiding over the reception of evidence, converting evidence into findings of facts, and applying the relevant law to the facts and (b) advice for writing opinions.

Separate treatment is necessary because trial and appellate opinions serve different functions. Trial court opinions are justificatory only. They are designed to explain the tribunal's decision. An opinion for an appellate court has a completely different purpose: the correction of errors of trial tribunals and applying, examining and evaluating the law of the jurisdiction.

In the common law tradition, the appellate court's ability to develop case law becomes legitimate because the decision is accompanied by a publicly recorded statement of reasons. Announcing a rule of law is the function of the appellate court, and is a by-product of the court's adjudicative function. If there were no reasons for public appellate opinions, the court's decision would merely resolve the particular dispute presented by the parties. In our great and noble tradition, the by-product of an appellate decision is critical; it survives long after the dispute between the litigants has been resolved. This by-product promulgates a legal precept, describing the legal consequence arising from the adjudicative facts set forth in the opinion.

By contrast, the purpose of a trial court opinion is much more limited. It is designed only to explain the tribunal's decision. Judicial officers who also find facts should prepare opinions to support all rulings on post-trial motions and where a complaint or claim has been dismissed without a hearing. This statement should be compulsory where judgment on the pleadings or summary judgment is entered. Moreover, a trial court opinion should be forthcoming in pretrial matters where evidence is suppressed or issues restricted and in all rulings on post-trial motions.

§ 13.2 Necessary Parts of a Trial Court Opinion

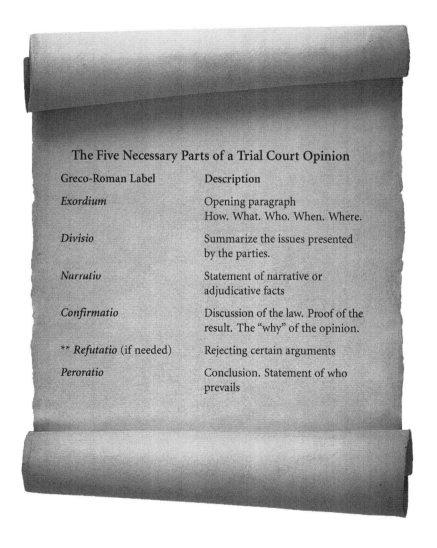

The Five Necessary Parts of a Trial Court Opinion

Greco-Roman Label	Description
Exordium	Opening paragraph How. What. Who. When. Where.
Divisio	Summarize the issues presented by the parties.
Narratio	Statement of narrative or adjudicative facts
Confirmatio	Discussion of the law. Proof of the result. The "why" of the opinion.
** *Refutatio* (if needed)	Rejecting certain arguments
Peroratio	Conclusion. Statement of who prevails

§ 13.3 Opening Paragraph

Writing the opening should discipline judges to focus on the central issues of the case. The opening paragraph should answer four questions: who, why, how, and what the court is going to do about it.

The paragraph should begin with identification of the parties. This provides the answer to "who." It should continue with a description of the type of action being brought, the relief sought and the issue presented. This tells the reader "why" the matter is present before the court. The paragraph should preview the court's holding, telling the reader "what" the court is going to do about the issue before it and allude to the reasons for doing so. The opening paragraph should also briefly explain the procedural history. This explains the cause of action explaining "how" the matter came before the court.

A statement of the court's jurisdiction should then follow. This is especially necessary in proceedings of federal district courts. The statutory basis for jurisdiction should be identified with specific reference to statutes.

Jurisdiction having been established and the legal basis for the complaint and defense having been asserted, the trial tribunal should then be in a position to summarize specific issues of law presented for disposition. Many trial court opinions begin with a statement of the *principal* issue to be discussed.

§ 13.4 Excerpts from Trial Court Opinions: Opening Paragraphs

Plaintiffs bring this action to recover on a products liability claim and a related claim for negligent infliction of emotional distress. They allege that the refrigerator in their apartment was negligently manufactured by defendant and that it suddenly burst into flames, destroying their personal property. Plaintiffs also seek damages for the emotional distress of Jodi Levit, which they claim is accompanied by physical manifestations. Defendant moves for partial summary judgment, arguing that plaintiffs failed to allege facts sufficient to permit recovery under Illinois law for the negligent infliction of emotional distress. We agree, and for the following reasons we grant summary judgment in favor of defendant on plaintiffs' emotional distress claim.[1]

---

1. Levit v. Gen. Motors Corp., 682 F. Supp. 386, 387 (N.D. Ill. 1988).

———————

Defendants, recently indicted on charges stemming from their arrest pursuant to a criminal complaint filed in December of 1982, move to dismiss the pending indictment. Defendants' arguments are predicated on an alleged violation of the Speedy Trial Act, 18 U.S.C. §3161(b) and the Due Process Clause of the Fifth Amendment to the United States Constitution. Notwithstanding the questionable conduct of the original Assistant United States Attorney assigned to this case, the Court holds that dismissal is not warranted by either ground urged by defendants. Accordingly, the motions to dismiss are denied.[2]

———————

Petitioner James Lavis ("Petitioner") seeks a writ of habeas corpus. He claims that the State of Illinois ("the State") violated his Fifth and Fourteenth Amendment rights by questioning him after he had requested counsel, and that the State appellate court erred in ruling that admitting his inculpatory statements into evidence constituted harmless error at his trial. For the reasons set forth below, the petition for habeas relief will be granted.[3]

———————

Petitioners Lloyd N. Paine III ("Paine") and Bernd Hoffman, a.k.a. Phillip B. Paine (collectively the "taxpayers") commenced this proceeding pursuant to 26 U.S.C. §7609(b)(2)(A) to quash two Internal Revenue Service summonses (the "Summonses") issued by the United States to third-party record keepers in possession of certain Paine's bank records. In response, the United States has moved, pursuant to the above-referenced statute, to compel compliance with the Summonses. For the reasons set forth below, the petitioners' motion to quash is denied and the government's motion to compel compliance with the Summonses is granted.[4]

———————

The Federal Deposit Insurance Corporation (FDIC) filed this action against former directors and officers of the Commercial State

———————

2. United States v. Oliver, 683 F. Supp 35, 36 (E.D.N.Y. 1988).

3. U.S. *ex rel.* Lavis v. O'Leary, 682 F. Supp. 375, 376 (N.D. Ill. 1988).

4. Paine v. United States, 682 F. Supp. 739, 739 (E.D.N.Y. 1987).

Bank of Afton (Bank), a failed Iowa-chartered bank taken over by the FDIC in 1985. Defendants Darrell S. Werner, Steven D. Werner, C. Frederick Booth, Robert M. Crandall, and Allan L. Kirkhart by motions to dismiss contend this court is without jurisdiction. They argue that the jurisdictional statute on which the FDIC relies, 12 United States Code section 1819 (Fourth), excepts from federal jurisdiction certain actions brought by the FDIC as a receiver, and this is such an action. The court concludes it has jurisdiction because the FDIC is here acting in its corporate capacity, not as receiver of the Bank. The defendants' motions to dismiss are denied.[5]

§ 13.5 Statement of Facts: Motions to Dismiss

A motion to dismiss usually asserts lack of jurisdiction over the subject matter, lack of jurisdiction over the person, improper venue, insufficiency of service of process, failure to state a claim upon which relief can be granted or failure to join a necessary party.[6] In most jurisdictions, in a motion to dismiss, the factual predicate for the motion on the pleadings must be contained within the four corners of the complaint. The averments of the plaintiff or claimant must be assumed to be true. This is especially important in motions under Rule 12(b)(6), asserting that no relief can be granted under the averred facts.[7] This motion relates to the common law demurrer that is predicated on the modern idiom: "I've heard the facts. So what?"

Where the tribunal grants a motion to dismiss, the better practice is to write an opinion. The judge should set forth the facts as broadly as possible, in accordance with the pleadings, in favor of the party adverse to the motion.

§ 13.6 Statement of Facts: Summary Judgment

Summary judgment is a different breed of cat. Facts recognizable by the court in a summary judgment proceeding range across a broader compass than

---

5. FDIC v. Kelly, 682 F. Supp. 427, 428 (S.D. Iowa 1988).

6. *See* FED. R. CIV. P. 12.

7. In some jurisdictions, this is called raising a demurrer, or a preliminary objection raising a question of law.

those considered on a motion to dismiss. Here the trial court may consider matters outside the pleadings including depositions, answers to interrogatories and admissions on file, if any, purporting to show that there is no genuine issue as to any material fact.

Here, too, the facts must be viewed in the light most favorable to the non-moving party. Unverified averments in the complaint or counterclaims are not sufficient to overcome depositions or affidavits supporting the motion for summary judgment. Where the party opposing the motion does not produce any evidentiary matter, or produces too little to establish that there is a genuine issue for trial, or rests solely on the averments of pleadings, the adverse party is apt to lose.[8] The modern view is that the adverse party in summary judgment must go forward with affidavits, interrogatories and answers to interrogatories, or with depositions to offset verified factual averments supporting the motion for summary judgment.[9]

Because an order granting summary judgment terminates the action, a statement of reasons should always be written. Where summary judgment is denied, no detailed statement is required. In setting forth reasons for granting summary judgment, it is extremely important to present the evidence supporting and the evidence contesting the motion, in order to demonstrate that there is not a genuine issue of material fact.

Caveat: The trial court may not—repeat, may not—serve as a fact finder in summary judgment. If the evidence on a material fact is controverted, summary judgment will not lie.

§ 13.7 The Trial Judge as Fact Finder

In the extremely important statement of reasons following a bench trial or hearing, it is necessary to "find" the facts. The judge should consider all the evidence presented and then make findings of fact based upon stipulations, uncontroverted relevant testimony and admissions in the pleadings. Or where the testimony, oral and documentary, is controverted, the judge must make a credibility determination. The findings of fact are necessary to inform the litigants, and to explain to any reviewing tribunal the factual predicate of the conclusion.

---

8. *See* Celotex Corp. v. Catrett, 477 U.S. 317 (1986); Anderson v. Liberty Lobby, Inc., 477 U.S. 242 (1986); Matsushita Elec. Indus. v. Zenith Radio Corp., 475 U.S. 574 (1986).

9. *See* Adickes v. S.H. Kress & Co., 398 U.S. 144, 160 (1970).

Judge Joyce J. George suggests that facts should be stated in the past tense and propositions of law stated in the present tense.[10] Should the statement of facts be presented by numbered paragraphs or by a narrative? It depends. If it is a lengthy proceeding where many relevant facts are controverted, it may be well to enumerate the findings. Many court rules provide that a narrative form is acceptable.

Rule 52(a) of the Federal Rules of Civil Procedure, provides:

(1) *In General.* In an action tried on the facts without a jury or with an advisory jury, the court must find the facts specially and state its conclusions of law separately. The findings and conclusions may be stated on the record after the close of the evidence or may appear in an opinion or memorandum of decision filed by the court. Judgment must be entered under Rule 58.

(2) *For an Interlocutory Injunction.* In granting or refusing an interlocutory injunction, the court must similarly state the findings and conclusions that support its action.

(3) *For a Motion.* The court is not required to state findings or conclusions when ruling on a motion under Rule 12 or 56 or, unless these rules provide otherwise, on any other motion.

. . . .

(6) *Setting Aside the Findings.* Finding of fact, whether based on oral or other evidence, must not be set aside unless clearly erroneous, and the reviewing court must give due regard to the trial court's opportunity to judge the witnesses' credibility.[11]

Relevant and material facts, however, must be more comprehensive in a trial court opinion than in an appellate opinion. You must remember that an appellate court opinion is based upon only the legal issues presented on appeal. Very often, the trial court addresses many more legal and factual issues than are asserted on appeal.

Findings based upon stipulations, uncontroverted evidence or pleading admissions should be so identified. Facts found from controverted evidence should be stated with an explanation of why certain evidence is accepted and other evidence is rejected. An explanation of credibility evaluations is always important because most appellate courts yield to the judge-fact-finder on issues of credibility.

---

10. Joyce J. George, Judicial Opinion Writing Handbook 44 (2d ed. 1986).

11. Fed. R. Civ. P. 52.

A subheading, "Statement of Facts," usually appears in opinions of tribunals of the first instance. In most cases, the facts should be presented in chronological order. Judge George has explained that only those facts necessary to the issue(s) should be set forth:

> Certain relevant facts are necessary to understand the analysis of the case and the result reached. Too much detail, however, is ineffective. For instance, when no question has been raised as to the timeliness of a filing, the judge accomplishes nothing by stating that the pleading, motion, or objection was timely made. Procedural defects which might decide some other case should not be discussed in a case where they are not in dispute. When details that have no bearing upon the outcome of the case are included, the reader is needlessly required to sort out and discard that which is unnecessary to the decision. This is a job no reader should be made to perform.
>
> To write an effective decision, you should set forth only facts that serve a useful purpose in understanding the conclusion. Legal descriptions, contracts, and statutes quoted in full, or testimony quoted at length, are rarely necessary to a disposition of the case. These should be summarized.[12]

§ 13.8 Fact? Or Disguised Conclusion of Law?

As Gertrude Stein might have said had she worn judicial robes, a fact is a fact is a fact.[13] Do not disguise a finding of fact as a conclusion of law; if you do, you may be assuming a legal conclusion, begging the question or arguing in a circle. In Latin, this fallacy is known as *petitio principii*. I use the term "legal conclusion" advisedly in order to distinguish it from "logical conclusion." A legal conclusion states a legal consequence; a logical conclusion is a permissible or compellable inference, and is a fact.

In fact finding, there are only two permissible types of facts:

- A basic fact, sometimes called a subordinate fact, is drawn from narrative or historical evidence.

---

12. Joyce J. George, Judicial Opinion Writing Handbook 47 (2d ed. 1986).

13. Gertrude Stein, "Sacred Emily," *in* Geography and Plays (1922) ("Rose is a rose is a rose is a rose.").

- An inferred fact is a logical factual conclusion drawn from basic facts or historical evidence. The key to a logical inference is the reasonable probability that the conclusion reached flows from the evidentiary data.

Basic facts:

A nickel-plated revolver was used in a bank holdup by a ski-masked robber who got away with $10,000 in marked money.

A nickel-plated revolver, a ski mask and $10,000 in marked money are found in the apartment of Dirty Dan, its sole occupant.

Proper fact finding: Our old friend Dan was the actor alluded to in the basic facts.

You will note that we did not conclude as a "fact" that Dan was guilty of the crime of bank robbery. That would be a legal conclusion and not a finding of fact. Consider the following:

Basic facts:

It is stipulated that Alpha and Bravo had previously entered into a binding contract for Bravo to paint Alpha's store on a stated Sunday for a sum certain. Bravo failed to appear to paint the store.

Proper fact finding: Bravo failed to perform on the date specified.

Improper fact finding: Bravo breached the contract.

The following examples help distinguish the difference between factual and legal conclusions:

Proper fact finding: Charley drove his car 60 miles an hour through a school crossing while children were in the crosswalk.

Improper fact finding: Charley drove his car negligently at the school crossing.

Basic fact finding: Ms. Foxtrot and Mr. Golf exchanged vows in a marriage ceremony at a nuptial mass on June 12 in front of 200 friends and relatives.

Improper fact finding: Ms. Foxtrot and Mr. Golf were legally married on June 12.

§ 13.9 Be Careful of the Proposed Findings of Fact

The trial judge must always be wary of statements of fact made by trial counsel. Has counsel stated biased impressions of the evidence? Has counsel inaccurately recited the evidence? Has counsel omitted evidence material to the ultimate decision? The answer to all three questions: probably. Therefore, the trial court's findings should always be stated with particularity. Do not simply state: "We adopt plaintiff's suggested findings of fact as findings of our own. *See* Brief for Plaintiff at 1, 3–5, and 7–10." This is an abdication of the judicial function. It makes appellate review frustrating and unnecessarily difficult, and creates the impression that the losing party was not given a fair shake.

§ 13.10 Discussion of the Law

In trial tribunals, discussion of the law is justificatory only. It is not designed to be error-correcting. Unless the case presents issues of first impression, the opinion need not be crafted with the same formality and dignity as one designed for precedential authority. Where it does discuss novel issues, however, its preparation should meet the standards and structure of a published appellate opinion.

Discussion of legal issues point by point should generally follow the procedure set forth in Chapter 10. The subheading "Discussion" should introduce the subject to the extent that treatment of each issue depends upon its importance and the state of the law at issue. If it is a novel question, an extended discussion may be necessary. If the point is well settled, the issue can be adequately treated by reference to one or two citations. If the state of the law is obvious, it may not be necessary to discuss the issue other than simply to identify it and to indicate that it has been raised and rejected.

Whether published or not, the trial tribunal's discussion of the law should address all issues presented by the parties. This is necessary to satisfy the litigants that their contentions have been considered and also to assure the reviewing court that a question raised on appeal had, in fact, been considered at the trial level. In this way, the reader will more clearly understand the "why" of the court's decision.

The discussion of law contains an aspect not present in appellate opinions—a statement of reasons why the fact finder deemed certain witnesses credible and others not. In the assignment of competencies in the judicial process, the fact finder is allowed the broadest discretion in credibility findings.

To save readers from the trouble of re-reading earlier parts of your opinion, you can explain and define terms that would not be recognizable to the average reader; in many cases it is not enough to define it once and expect readers to remember its meaning. Several experts of opinion writing for administrative law judges flatly state: "A better practice is to periodically repeat the information, especially when several pages have been covered since the last use of the term."[14]

Because the trial judge smells the smoke of battle, he or she deserves what Professor Maurice Rosenberg has called "the superiority of his nether position."[15] The cold printed record can never show considerations such as body language, hesitation when responding or constant looking to counsel for guidance.

§ 13.11 Conclusions of Law

Following your discussion of the facts, you proceed into another subdivision of the opinion entitled "Conclusions of Law." These are single statements culled from the previous subdivision, and applied to the Findings of Fact so that a Conclusion of Law is a combination of fact and law. What the master of jurisprudence Roscoe Pound defined as rules of law in the narrow sense is applicable here—"precepts attaching a definite detailed legal consequence to a definite detailed set of facts."

If set forth logically, your decision will have several sorts of conclusions, usually building one upon another. One conclusion may be established through inductive reasoning, by either enumerated instances or the method of analogy.[16] Such conclusions are preliminary. They, in turn, become the major premises in the categorical, hypothetical or disjunctive syllogisms you have used in your discussion in order to reach further conclusions through deductive reasoning.[17]

Whether achieved by induction or deduction in your "Discussion" subdivision, these conclusions are set forth by means of simple, unadorned propositions in the "Conclusions of Law" subdivision of the opinion.

---

14. Michael H. Frost and Paul A. Bateman, Writing Deskbook for Administrative Judges 39 (2010) (The authors are professors of Legal Analysis, Writing and Skills at Southwestern Law School in Los Angeles).

15. Maurice Rosenberg, *Judicial Discretion of the Trial Court, Viewed from Above*, 22 Syracuse L. Rev. 635, 663 (1971).

16. *See* Ruggero J. Aldisert, Logic for Lawyers: A Guide to Clear Legal Thinking 45–51, 89–113 (3d ed. 1997).

17. *See id.* at 145–68.

It is well to remember that lawyers and judges often express arguments with truncated propositions, omitting one of the premises or even the conclusion. This is called an enthymeme. In ordinary writing and speaking, the formal arrangements of argument often remain unobserved. Note the childhood restrictions:

Every good girl gets a star on her forehead.
Susie is a good girl.
Therefore, Susie gets a star on her forehead.

In normal speech, we would say that Susie got a star on her forehead because she was a good girl. Many legal briefs and opinions contain "enthymemes" (sometimes without the author being aware of it) because either the major or the minor premise is obvious or understood. Thus, in the "Discussion" subdivision, you may have said that the city was negligent for failure to inspect and maintain subterranean water mains. Your discussion may have omitted certain premises applying to the law of negligence: stating the duty of due care to maintain the water mains, breach of that duty, and the fact that it would have been foreseeable that plaintiff's property would be damaged in the event of a rupture of the lines. Your discussion may have omitted:

The major premise because it was self-evident.
The minor premise showing the breach.
The conclusion because it was set forth in earlier statements.

Not all good reasoning is stated in the order of formal correctness, as discussed in detail in §10.3.6. We learn also that a premise may be omitted from an argument: "All men are mortal, therefore, Socrates is a mortal" or "Socrates is a man, therefore, he is a mortal" or "All men are mortal. Socrates is a man." Thus, in examining your discussion for the statement of conclusion, you may not find the usual order of the major premise, followed by the minor premise and leading to the conclusion.

The conclusion may precede or come between the premises. In fact, the conclusion may only be implied. It is important to locate your conclusions in the discussion and state them explicitly in the "Conclusions of Law" subdivision.

§13.12 The Disposition

In a trial tribunal opinion, it is preferable to set forth the disposition under a separate subheading. This should be clearly stated, as free of ambiguity as possible; it should describe the decision reached and set forth the relief to be granted. The resolution of the litigation should be clear, concise and precise.

The opinion's disposition is not to be confused with the formal order of judgment, which is required by rule in certain jurisdictions. The federal practice requires that, in order to be effective, a formal order of judgment should be set forth in a separate document and should be properly entered.[18]

---

18. *See* Fed. R. Civ. P. 58.

CHAPTER FOURTEEN

Administrative Law Judge Opinions

§ 14.1 Overview

Most of the reading public is familiar with state and federal trial and appellate judges. The office of administrative law judge ("ALJ"), however, is a position that is less well known to the public, even though it constitutes an integral role in the many state and federal administrative agencies that possess administrative judicial hierarchies. The following lists demonstrate the prevalence of this important office:

§ 14.1.1 Federal Agencies with Administrative Law Judges

- Coast Guard
- Commodity Futures Trading Commission
- Department of Agriculture
- Department of Health and Human Services/Department Appeals Board
- Department of Health and Human Services/Office of Medicare Hearings and Appeals
- Department of Housing and Urban Development
- Department of the Interior
- Department of Justice/Executive Office for Immigration Review
- Department of Labor
- Department of Transportation
- Department of Veterans Affairs
- Drug Enforcement Administration
- Environmental Protection Agency
- Equal Employment Opportunity Commission

- Federal Aviation Administration
- Federal Communications Commission
- Federal Energy Regulatory Commission
- Federal Labor Relations Authority
- Federal Maritime Commission
- Federal Mine Safety and Health Review Commission
- Federal Trade Commission
- Food and Drug Administration
- International Trade Commission
- Merit Systems Protection Board
- National Labor Relations Board
- National Transportation Safety Board
- Nuclear Regulatory Commission
- Occupational Safety and Health Review Commission
- Office of Financial Institution Adjudication
- Patent and Trademark Office
- Postal Service
- Securities and Exchange Commission
- Small Business Administration
- Social Security Administration

§ 14.1.2 State Departments and Agencies with Administrative Law Judges

Some states, like California, follow the federal model of having a separate corps of ALJs attached to each agency that uses them. Others, like New Jersey, have consolidated all ALJs together into a single agency that holds hearings on behalf of all other state agencies. This type of state adjudicatory agency is called a "central panel agency." Still others use a type of central panel agency that does not handle all the hearings for every state agency.

The following is a representative list of state agencies that employ ALJs:

- Alabama Department of Revenue
- California Department of Consumer Affair
- California Department of Health Services
- California Department of Industrial Relations
- California Department of Social Services
- California Employment Development Department
- California Public Utilities Commission

- Florida Division of Administrative Hearings
- Georgia Office of State Administrative Hearings
- Illinois Human Rights Commission
- Industrial Commission of Arizona
- Iowa Department of Inspections and Appeals-Division of Administrative Hearings (holds hearings for some but not all state agencies)
- Iowa Workforce Development Department
- Louisiana Division of Administrative Law
- Maryland Office of Administrative Hearings
- Maryland Public Service Commission (hearings for public utility cases)
- Massachusetts Executive Office of Transportation
- Massachusetts Department of Environmental Protection
- Michigan State Office of Administrative Hearings and Rules
- Minnesota Office of Administrative Hearings (holds hearings for some but not all state agencies)
- New Jersey Office of Administrative Law (holds hearings for all state agencies)
- New York City Office of Administrative Trials and Hearings (holds hearings for all city agencies)
- New York City Taxi and Limousine Commission Taxicabs of the United States
- New York State Department of Environmental Conservation
- New York State Department of Labor
- Pennsylvania Department of Insurance
- Pennsylvania Department of Labor and Industry, Bureau of Workers' Compensation
- Pennsylvania Liquor Control Board
- Pennsylvania Public Utility Commission
- South Carolina Administrative Law Court (holds hearings for all state agencies)
- Texas Department of Banking
- Texas Finance Commission
- Texas Health and Human Services Commission
- Texas State Office of Administrative Hearings (holds hearings for only some state agencies)
- Traffic Violations Bureau of New York State DMV
- Washington Office of Administrative Hearings (holds hearings for all state agencies plus some local ones)

But why should these ALJs, who are purposefully set apart from state and federal judicial branches, be bothered to write an opinion? What should be included? And how does a reviewing court read these opinion on appeal? I address each question in turn.

§ 14.2 Why Write? The Rationale for an ALJ's Written Opinion

ALJs confront burdens slightly different from those faced by other judges. Most notably is the issue of an ALJ's audience. Professors Frost and Bateman are fond of using the expression "rhetorical influences" when discussing an ALJ's audience. In so doing, they pay fealty to the principal definition of "rhetoric," viz., "a. the study of principles and rules of composition formulated by ancient critics (as Aristotle and Quintilian) and interpreted by classical scholars for application to discourse in the vernacular."[1] They suggest that ALJs write for a variety of purposes to a variety of audiences under a variety of constraints and suggest that, although they are interdependent, three separate rhetorical influences affect most ALJs' writings:

- The audiences for the decision;
- The purposes for writing the decision; and
- The constraints on the decision writer.

As we indicated earlier in Chapter 2, judges write for both primary and secondary audiences. In the case of ALJs, however, the primary audience includes the litigants, a substantial number of whom are pro se, and their lawyers. Unlike general opinion-writing judges, included in the primary audience of the ALJs are their supervisors (if any), appeal boards (if any), and the reviewing courts. In the federal schema, most reviewing courts are the U.S. District or Appeals Courts. Some of these readers understand recurring legal concept vocabulary, agency shorthand and agency conventions. Others do not.

Secondary ALJ audiences include legislators, members of the public with an interest in subject and matter of the publishing state or federal administration, and the members of the media who read administrative decisions. Some cases have wide ranging implications for the general public such as public utilities cases and tax cases.

---

1. Webster's Third New International Dictionary Unabridged 1968.

Although the primary audiences are more familiar with the language, the secondary audience must still understand the decision. The presence of this secondary audience, alone, suggests that it is important for ALJs to follow the proper guidelines for writing decisions—looking specifically to the discussion in Chapter 2, regarding readership, and Chapters 5–10, regarding the anatomy of the opinion.

Added to that burden, administrative judges also grapple with a number of additional and sometimes-conflicting demands when writing a decision. Depending on the case, ALJs might be required to resolve a dispute, make findings of fact, reach conclusions of law, explain the rationale behind a decision, satisfy supervisors or supervising judges that the case was properly decided, create a record for appeal, set precedent, persuade litigants that the law supports the decision, educate litigators and the public about the law, or even reprimand litigants for improper behavior. All of this, the ALJs must do within the constraints of too-little time, binding precedent, agency conventions, readers' limited attention spans, personal schedules, court rules, and outdated technology.[2]

A federal ALJ, moreover, is responsible for conducting formal proceedings, interpreting the law, applying agency regulations, and carrying out the policies of the agency in the course of administrative adjudications. The ALJ must do all of these tasks independently, notwithstanding her status as an employee of the agency. To insulate the ALJ from agency pressure, therefore, the ALJ is not subject to most of the managerial controls applied to other employees of a federal agency. For example, ALJs are not subject to performance appraisals, and compensation is established by the Office of Personnel Management, independent of agency recommendations. Furthermore, the agency can take disciplinary action against the Judge only when good cause is established in proceedings before the Merit Systems Protection Board.

For proceedings required by statute to be determined on the record after notice and opportunity for an evidentiary hearing, an ALJ or other agency representative presides[3]—although it is not routine, an ALJ is not actually required if a statute specifically provides otherwise, usually via an official appeals "board."[4]

---

2. The preceding materials are set forth in MICHAEL H. FROST & PAUL A. BATEMAN, WRITING DESKBOOK FOR ADMINISTRATE LAW JUDGES: AN INTRODUCTION 4–9 & n.7 (2010).

3. *See* 5 U.S.C. § 556(b).

4. Some of the boards to which an appeal from an administrative law judge may be taken include the Board of Immigration Appeals, Federal Communications Commission Review Board, Social Security and Appeals Counsel, Department of Agriculture Nutrition Labeling; Department of Agriculture "Judicial Officer," various Department of the Interior appeal boards, Board of Indian Appeals, Board of Land Appeals, and Environmental Appeals Board.

At such a hearing, the ALJ or the agency board may: (1) administer oaths and affirmations; (2) issue subpoenas authorized by law; (3) rule on offers of proof and receive relevant evidence; (4) take depositions or have the depositions taken; (5) regulate the course of the hearing; (6) hold conferences for the settlement or simplification of the issues by the consent of the parties, or by the use of alternative means of dispute resolution; (8) dispose of procedural requests or similar matters; (9) make or recommend decisions in accordance with § 557 of the APA; and (10) take other action authorized by agency rule consistent with the APA.

As Morell E. Mullins notes in his vade mecum, *The Manual for Administrative Law Judges:*[5]

> Two important points should be emphasized with respect to this list. First, the Administrative Law Judge obviously is in many ways the functional equivalent of a trial judge in federal or state court. Receiving relevant evidence, ruling on offers of proof, holding conferences, disposition of procedural matters, and regulating the course of hearings obviously involve the very essence of the judicial function. Equally obvious, many of the functions require Administrative Law Judges to exercise judicial-type and judgment. When an oral decision is issued from the bench, the transcript pages upon which the oral decision appears constitute the official decision. No editing except typographical corrections should be made.

The complexity, size of the record, number of parties, and number of issues in most cases, however, make oral dispositions unwieldy.

§ 14.3 The Substance of the Opinion

As the primary method for memorializing the rationale behind a decision, this leaves a written opinion. The *Manual for Administrative Law Judges* suggests the following text format of an opinion that expands our previous discussion of "Necessary Parts of a Trial Tribunal's Opinion" in § 13.2:

> (a) The opening paragraphs should describe succinctly what the case is about. They may include a summary of the prior procedural steps and the applicable constitutional provisions, statutes, and regulations.

---

5. (2001 Interim Internet Edition) (hereinafter "Mullins, ALJ Manual").

(b) Although the relief requested by the parties may be described in the introduction, detailed contentions should not be recited. These lengthen the opinion unnecessarily since, if they are material and relevant, the must be set forth in detail in discussing the merits. Not observing this proscription is a common failing in opinion writing.

(c) If proposed findings and conclusions have been submitted, the ruling on each of them should be apparent from the decision, so the ALJ does not necessarily need to refer to each of them specifically. Likewise, insignificant or irrelevant issues raised by the parties need not be addressed specifically but can be disposed of with a statement that all other questions raised have been considered and do not justify a change in the result. However, an ALJ must be extremely careful in applying this principle. If the agency or a reviewing court disagrees about the significance of a particular issue, remand may result.

(d) The decision should include specific findings on all the major facts in issue without going into unnecessary detail.

(e) The ALJ should apply the law to the facts and explain the decision. Whether the facts, law, and conclusions should be combined or placed in separate sections of the decision depends on the agency's requirements, the ALJ's style and such other factors as the type of case and the nature of the record.

(f) The decision should end with a summary of the principal findings of fact and conclusion of law. In addition to making specific findings and conclusions, there should be ultimate findings framed in the applicable statutory or regulatory language.

(g) In a case involving many issues or complicated facts, the decision can be divided into labeled sections and subsections, with appropriate titles and subtitles. This will usually make reading, studying, and analysis of the decision easier and quicker. These divisions, with their titles, should be set forth in the table of contents.

(h) Frequently, adopting a framework, or outline, for the decision with appropriate headings before drafting the decision will make organizing the record, deciding the issues, and writing the conclusions easier and clearer. This outline can, and probably should, change as the decision-making progresses.

(i) Footnotes should be used for such material as citations of authority and cross-references, but rarely for substantive discussion. Footnotes on each page are preferable to a numerical listing of notes (endnotes) at the end of the opinion or in an appendix. The latter arrangement is inconvenient for the reader and hinders careful reading of the decision.

(j) Citations must be sufficiently detailed to enable the researcher to find the source without difficulty. This can be assured by using a standard reference work.

(k) Maps, charts, technical data, accounts, financial reports, forecasts, procedural details, and other germane background material too lengthy to be included in the test may be attached as appendices.

(l) In many cases the ALJ issues an order or proposed order. In some cases other actions are appropriate. For example, in franchise cases, a certificate must sometimes be issued or amended. Such documents should usually be added as supplements to the decision.[6]

Consider, as well, the authorized "bible" for New York State ALJs, *The Manual for Administrative Law Judges and Hearing Officers, 2011.*[7] "Chapter 6: The Decision" opens as follows:

The ALJ's decision or recommended report is the central element in all that has happened prior to its issuance and all that will happen after it is issued. It is the focus of the administrative adjudication or rate-making process and serves as notice to all involved — agency, party, citizen, the press and public — of the nature of the proceeding, its implications and importance, and its result. In so doing it provides a concrete example of how an agency works in the real world.

Elements of the decision and its form are set forth in state statutes and agency regulations. Of particular relevance to many New York state agencies is State Administrative Act § 307:

A final decision, determination or order adverse to a party in an adjudicatory proceeding shall be in writing or stated in the record and shall include findings of fact and conclusions of law or reasons for the decision, determination or order. Findings of fact, if set forth in statutory language, shall be accompanied by a concise statement of the underlying facts supporting the findings.

---

6. MULLINS, ALJ MANUAL 136–39.
7. (Hereinafter "NEW YORK MANUAL").

The manual cautions the judges to be aware that although lawyers and agency experts may be aware of shorthand expressions, the decision should be written in language understood by the public or the media. Thus, at all times, the ALJ should be aware of both primary and secondary readers.

Recall in § 5.2, we set forth "Five Parts Necessary for Any Opinion." The New York Manual follows the same general format. As the Manual notes, "the structure of the decision can either help or hinder its communicative purpose.... [A]dministrative decisions should consist of the following elements, included in the following order:"

1. An introductory procedural statement that a hearing was held, the parties who appeared, their representatives (noting professional stature, such as attorney or accountant, where appropriate), the witnesses, if any, and that testimony was taken and evidence accepted.

2. And introductory substantive statement that briefly outlines the issue heard and the conclusion reached.

3. A clear, concise but thorough statement of the issues presented.

4. The findings of fact, based on the entire record, including consideration of testimony, exhibits, official documents, and any other items within the record.

5. The conclusions of law or reasons of the decision, based on the material facts found and the applicable law, making clear where conclusions are based upon the lawful exercise of discretion.

6. The conclusion(s), based upon the conclusions of law or reason, indicating the final statement of the ALJ in deciding or recommending in the matter, and including where appropriate the relief, if any, that results from the conclusions.

The first two of these elements can be combined in one heading labeled the introductory paragraph, but numbers three through six should each be set out separately to allow for a well-structured, organized and understandable decision. Narrative decisions can be made more reader friendly if they are organized into sub-sections with appropriate headings. Such a technique allows the reader to follow the progression of the decision and its analysis, while providing the ALJ with a point of reference within each of the decision points.[8]

---

8. New York Manual 145–46.

The Five Necessary Parts of an ALJ Opinion

Greco-Roman Label	Description
Exordium	Opening paragraph How. What. Who. When. Where.
Divisio	Summarize the issues presented by the parties.
Narratio	Statement of narrative or adjudicative facts.
Confirmatio	Discussion of the law. Proof of the result. The "why" of the opinion.
** *Refutatio* (if needed)	Rejecting certain arguments.
Peroratio	Conclusion. Statement of who prevails.

§ 14.4 Idiosyncratic Problems of Immigration Judges

Most administrative law courts are not tribunals of general jurisdiction. As in the Social Security context, discussed below, ALJs paint with a narrow brush over limited areas of the law. Similarly, immigration judges ("IJs") deal almost solely with aliens who have entered the United States illegally and are then subject to removal.[9]

As such, IJs have far-reaching power. Indeed, they render final decisions on individual cases and make factual findings that reviewing courts can reverse only if those findings are "clearly erroneous." And that's only *if* there is an appeal: an overwhelming 90 percent of immigration judges' decisions in 2010 became final orders, with no appeal by either the respondents or the government.

Yet immigration judges encounter a special problem — an avalanche of cases — in reaching their conclusions and memorializing them in written opinions. Approximately 260 immigration judges preside in 59 courts throughout the United States and U.S. territories. Their caseload is simply awesome. In 2010 immigration judges completed 353,247 cases and the Board of Immigration of Appeals heard 35,787 appeals. Only 17% of the proceedings during that time, moreover, were conducted in English; 282 different languages were used for the balance.[10]

---

9. By statute and regulation the law can be synthesized as follows:

> An application for withholding of removal deportation requires a showing that there is a clear probability of persecution in the country to which an applicant will be removed. An application for asylum must establish only that the applicant is unable or unwilling to return to, and is unable or unwilling to avail himself or herself of the protection of, that country because of past persecution or a well-founded fear of future persecution on account of race, religion, nationality, membership in a particular social group, or political opinion. An applicant has a well-founded fear of persecution if there is a reasonable possibility that she will suffer it, and a showing of past persecution creates a rebuttable presumption of such a well-founded fear. The persecution must be committed by the government or forces the government is either unable or unwilling to control.

Garcia v. Att'y Gen., 665 F.3d 496, 502–03 (3d Cir. 2011) (internal quotation marks, citations and alterations omitted).

10. Office of Planning, Analysis, & Tech., EOIR, Dep't of Justice, FY2010 Statistical Yearbook F1 (Jan. 2011), *available at* www.justice.gov/eoir/stastpub/fy10syb.pdf.

To put [an immigration judge's] plight in context, it should first be noted that the average district judge has a pending caseload of 400 cases and three law clerks to assist him or her, whereas, in FY2010, each immigration judge completed an average of more than 1,500 cases, with the assistance of one law clerk shared with four judges at that time. By the end of 2011, the number of cases pending before the immigration courts reached an all time high of more than 297,551 — a 60 percent increase since the end of FY2008. In the first 10 months of FY2011, cases remained pending 30 percent longer than the average disposition time in FY2009. Under these circumstances, it is not surprising that ... immigration judges suffer from greater stress and burnouts than prison wardens or doctors in busy hospitals.[11]

Accordingly, crafting a written opinion for each disposition proves to be a task of Herculean proportions. Long-time Immigration Judge Dana Leigh Marks sums up the dire situation thusly:

At the conclusion of hours of painstaking direct and cross-examination, immigration judges render an extemporaneous oral decision, often lasting 45 minutes or more. These decisions are generally handed down without the benefit of a judicial law clerk's research or drafting assistance because the ratio of judges to law clerks remains inadequate for the task. Today, because three judges routinely share one clerk, most immigration judges have access to only a third of a judicial law clerk's time. Immigration judges cannot refer to a transcript when making their decisions, because written transcripts of the proceedings are created only after the decision is appealed. Immigration judges must rely not only on their notes to remember the testimonial evidence presented by the parties but also on their knowledge of the law, because prehearing briefs are the exception, not the norm. Each week, immigration judges generally spend 36 hours in court and on the bench, leaving them little time to devote to adjudicating motions, preparing cases, or staying abreast of legal precedent in this highly fluid area of the law.[12]

---

11. Dana Leigh Marks, *Still a Legal "Cinderella"? Why the Immigration Courts Remain an Ill-Treated Stepchild Today*, FED. LAWYER, March 2012, at 25, 27.

12. *Id.* at 26.

Even though these strictures mean that most IJ opinions are delivered orally and later transcribed, I strongly recommend that those oral opinions nevertheless adhere to our discussion above in § 14.3. If nothing else, including in the oral dictation the five essential parts of an opinion — an opening, a summary of issues, a statement of facts, a discussion of the applicable law, and a conclusion — will lend structure to the opinion and make the subsequent levels of appellate review far more efficient. This is especially important because:

> Where ... the BIA affirms the IJ's decision without opinion, we review the IJ's opinion and scrutinize its reasoning. Review of an IJ decision is conducted under the substantial evidence standard which requires that administrative findings of fact be upheld "unless any reasonable adjudicator would be compelled to conclude to the contrary."[13]

Moreover, because "[a]dverse credibility determinations are factual findings subject to substantial evidence review[,] [w]e will defer to and uphold the IJ's adverse credibility determinations if they are supported by reasonable, substantial, and probative evidence on the record considered as a whole."[14] Hence, an IJ's opinion must be able to bear the scrutiny of not just BIA review, but, in some cases, review by a U.S. Court of Appeals. That review is far more efficacious when it is clear from the opinion — whether rendered orally or crafted meticulously — upon what facts the IJ relied and with what precedents the IJ reached a conclusion.

§ 14.5 ALJ Review Boards

Author's Note: *The following section is excerpted from* Department of Justice "Fact Sheet" *and* Practice Manual, Department of Justice, Executive Office for Immigration Review.[15] *Although these sources discuss the Board of Immigration Appeals ("BIA") — the administrative agency that conducts the first review of the Immigration Judges — much of what is said in these pages about the BIA is ap-*

---

13. Chen v. Gonzales, 434 F.3d 212, 215–16 (3d Cir. 2005) (quoting 8 U.S.C. § 1252(b)(4)(B)).

14. *Id.* (internal quotation marks and citations omitted).

15. Both sources are available at www.justice.gov/eoir.

plicable also to those state and federal administrative boards or commissions that conduct the administrative reviews.

The Board of Immigration Appeals has been given nationwide jurisdiction to review the orders of Immigration Judges and certain decisions made by the Department of Homeland Security (DHS), and to provide guidance to the Immigration Judges, DHS, and others, through published decisions. The Board is tasked with resolving the questions before it in a manner that is timely, impartial, and consistent with the Immigration and Nationality Act and regulations, and to provide clear and uniform guidance to DHS, Immigration Judges, and the general public on the proper interpretation and administration of the Act and its implementing regulations.[16]

The Office of the Chief Immigration Judge (OCIJ) oversees the administration of the Immigration Courts nationwide and exercises administrative supervision over IJs. The Immigration Judges, as independent adjudicators, make determinations of removability, deportability, and excludability, and adjudicate applications for relief. The Board, in turn, reviews the decisions of the Immigration Courts.[17] The decisions of the Board are binding on the Immigration Courts, unless modified or overruled by the Attorney General or a federal court.

The majority of cases at the Board are adjudicated by a single Board Member. In general, a single Board Member decides the case unless the case falls into one of the categories that require a decision by a panel of three Board Members.

The BIA uses three-member review in cases that require the Board to correct clear errors of fact, interpret the law, and provide guidance regarding the exercise of discretion. This enables the Board to resolve simple cases efficiently,

---

16. *See* 8 C.F.R. § 1003.1(d)(1).

17. The Board generally has the authority to review appeals from the following: decisions of Immigration Judges in removal, deportation, and exclusion proceedings (with some limitations on decisions involving voluntary departure, pursuant to 8 C.F.R. § 1003.1(b)(2), (3)); decisions of Immigration Judges pertaining to asylum, withholding of deportation, withholding of removal, Temporary Protected Status, the Convention Against Torture, and other forms of relief; decisions of Immigration Judges on motions to reopen where the proceedings were conducted in absentia; some decisions pertaining to bond, parole, or detention, as provided in 8 C.F.R. part 1236, subpart A; decisions of DHS on family-based immigrant petitions, the revocation of family-based immigrant petitions, and the revalidation of family-based immigrant petitions (except orphan petitions); decisions of DHS regarding waivers of inadmissibility for nonimmigrants under § 212(d)(3) of the Immigration and Nationality Act; and decisions of Immigration Judges in rescission of adjustment of status cases, as provided in 8 C.F.R. part 1246.

while reserving its limited resources for more complex cases and the development of precedent to guide the immigration judges and the parties. Three-member panels focus on:

- Complex Cases
- Settling inconsistencies among the rulings of different immigration judges;
- Establishing precedent construing the meaning of laws, regulations, or procedures;
- Reviewing decisions by immigration judges or the Immigration and Naturalization Service (INS) that are not in conformity with the law or with applicable precedents;
- Resolving cases or controversies of major national import; and
- Reviewing clearly erroneous factual determinations by immigration judges.

The BIA applies the deferential "clearly erroneous" standard in its review of immigration judges' fact findings. Under the "clearly erroneous" standard, the Board may not disturb an immigration judge's fact findings unless they were so clearly wrong that they must be overturned. Indeed, the Board considers only that evidence that was admitted in the proceedings below. It does not consider new evidence on appeal. If new evidence is submitted, that submission may be deemed a motion to remand proceedings to the Immigration Judge for consideration of that evidence and treated accordingly. The Board may, however, at its discretion, take administrative notice of commonly known facts not appearing in the record. For example, the Board may take administrative notice of current events and contents of official documents, such as country condition reports prepared by the State Department.

The BIA's published decisions are binding on the parties to the decision. Published decisions also constitute precedent that binds the Board, the Immigration Courts, and DHS. The vast majority of the Board's decisions are unpublished, but the Board periodically selects cases to be published.[18] This oc-

---

18. *See* 8 C.F.R. § 1003.1(g). When a decision is selected for publication, it is prepared for release to the public. Headnotes are added, and an I&N Decision citation is assigned. Where appropriate, the parties' names are abbreviated, and alien registration numbers ("A numbers") are redacted. The decision is then served on the parties in the same manner as an unpublished decision. In the past, the Board issued precedential decisions as slip opinions, called "Interim Decisions," before publication in a bound volume. While precedential decisions are still assigned an "Interim Decision" number for administrative reasons, the proper citation is always to the volume and page number of the bound volume. The use of the Interim Decision citation is greatly disfavored by the Board

curs when the opinion resolves an issue of first impression; alters, modifies, or clarifies an existing rule of law; reaffirms an existing rule of law; resolves a conflict of authority; or discusses an issue of significant public interest. The BIA's unpublished decisions are binding on the parties to the decision but are *not* considered precedent for unrelated cases. Whether published or not, decisions of the Board are reviewable by the Attorney General and may be referred to the Attorney General, at the request of the Attorney General, DHS, or the Board. The Attorney General may vacate decisions of the Board and issue his or her own decisions.[19] The decisions of the Board are also reviewable in certain federal courts—District and Courts of Appeals—depending on the nature of the appeal.

§ 14.5.1 Other State and Federal Review Tribunals

The practice in and for the BIA takes primary emphasis in discussing administrative reviews of ALJ's opinions because of the sheer number of appeals taken from the trial tribunals, and also because of the high incidence of IJ opinions. Other federal review boards include the Federal Communications Commission Review Board, Social Security and Appeals Council, Department of Agriculture Nutrition Labeling; Department of Agriculture "Judicial Officer," various Department of the Interior appeal boards, Board of Indian Appeals, Board of Land Appeals, and Environmental Appeals Board.

It must be emphasized that although all state and federal review boards resemble in part the BIA experience, each board is idiosyncratic in its procedure and jurisdiction. These are promulgated by agency regulation and statute. Newly appointed members of review agencies should acquaint themselves immediately with the regulations that govern, and, if these are sparse, a study should be made of past procedures in opinion writing.

---

19. *See* 8 C.F.R. § 1003.1(d)(1)(i), 1003.1(h). Decisions of the Attorney General may be published as precedent decisions in *Administrative Decisions Under Immigration and Nationality Laws of the United States* ("I&N Decisions").

§ 14.6 The ALJ Opinion on Review

ALJs must be aware that they write for more than the reviewing board or a high-ranking official of the administrative agency. Appeals to a reviewing court, usually the intermediate appellate courts, are taken from only the final order of the agency. It is the reviewing board's final order that confers jurisdiction in the reviewing court, and appellate judges rely heavily on the board's opinion. But often the board will justify its order on the bases of the ALJ's opinion; or even if the board has prepared its own opinion, its statement of reasons often makes generous references to the ALJ's opinion, especially on matters of controlling issues related to findings of fact or deciding matters of credibility.

As examples of this phenomenon, consider two recent immigration cases from my home Court, the Court of Appeals for the Third Circuit. In *Lin Lee v. Attorney General*,[20] a change in our Court's immigration law jurisprudence led us to reverse the Board of Immigration Appeals's ("BIA") order of removal for an immigrant seeking asylum. Although we ultimately reversed the Board's decision, we relied entirely on the Board's statement of facts, which, in turn, relied entirely on the immigration judge's statement of facts. One phrasing, in fact, remained almost identical throughout all three stages of review:

> Respondent is a native and citizen of China. She first entered the United States on or about May 13, 2000....[21]

became:

> Respondent is a 33-year-old native and citizen of China, who first entered the United States on or about May 13, 2000....[22]

which, in turn, became:

> Lee, a native and citizen of China, entered the United States on May 13, 2000.[23]

---

20. No. 11-1524, 2011 WL 4599666 (3d Cir. Oct. 6, 2011).

21. *In re* Lin Lee, No. A 077-950-685, Order on Motion to Reopen, at 1 (Immigration Ct., N.J., Aug. 24, 2009).

22. *In re* Lin Lee, No. A077 950 685, Appeal of Motion to Reopen, at 1 (B.I.A. Feb. 9, 2011).

23. Lin Lee v. Att'y Gen., No. 11-1524, 2011 WL 4599666, at *1 (3d Cir. Oct. 6, 2011).

The rest of the Court's opinion drew heavily from the facts found and law applied by the immigration judge and the BIA.

The progression of *Johnson v. Attorney General*,[24] exhibits a similar pattern. The immigration judge did not find many facts, leaving the BIA to explain the basis for its reversal in greater detail. In so doing, the BIA wrote:

> respondent is a native and citizen of Jamaica who entered the United States in 1981 as a lawful permanent resident. In March 1986, he was convicted in Florida for importation and possession of a controlled substance.[25]

On appeal, we wrote:

> Johnson, a native and citizen of Jamaica who suffers from bipolar disorder, entered the United States as a lawful permanent resident in 1981. In 1986, a Florida state court convicted him of importing and possessing a controlled substance.[26]

The remainder of Johnson's appeal required our Court to dissect, in detail, the IJ's and BIA's decisions.

Although these similarities may seem trivial, their import on appeal is significant. Although an appellate court may still find additional facts in the record, the initial reviewing court's determinations of fact—and often, even their *phrasing* of facts—is usually adopted *in toto* on appeal. Accordingly, a correct and comprehensive finding of facts makes a reviewing court's job much easier. An incorrect, incomplete, or clouded finding, on the other hand, frustrates and delays appellate review, often to the detriment of litigants pursuing ends of paramount importance—like immigration asylum or the restoration of social security benefits, for instance. A clear and readable ALJ opinion, therefore, is an indispensible element of proper appellate review.

§ 14.6.1 An Example of How Appellate Courts Review ALJ Opinions

I include an example of what we, on the Court of Appeals, look for from an ALJ on appellate review. In *Malloy v. Commissioner of Social Security*,[27] we

---

24. 358 F. App'x 369 (3d Cir. 2009) (per curiam).

25. *In re* Johnson, No. A037 331 916, Appeal of Deferral of Removal under the Convention Against Torture, at 1 (B.I.A. Sept. 26, 2008).

26. 358 F. App'x at 370.

27. 306 F. App'x. 761, 763–64 (3d Cir. 2009).

set forth a summary of the law that governs Social Security cases. Most other administrative agencies—with the notable exception discussed above—follow the same pattern, referring to decisions of review boards, regulations, and decisions of courts with jurisdiction to review petitions for review.

Claimants for disability benefits must demonstrate that they meet certain criteria under the Act. The Act grants the Secretary of Health and Human Services authority to adopt rules and regulations implementing the disability benefits program. *Rosetti v. Shalala*, 12 F.3d 1216, 1218 (3d Cir. 1993). In utilizing this authority, the Social Security Administration implements a five-step sequential evaluation procedure for the assessment of disability claims. *See* 20 C.F.R. § 404.1520. The U.S. Supreme Court has described the operation of this process as follows:

> The first two steps involve threshold determinations that the claimant is not presently working and has an impairment which is of the required duration and which significantly limits his ability to work. *See* 20 C.F.R. §§ 416.920(a) through (c). In the third step, the medical evidence of the claimant's impairment is compared to a list of impairments presumed severe enough to preclude any gainful work. *See* 20 C.F.R. pt. 404, subpt. P, App. 1 (pt. A). If the claimant's impairment matches or is "equal" to one of the listed impairments, he qualifies for benefits without further inquiry. § 416.920(d). If the claimant cannot qualify under the listings, the analysis proceeds to the fourth and fifth steps. At these steps, the inquiry is whether the claimant can do his own past work or any other work that exists in the national economy, in view of his age, education, and work experience. If the claimant cannot do his past work or other work, he qualifies for benefits. §§ 416.920(e) and (f).

Sullivan v. Zebley, 493 U.S. 521, 525–26 (1990).

The claimant bears the burden of persuasion in the first four steps of the analysis. Only if the claimant demonstrates that the impairment precludes performing his or her past work does the burden shift to the Commissioner, to prove that the claimant still retains a residual functional capacity to perform some alternative, substantial, gainful activity present in the national economy. *Kangas v. Bowen*, 823 F.2d 775, 777 (3d Cir. 1987).

Whether a claimant is disabled as defined by the Act is a decision which is reserved to the Commissioner. Under the Commissioner's regulations, the [ALJ] has the responsibility for determining a claimant's residual functional capacity after evaluating all the evidence of record regarding the claimant's impairments and resulting functional limitations. 20 C.F.R. §§ 404.1546(c), 416.946(c). Although the Commissioner considers opinions from treating and examining medical sources on this issue, the final responsibility for the decision is reserved to the Commissioner. 20 C.F.R. §§ 404.1527(e)(1)-(3), 416.927(e)(1)-(3).

Courts may review the Commissioner's factual findings only to determine whether they are supported by substantial evidence. *See* 42 U.S.C. § 405(g) ("The findings of the Commissioner of Social Security as to any fact, if supported by substantial evidence, shall be conclusive...."). The statutory standard of substantial evidence requires more than a mere scintilla of evidence, but less than a preponderance. *Plummer v. Apfel,* 186 F.3d 422, 427 (3d Cir. 1999). It "does not mean a large or considerable amount of evidence, but rather 'such relevant evidence as a reasonable mind might accept as adequate to support a conclusion.'" *Pierce v. Underwood,* 487 U.S. 552, 565 (1988) (quoting *Consol. Edison Co. v. NLRB,* 305 U.S. 197, 229 (1938)).

The presence of evidence in the record that supports a contrary conclusion does not undermine the Commissioner's decision so long as the record provides substantial support for that decision. *See Blalock v. Richardson,* 483 F.2d 773, 775 (4th Cir. 1972). The reviewing court looks to the record as a whole to assess whether substantial evidence supports the Commissioner's decision. *Taybron v. Harris,* 667 F.2d 412, 413 (3d Cir. 1981). In assessing the extent to which the record supports the Commissioner's conclusions, the court reviews objective medical facts, diagnoses or medical opinions based on those facts, subjective complaints of pain or disability, and the claimant's age, education, and work history. *See Jones v. Harris,* 497 F. Supp. 161, 167 (E.D. Pa. 1980).

§ 14.7 Conclusion

My own experience with state hearing officers in the late 1940s and throughout the 1950s came about through my trying a case before lay persons who very seldom had neither the inclination nor the ability to write opinions, much less even deliver oral reasons for the decision. All this was the product of state patronage.

But things have changed. As the decades passed, in both state and federal agencies, highly professional, legally trained career men and women have come to serve as ALJs. We all are the beneficiaries of the creation of a corps of dedicated and competent administrative law judges.

CHAPTER FIFTEEN

ARBITRATION PROCEDURES AND OPINION WRITING

§ 15.1 Overview

The preceding chapters have discussed opinion writing by trial judges in both the judicial and administrative systems. Although there may be certain differences between the two—the trial judge and the administrative law judge—they both have one thing in common: they are part of a *public* judicial hierarchy. We now turn to procedures of *private* resolution of disputes coming within the general rubric of arbitration.

Although the practice of using arbitrators in place of judges has undergone significant changes of late, increasing both in numbers and in the amount and size of requested rewards, arbitration procedures themselves have a long history. From a global perspective, the use of arbitration has been with us for centuries, tracing back to the law merchant origins in the city states of medieval Europe and elsewhere. Even at the local level, in the state of Pennsylvania—where I was born, practiced law, served as a judge on the Court of Common Pleas, and for over four decades, have served as a judge on the U.S. Court of Appeals for the Third Circuit—we have a history of mandatory arbitration of cases harking back to 1705.[1]

"Private court adjudication" is what arbitration is all about. In addition to the decision-making apparatus being private, arbitration is unique because the process is generally based on a contract—which sets forth the metes and bounds of the subsequent arbitration procedures—and the award is commercial in nature. The major objective of arbitration is to create a dispute-set-

---

1. RAYMOND D. RUBENS, PENNSYLVANIA ARBITRATION GUIDE 28 (1974). The present Act, 42 PA. CON. STAT. ANN. § 7361, last amended in 2006, provides for amounts of $50,000 or less in Philadelphia and Allegheny counties and $35,000 or less in all other counties. By rule, the Common Pleas Court of Allegheny County limits the amount to $35,000 or less.

tling mechanism that is far removed from the expense and delay inherent in judicial trial and appellate court procedures. It goes without saying that today's tragically high cost of delivering legal services in the United States—and formerly in England and Wales—is caused by abuses of depositions and the discovery process as a whole. England and Wales were able to revive their seemingly debilitated judicial system during the late 20th century by revamping it altogether. The new Civil Procedure Rules ("CPR") for England and Wales became effective on April 28, 1999, and largely replaced the Rules of the Supreme Court and the County Court Rules.[2] This wholesale revision of the civil procedures was designed to: (1) improve access to justice and reduce the costs of litigation; (2) reduce the complexity of the rules and modernize terminology; and (3) remove unnecessary distinctions between practice and procedure.[3] The CPR revisions are salutary developments, and I cannot resist pointing out that what our moribund federal rules really need is a good dose of CPR. But until then, we will continue to see an increasing number of matters settled through the private channels of arbitration.

§15.2 Arbitration Awards

Once the arbitrators have heard the parties and considered the issues presented, a decision must be rendered. This decision is known as the "award"—even if all of the claimant's contentions fail and no money is paid or owed to either party. A binding arbitration means that the winning party can take the arbitration award to the court and enforce it if the losing party does not comply. This finality is attractive because once a decision is rendered, the case is over. And the losing party does not have the right to re-litigate the matter at the usual cost of trial court proceedings on motions to enforce or to vacate the

---

2. The foregoing discussion on the new English rules is taken from Ruggero J. Aldisert, *Alright, Retired Judges, Write*, 8 J. App. Prac. & Process 227 (2006).

3. As a result of the CPR, freewheeling deposition-taking—the major cause for increased litigation costs in American courts—is no longer available in England and Wales. Now, one must get a court order for cause shown to obtain a deposition, and when permitted, it must be conducted under strict court supervision. CPR 34.8 provides that a party may apply to the court for a person (the "deponent") to be examined before the hearing. Evidence from this process is referred to as a "deposition." The deposition must be taken before (1) a judge, (2) an examiner of the court, or (3) such other persons the court appoints. Moreover, if the party intends to introduce the deposition evidence at the hearing, he or she must serve the notice 21 days before the day fixed by the hearing.

award and accompanying appeal thereafter. It is for these reasons that arbitration agreements are included in many commercial transactions today and why many medical providers today require that patients sign an arbitration clause.

§ 15.2.1 The Conflict between Federal and State Arbitration Acts

In crafting an award, arbitrators are mindful of the role reviewing courts play in the arbitration process. "It is the arbitrator's construction which was bargained for and insofar as the arbitrator's decision concerns construction of the contract, the courts have no business overruling him because their interpretation of the contract is different from his."[4] *Enterprise* enunciated a basic philosophy that was to apply to all labor arbitration cases, and indirectly to most commercial cases. It elevated the arbitrator to an exalted status, emphasizing that there would be no interference with his award simply because the reviewing court differed in interpreting a provision of the contract.

What has troubled many courts is the uncertainty as to which body of law governs judicial review of a disputed award—whether it be the Federal Arbitration Act, 9 U.S.C. §1 ("FAA") or the state's Uniform Arbitration Act ("UAA"). The difference between the scope of judicial review of an arbitration award pursuant to the FAA and the scope of review under state law has commanded the attention of U.S. Courts of Appeals for over 60 years. Briefly stated, the FAA standard still rigorously limits judicial intervention, except for dishonorable conduct of the arbitrator. By contrast, under the UAA, a court may modify an award that is "contrary to law."[5] Deciding which statute applies turns on the language of the arbitration provision in the parties' agreement. The default rule is to apply the FAA. This presumption will be overcome only if the applicable provision in the arbitration agreement evidences a "clear intent" to impose a state act permitting a review of the award. The "clear intent" standard protects parties' rights to contract for applicable law:

> The rule we announce will preserve and facilitate the ability of parties to *contract around* the default federal standard. Sophisticated parties (i.e. those who employ experienced lawyers to draft their contract) will soon learn that its generic choice of law clause is not enough. Assuming that both parties *genuinely* wish to be governed by standards

---

4. United Steelworkers of Am. v. Enter. Wheel & Car Corp., 363 U.S. 593, 599 (1960).
5. 42 Pa. Cons. Stat. Ann. §§7301(d)(2) and 7314(a).

other than the FAA's requiring something more will impose minis-
cule requiring transaction costs. It is not particularly difficult, for example to provide "a controversy shall be settled by arbitration in
accordance with the terms of the Pennsylvania Uniform Arbitration Act."[6]

Judges will differ in interpreting an agreement's language. For example, in
a dissent, my view stated that the following provision in an arbitration agreement was sufficient to trump the default FAA, thus allowing for the application of the state law of vacatur:

> Any dispute or difference between the Reinsured and the Reinsurers
> relating to the interpretation or performance of this Agreement ... or
> any transaction under this Agreement ... shall be subject to binding
> arbitration ... in accordance with the rules and procedures established
> by the Pennsylvania Uniform Arbitration Act.[7]

The Majority held otherwise.

Because so much rides on whether a certain statute governs the arbitration
process, arbitrators should be mindful to include a statement of the governing arbitration law in their awards. The necessary parts of a binding arbitration award are discussed more thoroughly in the remainder of this chapter.

§ 15.3 Crafting a Binding Award

Because an award is generally final and binding on the parties involved in
the matter, the construction of an award is a crucial aspect of an arbitrator's
duties, to which great attention is due. In *The Arbitrator's Handbook*, Professor John W. Cooley,[8] America's expert in arbitration, explains the formal requisites of a binding award. First, the formalities: the award should always be
in writing, signed by the arbitrators on the panel, and, if required by the rules
or the parties' agreement, notarized and witnessed.[9] It goes without saying that

---

6. Ario v. Underwriting Members of Syndicate 53, 618 F.3d 277, 299 (3d Cir. 2010)
(Aldisert, J, dissenting) (quoting Roadway Package Sys., Inc. v. Kaysey, 257 F.3d 287, 297
(3d Cir. 2001)).

7. *Id.*

8. Professor Cooley has served as an arbitrator and mediator in complex commercial
disputes, a trainer in dispute resolution, and a consultant in dispute system design.

9. John W. Cooley, The Arbitrator's Handbook 180 (2d ed. 2004).

IS THIS A MODEL ARBITRATOR?

**THE PARTIES PAID YOU TO DECIDE THIS
CASE—YOU OWE IT TO THEM TO EXPLAIN WHY**

the award should be clear and concise, and while it normally does not include a written opinion explaining the arbitrators' reasoning, the award must contain a ruling on all claims (principal claims, counter-claims, cross-claims, third-party claims, etc.) and damage requests (compensatory, consequential, punitive, etc.) at issue.[10] Finally, the award must: name the winning party on each claim and the party against whom the award is rendered; specify the precise dollar amount of the award on each claim; and apportion all administrative fees and expenses at the hearing and assess the arbitrators' fees and attorney's fees, if appropriate.[11]

---

10. *Id.*
11. *Id.*

Professor Cooley teaches that the "form, format and length of an arbitrator's statement of reasons supporting an award will be governed largely by its purpose, the agreement of the parties, the applicable rules and the nature of the case."[12] Generally, findings of fact or conclusions of law must accompany an award *only* when the rules require, the arbitrator decides or the parties agree. If the parties have pre-agreed to an "equitable decision," then the opinion can simply describe the arbitrator's reasoning without citing or analyzing case law. Thus, in a simple personal injury case, for example, the opinion might simply consist of a very short explanation—one to three pages—communicating factual findings, liability determinations, and how the arbitrator arrived at the damage amount. It is only when arbitrators are required to draft a comprehensive legal opinion that it should resemble an appellate court opinion in form, content and style.[13]

I am not in total agreement with this philosophy. I believe that there should be a statement of reasons (the equivalent of an opinion in the public judicial forum) with findings of fact and conclusions of law justifying *any* award. The parties to any arbitration—winners or losers—deserve an explanation as to why a particular award is announced. This is not too much to require. It goes with the territory. The five parts of a statement of reasons—identical to the necessary parts of a trial court opinion—are rather minimal: (1) an orientation paragraph indentifying the parties and an explanation of the action, (2) a summary of the issues to be discussed, (3) a finding of facts, (4) a statement of controlling law for each issue, and (5) the award. I would also include two additional parts, one of which may be expressed in one acronym. First, the governing arbitration law—FAA or UAA. Second, a statement explaining the power and authority of the arbitrator set forth in the agreement (usually one to three sentences). Whether the facts are simple or convoluted, the issues few or many, to create an award, the arbitrator should follow the construction of judicial opinions. To reduce this to a few pages in a simple case is to translate thoughts to words. To do this is to inform the parties to whom, and why, the award is issued. Not to do this is never justified. Justice demands a written opinion in every instance where a party is granted an award.

Without a written statement of reasons in a case brought under the FAA, an arbitrator essentially ensures that the courts will never overturn the determination. More important, there must be satisfaction that the arbitrators were

---

12. *Id.* at 184.

13. *Id.* If you are sitting as a hearing arbitrator in a typical evidentiary-type arbitration proceeding, then your opinion should resemble a trial court opinion.

absolutely neutral in the consideration of the matter, actually performing in a completely disinterested fashion. Upon his retirement from the Supreme Court, Justice Felix Frankfurter wrote to his colleagues:

> The nation is merely warranted in expecting harmony of aims among those who have been called to the Court. This means a pertinacious pursuit of the processes of Reason in the disposition of controversies before the court. This pre-supposes intellectual disinterestedness in the analysis of the factors involved in the issues that call for decision. This in turn requires rigorous self-scrutiny to discover, with the view to curbing, every influence that may deflect from such disinterestedness.[14]

Justice Frankfurter was later quoted: "Fragile as reason is and limited as law is to the expression of the institutionalized medium of reason, that's all we have standing between us and the tyranny of mere will and the cruelty of unbridled, unprincipled, undisciplined feeling."[15] Although Justice Frankfurter was discussing the preservation of fairness and reason in public judicial forums, the same standard should be expected of those who preside over private adjudications. In arbitration proceedings—whether the sum involved is $500 or $50,000—the only guarantee that the award was dictated by disinterested reason and not "the cruelty of unbridled, unprincipled, undisciplined feeling" is the written statement of reasons for granting the award.[16]

§ 15.4 Parts Necessary for an Arbitration Award

Author's Note: *Section 5.2 outlined the necessary parts of an appellate opinion, starting with the categorization originated by Greco-Roman rhetoricians. This outline has been adjusted for opinions of a trial court, and also for administrative law judges. In both, we made references to Part Two (The Anatomy of an Opinion) of this book. We repeat this advice for constructing arbitration opinions, with one caveat—an arbitrator's opinion requires additional parts that are*

---

14. Retirement of Mr. Justice Frankfurter, 371 U.S. vii, x (1962).

15. *Id.* at ix–x.

16. *See* David L. Shapiro, *In Defense of Judicial Candor,* 100 Harv. L. Rev. 731, 737 (1987) ("A requirement that [arbitrators] give reasons for their decisions—grounds of decision that can be debated, attacked, and defended—serves a vital function in constraining the judiciary's exercise of power.").

not necessary in other trial court or appellate opinions. We now include them as necessary parts of these opinions.

The Seven Necessary Parts of an Arbitration Opinion

Greco-Roman Label	Description
Exordium	Opening paragraph. How. What. Who. When. Where.
Governing Statute†	Federal Arbitration Act (FAA) or the State Uniform Arbitration Act (UAA).
Authority†	Description of the general powers and authority of the arbitrators as set forth in the arbitration clause of the agreement of the parties.
Divisio	Statement of issues to be discussed.
Narratio	Statement of narrative or adjudicative facts.
Confirmatio	Discussion of the law. Proof of the result. The "why" of the opinion.
** *Refutatio* (if needed)	Refutation of rejected arguments.
Peroratio	The Award.

† Signifies the additional parts necessary for an arbitrator's opinion.

§ 15.5 Excerpts from Arbitration Awards

§ 15.5.1 Effective Statements of Reasons

The Porter Insurance Trust contends that it is not bound by any knowledge Zey had about the loan because he had an interest adverse to the Porters' interest, his commission of 90% of the first year premium, $345, 060, and LIF received 20% of Zey's commission, $69,012. Witkin, Summary of California Law (10th ed.) Vol. 3, Agency and Employment, sec. 156, p. 200 (2005). The arbitrator accepts this position. None of the Porters and the Porter Insurance Trust are bound by Zey's knowledge.

The Porter defense is based on fraud in the execution, or fraud in the inception, irrespective of NBCal's intent. The case of *Duick v. Toyota Motor Sales, USA*, 198 Cal. App. 4th 1316 (2011), supports this position, as does *Betty Crick v. Louis Silviera Jr.*, 2011 WL 3106704 (Cal App. 3d Dist. 2011).

The arbitrator finds that the loan agreement is not enforceable because of fraud in the execution, or inception. The Porter Trust is the prevailing party.[17]

The Supreme Court of the United States in the [c]ase of *Harris v. Forklift Sys. Inc.*, 510 U.S. 17 [(1993)], stated that a hostile or abusive environment exists when a reasonable person would find that the atmosphere is sexually severe and pervasive.

To prevail the complainant must show that she was subjected to unwelcome sexual harassment that affected a term, condition, or privilege of her employment, *Beard v. Flying J. Inc.*, 266 F.3d 792, 297–98 (8th Cir. 2001).

As in Harris, 51 U.S. at 21–22, the issue here is whether the conduct was severe or pervasive enough considering the frequency of the conduct, its severity, whether it was humiliating, whether it unreasonably interfered with an employee's work performance or was mere offensive utterances that were sporadic use of sexually abusive language, *Farragher v. City of Boca Raton*, 524 U.S. 775, 788 (1998).

The Arbitrator concludes that, given all the circumstances [set out above in the Finding of Facts], a reasonable person would conclude

---

17. Nat'l Bank of Cal. v. Porter, No. 72-148-Y-00512-11 (February 13, 2012) (Newman, Arb.).

that the supervisor's statement were a form of hostile environment sexual harassment that unreasonably interfered with Claimant's work performance.

§ 15.5.2 Effective Statement of the Governing Arbitration Law

The Purchase Agreement states that "[t]he laws of the State of Nevada shall apply to this Agreement." (Parag. 25.10; see also Parag. 21)[.] Claimants assert that their claims arise under federal statutes as well.

The Purchase Agreement contains an arbitration clause,[] which provides that the arbitration "shall be conducted under the Dispute Resolution Rules of the American Arbitration Association ("AAA") as modified herein." (Parag. 25.10)[.] The parties agree that this reference is to the AAA Commercial Arbitration Rules and Mediation Procedures as amended and effective June 1, 2009. The parties also agree that the AAA Large Complex Case Rules are applicable "to the extent not in conflict with the preceding rules." (Scheduling Order #1, Parag. 5)[.]

As Scheduling Order #1 provides, the AAA Class Rules, effective October 8, 2003, also apply in this case....[18]

* * *

What has been said heretofore is but an extension of the basic definition of the word: arbitration is a form of alternative dispute resolution that resolves conflicts outside of the public court system. At bottom, it is a kind of settlement technique in which a third party reviews the case and imposes a decision that is legally binding on both parties. It is designed to be faster and cheaper than a matter in the trial courts, and is not subject to a lengthy and expensive appellate review. For these reasons, the use of arbitration has been rapidly increasing over the years and shows no signs of slowing. For one who has been a state trial judge and a federal appellate judge for over 50 years, I am a very staunch supporter of arbitration.

---

18. Spradlin et al. v. Trump Ruffin Tower I, LLC, No. 11-115-Y-01846-09 (August 10, 2010) (LaMothe, Arb.).

PART THREE

WRITING STYLE

CHAPTER SIXTEEN

Writing Style

§ 16.1 Footnotes

Anyone who reads a footnote in a judicial opinion would answer a knock at his hotel door on his wedding night.

This was a frequent pronouncement by Burton S. Laub, a distinguished writer on legal matters and a charming raconteur, who retired as a Pennsylvania Common Pleas judge (Erie County) and then became dean of Dickinson Law School. The footnote situation has worsened since he first spoke those words. The time has come to re-examine the legitimacy of the ubiquitous footnote, which has proliferated to intolerable levels, especially in the federal courts.

At one extreme is the U.S. Supreme Court, an institution that gorges on the unnecessary and spits out footnotes in a sort of postgraduate show-and-tell. If the purpose of an opinion is to explain and clarify, that purpose is often defeated by a style that forces the reader's eye to yo-yo up and down from the text to the bottom of the page and dizzily upward again, over and over. Footnotes obfuscate as much as they illuminate, creating muddlement and even generating additional litigation, for which I detect no overwhelming national demand except among a professional set that shall be nameless here. At the other extreme is the Supreme Court of Illinois, which by long tradition aims to use the ideal number of footnotes: none.

§ 16.2 Guidelines to "Middle Ground" Footnoting

For many years, I attempted a middle ground between the two extremes, influenced largely by discussions at judicial seminars. I have developed the following guide to "middle ground" footnoting throughout the years.

§ 16.2.1 Proper Footnote Use

- ✓ To authenticate a statement where the citation is not important enough to include in the text.
- ✓ To set forth multiple citations in order to support a single proposition in the text.
- ✓ To quote extensive text of a rule, statute, regulation, will, contract or other document essential to the opinion.
- ✓ To dispose of collateral issues, controlled by precedent, that would disrupt flow or organization of the text.
- ✓ To record related issues not reached.
- ✓ To set forth trial testimony that supports facts in the text.
- ✓ To respond to concurring or dissenting opinions.
- ✓ To incorporate contributions of other members of the court whose ideas interfere with organization of the text or whose writing styles do not conform with the writer's.
- ✓ To track *all* contentions in a direct or collateral criminal appeal not discussed in the opinion so that there will be a record of the contentions for *res judicata* purposes.

§ 16.2.2 Improper Footnote Use

- ✗ To respond to a very sophisticated argument that might have been made—but was not.
- ✗ To distinguish a case that could have been cited—but was not.
- ✗ On the other hand, there is the view expressed with both charm and force by Abner Mikva, distinguished retired judge of the District of Columbia Circuit, here set forth at length:

§ 16.2.3 Goodbye to Footnotes[1]

By Abner J. Mikva
U.S. Circuit Judge, District of Columbia Circuit

In the almost fifty years since Fred Rodell wrote his classic piece *Goodbye to Law Reviews*, 23 Va. L. Rev. 38 (1936), some important things have not happened to legal writing.

---

1. Abner J. Mikva, *Goodbye to Footnotes*, 56 U. Colo. L. Rev. 647 (1985). Reprinted with permission of the University of Colorado Law Review.

1. The law reviews have not changed.
2. Judicial opinions (at which Professor Rodell took a very hefty side-swipe) have not changed except to become even longer and more numerous.
3. Professor Rodell did not even keep his promise not to write any more law review articles—he succumbed on numerous occasions, including a brilliant reprise, *Goodbye to Law Reviews—Revisited*, 48 VA. L. REV. 279 (1962).
4. The use of footnotes in legal writing has not been contained. Instead it has spread like a fungus and has magnified all of the shortcomings of legal writing so deftly denounced by Rodell.

Rodell himself called footnotes "phony excrescences." Since I cannot improve on that summation, you now have my thesis. I predict that this diatribe against footnotes in judicial opinions will bear no more fruit than have Fred Rodell's complaints about legal writing in general, but here goes anyway.

First, a few more words about Professor Rodell's original *Goodbye*. I give reprints to all my clerks at the beginning of each term as a partial antidote to their Law Review or other legal writing experiences. Rodell's diagnosis was pithy: "There are two things wrong with almost all legal writing. One is its style and the other is its content." Although he sniped at footnotes in both of his articles, Rodell aimed his main assault at the whole institution of legal writing—a scattershot attack on a venerable institution which dates back at least to the Ten Commandments.

My aim is much lower and narrower. I consider footnotes in judicial opinions an abomination. While much of what I have to say may apply to footnotes wherever they may be found, my emphasis, both as to problems and solutions, is on judicial opinions.

Let me start with the physical properties of footnotes and the difficulties they cause. By definition, a footnote is below the text to which it refers. (In other types of writing there is a device called "chapter notes" which appear at the end of the writing; the problems with chapter notes are substantially similar to those with footnotes.) When reading a footnoted opinion one's eyes are constantly moving from text to footnotes and back again. The distraction and the time waste are substantial. If footnotes were a rational form of communication, Darwinian selection would have resulted in the eyes being set vertically rather than on an inefficient horizontal plane....

How did footnotes ever come about? The most likely first use was as a citation to authority. In the pure application, a footnote that merely cites a case or other writing is the easiest to defend—and the least troublesome. Judges ought to refer to precedents in their opinions, and it helps to know exactly where to find the referenced case. Unfortunately, it was all too easy to move from the pure citation to a description of what the cited authority was about. From there it was only a small step to explaining how the cited authority was distinguishable from the case under consideration, or describing what some other authority had to say about the cited authority, which is distinguishable from what some other authority said about the cited authority, which is … ad very nauseam. This evolutionary process of footnoting did more than add to the length and complexity of footnotes; it led to footnotes becoming substantive. Distinguishing a case can be a subtle way of undercutting it or overruling it. The footnote thus acquired its full capacity for mischief. Meat began to fall from the text and into the footnotes.

The use of footnotes that most perverts judicial opinions is the *obiter dictum* avoidance technique. A judge is reluctant to excise some beautiful prose or sage advice that colleagues or clerks have challenged as superfluous to the decision. What to do? Put it in a footnote.

The rules about the precedential significance of judicial footnotes are very fuzzy. Many legalists insist that footnotes are part of the opinion and entitled to full faith and credit; others insist that they are just footnotes. What is clear is that *obiter dictum* footnotes are used with reckless abandon and frequently overwhelm the text. All too often, yesterday's *obiter dictum* becomes tomorrow's law of the land....

The meatiest footnotes are the adversarial ones. Both majority opinions and dissents are replete with examples of black letter law being made or refined in footnotes. Even after all these years, I am still somewhat disconcerted to find a judge answering the opposition with footnote thunderbolts. I realize that it is more convenient to respond to conflicting points of view in footnotes than to disturb the symmetry of the text. But if the conflict is central to the case, battling it out below the line seems a strange way to fashion precedent....

Which cases hold the records? Well, if it is not unfair to include patent cases, in which footnotes invariably take on a life of their own, there is *United States v. E.I. du Pont de Nemours & Co.*, 118 F. Supp. 41 (D. Del. 1953), with 1,715 footnotes. My own court has done pretty well for appellate opinions. There is *Public Service Commission v. FPC*,

543 F.2d 757 (D.C. Cir. 1974), with 676 footnotes. In *Tel-Oren v. Libyan Arab Republic*, 726 F.2d 774 (D.C. Cir. 1984), three judges used 60 weighty footnotes (and 53 pages of text) to disagree about the basis of their unanimous one page *per curiam* order dismissing the case for lack of jurisdiction.

The beat goes on. There are numerous examples of judges using footnotes to fight battles among themselves — not battles of style, but battles about the very warp and woof of the law (even if it is not the law central to the case) — all relegated to the footnote category in order to keep the opinion itself uncluttered.

One of the by-products of the *obiter dictum* footnote is the length of opinions. As the footnotes and their unnecessary-to-the-opinion subject matter proliferate, so do the pages of the opinions. Point-counterpoint, countered-counter-point — the majority and dissenters hurl footnotes at each other, sometimes becoming so provocative as to require answers in the body of the opinion itself.

And the pages mount. I was appointed to the court in 1979, and my name first appeared in volume 602 of Fed Second. Less than six years later, in July 1985, we are at volume 762 and still counting. While there are a number of reasons for our epexegesis, footnotes contribute substantially.

The *obiter dictum* footnote has its variations. Sometimes the judges cannot agree on the *ratio decidendi* of a case. Rather than ventilate or, better yet, resolve the dispute, the judges bury it in some footnotes, and put a merely "provisional" explanation of the holding in the text. Sometimes the writing judge cannot decide when to stop either the stream of prose or the string of authorities. What to do? Put the excess in footnotes. At other times the judges (or their clerks) worry that they have not made the point clearly or forcefully enough in the text. Where to billet the reinforcements? Footnotes, of course.

Footnotes are used to handle the "kitchen sink" approach that many lawyers take to advocacy. Rather than limit the case or appeal to the best shot, the lawyer throws in everything but the kitchen sink in the hope that some judge will bite on one or another of the throwaways. The judge all too often operates on the premise that any unanswered point made by the losing side is a potential *causa reversa*. Rather than clutter up the text with such flotsam and jetsam (or simply bite the bullet by saying, "We have considered the other points raised and they need no discussion"), the author relies upon footnotes as the repository for unnecessary answers to frivolous contentions....

I quit using footnotes in my opinions several years ago. I quit cold-turkey and it was—and sometimes still is—very painful. When I decided to quit, I called in my clerks to tell them the hard news. After our discussion they caucused among themselves and asked to discuss it with me further. They strongly urged me not to make such a rash decision, pointing out that I was a new judge, whose reputation as a jurist was still being measured, and that it would not sit well at the law schools and other measuring places for me to write such unusual opinions. "Nonsense," I said. "Footnotes are not that well regarded. Besides, Judge Stephen Breyer of the First Circuit has also abandoned footnotes, and if he can do it, so can I." "Yes," came the rejoinder, "but Professor Breyer is a schol—" and they stopped one syllable short of contumely.

It has become a little easier with the passage of time. Some of the pain is the product of the very process of opinion writing that I was discussing above. When the time comes to edit and revise the first draft, it is very hard to decide what to keep and what to throw away. Gone is the comforting option of dropping the marginal point to a footnote. It is either up or out.

Such a process clearly makes for shorter opinions—but it is not as easy to excise one's own purple prose as it is to tell some other writer about his excesses. It is also easier to tell another judge about the self-assurance necessary to give short-shrift to the unimportant points raised on appeal. But once you have been reversed or en banced on some throw-away point (and all of us think we have), it is hard to ignore totally any point urgently pressed by counsel, no matter how sure you are of your ground. It is still tempting to consider a footnote or two....

The biggest problem has to do with citations of authority. If I thought I was fully cured and that my crusade was catching on, I would use footnotes just for authority citations. If footnotes were confined to that use solely, readers could make up their own minds whether they were reading for profit or pleasure. A reader who just wanted to know what the judge was saying about the case being decided could ignore the footnotes altogether. The reader who wanted to wade in more deeply—check the authority, or distinguish it for future cases—could turn to the footnotes. As it is, because I am still full of footnote toxin, I put my authority citations right in the text. The result is hardly conducive to a flowing style of writing.

Let me discuss one other point that Fred Rodell made in his first *Goodbye.* He said that "every legal writer is presumed to be a liar until he proves himself otherwise with a flock of footnotes." I do not see why legal writers, including judges, should have to indulge that presumption. Obviously, if there is a direct quotation from a case or other authority, it is helpful to share that source with the reader. This is especially true when a judge is vouchsafing a view by relying on prior cases. But is it really necessary to have to put a touchstone after every reference? We all have seen the erudite opinions in which the author uses a few authorities over and over again—and each reference is footnoted with an "*Id.*" I sometimes wonder whether that really is shorthand for *idem*, or whether it refers to the presumed ego of the authority, author, or editor. (*United States v. Dallas County Commission*, 548 F. Supp. 794 (S.D. Ala. 1982) is surely the leading example of this compulsion run riot. Of its 415 footnotes, fully 112 consist of the single abbreviation *Id.*)

So if I wrote the Blue Book and substantive footnotes were outlawed, I would make the whole citation process much more permissive. I would say that the number of footnotes should be limited; the legal writer should write primarily for the non-researcher, putting in only enough citation so that his authorities could be checked by those needing to know the source but not so many as to overwhelm the reader.

I hate to read footnotes. I always lose my place in the text and miss the train of thought the author is trying to get me on. But I am afraid that the footnote I fail to read is the key to the whole thing, and so I sneak a peek at some, but not all (I always read footnotes numbered 4). I feel guilty about the ones that I skip over. In my early days on Law Review I was told that the footnotes are the real measure of worth in legal writing. Intellectually, I do not believe it, but then I think of all the footnotes that law students and lawyers and judges have written since the beginnings of law. (Not quite the beginnings: there is not a single footnote to the original version of the Ten Commandments.) Can all those exemplars be wrong?

I think they are.[4]

§ 16.2.4 A Letter to a Law Review Editor

Forty years ago, I wrote a book review for the *Duquesne Law Review*. The book review editor requested that I authenticate many statements with footnotes. I replied as follows:

December 31, 1969

Mr. Stephen G. Walker
Duquesne Law Review
Duquesne University School of Law
Pittsburgh, Pennsylvania 15219

Dear Mr. Walker:

I[1] acknowledge[2] receipt[3] of[4] your[5] letter.[6] I[7] hate[8] footnotes.[9]

Please let me do my thing. Like, dig: the chart I wrote—without the footnote bag. Like Aquarius, not William Jennings Bryan and celluloid collars. Are we together?

Sincerely,

Ruggero J. Aldisert

---

[1] Ruggero J. Aldisert. *See* note 7 *infra*; *cf.* Descartes: "I think, therefore I am."

[2] This word is employed in the lay sense, not as a legal term of art, *e.g.*, to acknowledge an instrument to be recorded.

[3] Receipt was had in the first instance by my secretary (see initials in this cover letter): the letter was then hand-delivered to me in chambers.

[4] Used as a function word to indicate the object of an action denoted or implied by the preceding noun. *See* WEBSTER'S SEVENTH NEW COLLEGIATE DICTIONARY (1967); *see also* THE OXFORD UNIVERSAL DICTIONARY (1955).

[5] "Your" meaning the author of the letter individually and also in his capacity as Book Review Editor of the *Duquesne Law Review* of Duquesne University. For antecedent organizations, see College of the Holy Ghost. *Compare* "Holy Ghost" *with* "Holy Spirit." *Contra* the Church of Universal Brotherhood, which makes no distinction.

[6] Letter from Stephen G. Walker to Hon. Ruggero J. Aldisert, December 17, 1969.

[7] Circuit Judge, United States Court of Appeals for the Third Circuit. *See* note 1, *supra*.

[8] Used to convey a feeling of enmity, without approaching connotations of words such as "detest," "loathe," "abhor," or "abominate." *See generally* the Abominable Snowman.

[9] *See* notes 1–7, *supra*; *see also* text of book review galley 2, ¶ 1(enclosure): "But the book is worth reading. There is an easy pace to it. The Jackson selections are delightful to read, a refreshing change from the ponderous tomes afflicted with 'footnote-itis' which seems to obfuscate most appellate opinions today—my own included."

§ 16.3 Writing Style

This book is not primarily designed to address writing style. The literature abounds in excellent works and critiques: "Use active voice." "Avoid multisyllabic words." "Avoid Latin expressions." (Even so, I love them. They can be useful as shorthand substitutes for long rambling sentences.) "Align verbs with key actions within sentences." "Revise noun-dominated sentences." "Don't let too many words separate subject and predicate." "Make sure 'only' and 'also' lie where logic dictates." "Except in special cases, do not begin a sentence with a conjunction."[2] It is only for the sake of completeness that I volunteer some observations by authorities I respect very much. I cannot tell you why so much legal writing is so stilted. It may start with upper-class students who forget about the niceties of first-year composition classes and lapse into the pedantic style used by academics. It may be the exposure to certain law school casebook opinions, where a decent writing style is seldom paramount and indeed may be perceived as indicating frivolousness or a substitute for scholarship. It may be the law review syndrome, which sees student writers and untenured professors who are desperate to be published, but have no confidence in their own views, and therefore retire to the shelter of overly timid writing polluted with points and counterpoints, thrusts and parries, completely drenched with footnotes and lovely "*but sees.*"

As the appellate case loads have increased, so has the judges' dependence upon law clerks. Law review graduates seem to be preferred because of their editorial experience. Unfortunately, that experience too often has been gained in the production of prose that only foreshadows a transfer of literary shortcomings, whole and unaltered, to the writing of opinions. Flawed jewels shine no more brightly in elegant settings.

Effective writing has a beat, or rhythm. We need this device especially in legal writing. Great speaking and great writing require much advance preparation. When addressing a jury or a court, great advocates develop a rhythm that commands attention and persuades. Yet many eloquent speakers—judges, lawyers and law professors—abandon this style when it comes to writing. The beat that captivated and moved the audience is gone when pen comes to hand. The pen becomes mired in glue and what should be written rhetoric becomes as stultifying as an Internal Revenue Service ruling.[3]

> While a certain amount of rhythm in one's prose is desirable, rhyming is not. Economy of the reader's attention requires that we

---

2. *See* Joyce J. George, Judicial Opinion Writing Handbook (2d ed. 1986); *see also* Henry Weihofen, Legal Writing Style (1961); Charles G. Douglas, III, *How to Write a Concise Opinion,* Judges' J., Spring 1983, at 3; Elizabeth A. Francis, *A Faster, Better Way to Write Opinions,* Judges' J., Fall 1988, at 26 (Fall 1988); James D. Hopkins, *Notes on Style in Judicial Opinions,* 8 Trial Judges' J. 49 (1969).

3. For a classic exemplar of a great writer's use of rhythm, consider the work of the master, Winston S. Churchill. *See* William Manchester, The Last Lion: Winston Spencer Churchill, Alone: 1932–1940, 32–34, 210 (1988).

minimize friction in the process of communication between writer and reader. We want no distracting stimuli that will interfere with smooth transmission. The unexpected appearance of rhyme in prose— like grammatical error, misspelling, and wrong choice of words—is a distraction. One should therefore try to avoid having too many words in the same sentence that rhyme or contain the same sound. Several such words in close proximity to each other offend the inner ear, even when absorbed only through the eye. Lawyers use many abstract words, which often end in "ation," "otion," "ty," or "ship." Two or three such words in a sentence give a jingling effect.[4]

The [judge] may feel that this talk of rhythm and cadence is over-refined, that a busy [judge] has no time for such concern with sensitivity. Too often this is true; the [judge] working under pressure cannot give the time he would like to give, not only to his writing, but also to the investigation of facts and legal research. But this means he is not performing at his highest level of competence, and it hurts [the] case. Able [judges] know the importance of expressing their thoughts in the most effective way possible, and they devote time and effort to putting them into the best form they can.[5]

§ 16.4 Literature and Poetry

Literature, poetry, popular culture and other art forms can be worked effectively into opinion writing. Not only are they expressive and engaging, but they reflect the mores and customs of the culture of which they are a part. Consider the following:

> There have been cases which have used the word "fine" to refer to civil damages assessed by statute. As the partial dissent notes, two cases decided 70 years after the Excessive Fines Clause was adopted considered the term "fines" to include money, recovered in a civil suit, which was paid to government.... These cases, however, provide no support for petitioners' argument that the Eighth Amendment is applicable in cases between private parties. As to the dissent's reliance on the Bard ... we can only observe:

---

4. Henry Weihofen, Legal Writing Style 287 (1961).
5. *Id.* at 292.

Though Shakespeare, of course,
Knew the Law of his time,
He was foremost a poet,
In search of a rhyme.[6]

The following is the partial dissent that prompted the preceding response:

William Shakespeare, an astute observer of English law and politics, did not distinguish between fines and amercements in the plays he wrote in the in the late 16th Century. In Romeo and Juliet, published in 1597, Prince Escalus uses the words "amerce" and "fine" interchangeably in warning the Montagues and the Capulets not to shed any more blood on the streets of Verona:

"I have an interest in your hate's proceeding,
My blood for your rude brawls doth lie a-bleeding;
But I'll amerce you with so strong a fine,
"That you shall all repent the loss of mine."

Act III, scene 1, lines 186–189.[7]

* * *

Music is one of the oldest forms of human expression. From Plato's discourse in the Republic to the totalitarian state in our own times, rulers have known its capacity to appeal to the intellect and to the emotions, and have censored musical compositions to serve the needs of the state. See 2 DIALOGUES OF PLATO, REPUBLIC, bk. 3, pp. 231, 245–248 (B. Jowett transl., 4th ed. 1953) ("Our poets must sing in another and a nobler strain"); *Musical Freedom and Why Dictators Fear It*, N.Y. TIMES, Aug. 23, 1981, §2, p. 1, col. 5; *Soviet Schizophrenia toward Stravinsky*, N.Y. TIMES, June 26, 1982, §1, p. 25, col. 2; *Symphonic Voice from China Is Heard Again*, N.Y. TIMES, Oct. 11, 1987, §2, p. 27, col. 1. The Constitution prohibits any like attempts in our own legal order. Music, as a form of expression and communication, is protected under the First Amendment.[8]

---

6. Browning-Ferris Indus. of Vt., Inc. V. Kelco Disposal, Inc., 492 U.S. 257 (1989).

7. *Id.* at 290 (O'Connor, J., dissenting).

8. Ward v. Rock Against Racism, 491 U.S. 781, 790 (1989).

§ 16.5 Favorite Opinion Writers

I have certain favorite opinion writers. Among the all-time greats, Oliver Wendell Holmes comes to mind, along with Benjamin Cardozo, Learned Hand, Robert Jackson, William J. Brennan, Jr., Hugo Black, William H. Hastie and Albert Branson Maris. Of more recent vintage, opinions from John Roberts, Alex Kozinski, Diane Wood, Margaret McKeown, Richard Posner, and Terence Evans have been especially noteworthy for their clarity and wit. Examine these fragments, beginning—as any prudent opinion reader must—with the unmatched trio of Justice Holmes, Judge Cardozo, and Judge Hand:

> When an uncopyrighted combination of words is published there is no general right to forbid other people repeating them—in other words there is no property in the combination or in the thoughts or facts that the words express. Property, a creation of law, does not arise from value, although exchangeable—a matter of fact. Many exchangeable values may be destroyed intentionally without compensation. Property depends upon exclusion by law from interference, and a person is not excluded from using any combination of words merely because someone has used it before, even if it took labor and genius to make it. If a given person is to be prohibited from making the use of words that his neighbors are free to make some other ground must be found. One such ground is vaguely expressed in the phrase unfair trade. This means that the words are repeated by a competitor in business in such a way as to convey a misrepresentation that materially injures the person who first used them, by appropriating credit of some kind which the first user has earned. The ordinary case is a representation by device, appearance, or other indirection that the defendant's goods come from the plaintiff. But the only reason why it is actionable to make such a representation is that it tends to give the defendant an advantage in his competition with the plaintiff and that it is thought undesirable that an advantage should be gained in that way. Apart from that the defendant may use such unpatented devices and uncopyrighted combinations of words as he likes. The ordinary case, I say, is palming off the defendant's product as the plaintiff's, but the same evil may follow from the opposite falsehood—from saying, whether in words or by implication, that the plaintiff's product is the defendant's, and that, it seems to me, is what has happened here.
>
> Fresh news is got only by enterprise and expense. To produce such news as it is produced by the defendant represents by implication that it has

been acquired by the defendant's enterprise and at its expense. When it comes from one of the great news-collecting agencies like the Associated Press, the source generally is indicated, plainly importing that credit; and that such a representation is implied may be inferred with some confidence from the unwillingness of the defendant to give the credit and tell the truth. If the plaintiff produces the news at the same time that the defendant does, the defendant's presentation impliedly denies to the plaintiff the credit of collecting the facts and assumes the credit to the defendant. If the plaintiff is later in western cities it naturally will be supposed to have obtained its information from the defendant. The falsehood is a little more subtle, the injury a little more indirect, than in ordinary cases of unfair trade, but I think that the principle that condemns the one condemns the other. It is a question of how strong an infusion of fraud is necessary to turn a flavor into a poison. The dose seems to me strong enough here to need a remedy from the law. But as, in my view, the only ground of complaint that can be recognized without legislation is the implied misstatement, it can be corrected by stating the truth; and a suitable acknowledgment of the source is all that the plaintiff can require. I think that within the limits recognized by the decision of the Court the defendant should be enjoined from publishing news obtained from the Associated Press for hours after publication by the plaintiff unless it gives express credit to the Associated Press; the number of hours and the form of acknowledgment to be settled by the District Court.[9]

The plaintiff, a Russian bank, chartered in 1869 by the Imperial Russian government, has deposit accounts with the defendant opened in 1911 and 1915, with a balance of $66,749.45 to its credit at the trial.

Following the Soviet revolution of November, 1917, the assets of the bank of Russia were seized by the revolutionary government and the directors driven into exile. By decrees of the Russian Soviet Republic in 1917, the bank was declared to be merged in the People's or State Bank, its assets were confiscated, its liabilities canceled, and its shares extinguished, and by a later decree, in January, 1920, the People's or State Bank was itself abolished, a banking system having been found to be unnecessary to the new economic life.

---

9. Int'l News Serv. v. Assoc. Press, 248 U.S. 215, 246–48 (1918) (Holmes, J., concurring).

The terms of the plaintiff's charter or "statutes" are printed in the record. The governing body was to be a directorate consisting of seven members, of whom three were to form a quorum. One of the directors lost his life in the revolution. The other six made their way to Paris, where they held meetings from time to time, and did such business as they could. All six were alive in October, 1925, when this action was begun. Three have since died, but a quorum, three, survive....

We think the plaintiff [the bank] is not dissolved, but is still a juristic person with capacity to sue....

Exhibitions of power may be followed or attended by physical changes, legal or illegal. These we do not ignore, however lawless their origin, in any survey of the legal scene. They are a source at times of new rights and liabilities. Ex facto jus oritur. Exhibitions of power may couple the physical change with declarations of the jural consequences. These last we ignore, if the consequences, apart from the declaration, do not follow from the change itself....

The everyday transactions of business or domestic life are not subject to impeachment, though the form may have been regulated by the command of the usurping government.... To undo them would bring hardship or confusion to the helpless and the innocent without compensating benefit. On the other hand, there is no shelter in such exceptions for rapine or oppression. We do not recognize the decrees of Soviet Russia as competent to divest the plaintiff of the title to any assets that would otherwise have the protection of our law. At least this must be so where the title thus divested is transferred to the very government not recognized as existent. For the same reason we do not admit their competence in aid of a like purpose to pass sentence of death on the expropriated owner. Death, if it has followed, is not death by act of law....

There is a distinction not to be ignored between the life of a human being and the life of a personal ficta, the creature of the state. When a human being dies, his death is equally a fact whether it is brought about legally or illegally, whether he has died of illness in his bed or has been murdered on the highway. The event is not conditioned by the juristic quality of the cause. But in respect of juristic beings, the quality of the cause may determine the event as well. The personality created by law may continue unimpaired until law rather than might shall declare it at an end. Conceivably, the law *will* declare it at an end when marauders have brought frustration to the purpose for which personality was given. That is another question. What is not to be lost sight of is that even so it is the law and not merely an assassin that must pronounce the words of doom....

The case comes down to this: A fund is in this state with title vested in the plaintiff at the time of the deposit. Nothing to divest that title has ever happened here or elsewhere. The directors who made the deposit in the name of the corporation or continued it in that name now ask to get it back. Either it must be paid to the depositor, acting by them, or it must be kept here indefinitely. Either they must control the custody, or for the present and the indefinite future it is not controllable by any one. The defendant expresses the fear that the money may be misapplied if the custody is changed. The fear has its basis in nothing more than mere suspicion. The directors, men of honor presumably, will be charged with the duties of trustees, and will be subject to prosecution, civil or criminal, if those duties are ignored. The defendant is not required to follow the money into their hands and see how they apply it. Its duty is to pay.[10]

The plaintiff, a corporation, is a manufacturer of silks, which puts out each season many new patterns, designed to attract purchasers by their novelty and beauty. Most of these fail in that purpose, so that not much more than a fifth catch the public fancy. Moreover, they have only a short life, for the most part no more than a single season of eight or nine months. It is in practice impossible, and it would be very onerous if it were not, to secure design patents upon all of these; it would also be impossible to know in advance which would sell well, and patent only those. Besides, it is probable that for the most part they have no such originality as would support a design patent. Again, it is impossible to copyright them under the Copyright Act (17 USCA § 1 et seq.), or at least so the authorities of the Copyright Office hold. So it is easy for any one to copy such as prove successful, and the plaintiff, which is put to much ingenuity and expense in fabricating them, finds itself without protection of any sort for its pains.

Taking advantage of this situation, the defendant copied one of the popular designs in the season beginning in October, 1928, and undercut the plaintiff's price. This is the injury of which it complains. The defendant, though it duplicated the design in question, denies that it knew it to be the plaintiff's, and there thus arises an issue which might

---

10. Petrogradsky Mejdunarondy Kommerchesky Bank v. Nat'l City Bank, 170 N.E. 479 (N.Y. 1930) (Cardozo, C.J.).

be an answer to the motion. However, the parties wish a decision upon the equity of the bill, and, since it is within our power to dismiss it, we shall accept its allegation, and charge the defendant with knowledge.

The plaintiff asks for protection only during the season, and needs no more, for the designs are all ephemeral. It seeks in this way to disguise the extent of the proposed innovation, and to persuade us that, if we interfere only a little, the solecism, if there be one, may be pardonable. But the reasoning which would justify any interposition at all demands that it cover the whole extent of the injury. A man whose designs come to harvest in two years, or in five, has prima facie as good right to protection as one who deals only in annuals. Nor could we consistently stop at designs; processes, machines, and secrets have an equal claim. The upshot must be that, whenever any one has contrived any of these, others may be forbidden to copy it. That is not the law. In the absence of some recognized right at common law, or under the statutes—and the plaintiff claims neither—a man's property is limited to the chattels which embody his invention. Others may imitate these at their pleasure....

This is confirmed by the doctrine of "non-functional" features, under which it is held that to imitate these is to impute to the copy the same authorship as the original.... These decisions imply that, except as to these elements, any one may copy the original at will. Unless, therefore, there has been some controlling authority to the contrary, the bill at bar stands upon no legal right and must fail.

Of the cases on which the plaintiff relies, the chief is *International News Service v. Associated Press*, 248 U.S. 215. Although that concerned another subject-matter—printed news dispatches—we agree that, if it meant to lay down a general doctrine, it would cover this case; at least, the language of the majority opinion goes so far. We do not believe that it did. While it is of course true that law ordinarily speaks in general terms, there are cases where the occasion is at once the justification for, and the limit of, what is decided. This appears to us such an instance; we think that no more was covered than situations substantially similar to those then at bar. The difficulties of understanding it otherwise are insuperable. We are to suppose that the court meant to create a sort of common-law patent or copyright for reasons of justice. Either would flagrantly conflict with the scheme which Congress has for more than a century devised to cover the subject-matter.

Qua patent, we should at least have to decide, as tabula rasa, whether the design or machine was new and required invention; further, we must ignore the Patent Office whose action has always been a condition upon the creation of this kind of property. Qua copyright, although it would be simpler to decide upon the merits, we should equally be obliged to dispense with the conditions imposed upon the creation of the right. Nor, if we went so far, should we know whether the property so recognized should be limited to the periods prescribed in the statutes, or should extend as long as the author's grievance. It appears to us incredible that the Supreme Court should have had in mind any such consequences. To exclude others from the enjoyment of a chattel is one thing; to prevent any imitation of it, to set up a monopoly in the plan of its structure, gives the author a power over his fellows vastly greater, a power which the Constitution allows only Congress to create....

True, it would seem as though the plaintiff had suffered a grievance for which there should be a remedy, perhaps by an amendment of the Copyright Law, assuming that this does not already cover the case, which is not urged here. It seems a lame answer to such a case to turn the injured party out of court, but there are larger issues at stake than his redress. Judges have only a limited power to amend the law; when the subject has been confided to a Legislature, they must stand aside, even though there be an hiatus in completed justice. An omission in such cases must be taken to have been as deliberate as though it were express, certainly after long-standing action on the subject-matter.... Our vision is inevitably contracted, and the whole horizon may contain much which will compose a very different picture.[11]

* * *

In keeping with the tradition of the "greats," Justice Jackson wrote with a golden pen. Here are two of my favorites—the first crystallizes one of the most-repeated bon mots about the Supreme Court; the second represents one of the most eloquent defenses of First Amendment liberties ever to grace the pages of a judicial reporter:

Conflict with state courts is the inevitable result of giving the convict a virtual new trial before a federal court sitting without a jury. Whenever decisions of one court are reviewed by another, a percentage of them are reversed. That reflects a difference in outlook normally found between personnel comprising different courts. However, reversal by a higher court is not proof that justice is thereby better

---

11. Cheney Bros. v. Doris Silk Corp., 35 F.2d 279 (2d Cir. 1929) (Hand, J.).

done. There is no doubt that if there were a super-Supreme Court, a substantial proportion of our reversals of state courts would also be reversed. We are not final because we are infallible, but we are infallible only because we are final.[12]

There is no doubt that, in connection with the pledges, the flag salute is a form of utterance. Symbolism is a primitive but effective way of communicating ideas. The use of an emblem or flag to symbolize some system, idea, institution, or personality, is a short cut from mind to mind. Causes and nations, political parties, lodges and ecclesiastical groups seek to knit the loyalty of their followings to a flag or banner, a color or design. The State announces rank, function, and authority through crowns and maces, uniforms and black robes; the church speaks through the Cross, the Crucifix, the altar and shrine, and clerical raiment. Symbols of State often convey political ideas just as religious symbols come to convey theological ones. Associated with many of these symbols are appropriate gestures of acceptance or respect: a salute, a bowed or bared head, a bended knee. A person gets from a symbol the meaning he puts into it, and what is one man's comfort and inspiration is another's jest and scorn....

It is also to be noted that the compulsory flag salute and pledge requires affirmation of a belief and an attitude of mind. It is not clear whether the regulation contemplates that pupils forego any contrary convictions of their own and become unwilling converts to the prescribed ceremony or whether it will be acceptable if they simulate assent by words without belief and by a gesture barren of meaning. It is now a commonplace that censorship or suppression of expression of opinion is tolerated by our Constitution only when the expression presents a clear and present danger of action of a kind the State is empowered to prevent and punish. It would seem that involuntary affirmation could be commanded only on even more immediate and urgent grounds than silence. But here the power of compulsion is invoked without any allegation that remaining passive during a flag salute ritual creates a clear and present danger that would justify an effort even to muffle expression. To sustain the compulsory flag salute we are required to say that a Bill of Rights which guards the individual's right

----

12. Brown v. Allen, 344 U.S. 443, 540 (1952) (Jackson, J., concurring)

to speak his own mind, left it open to public authorities to compel him to utter what is not in his mind.

Whether the First Amendment to the Constitution will permit officials to order observance of ritual of this nature does not depend upon whether as a voluntary exercise we would think it to be good, bad or merely innocuous. Any credo of nationalism is likely to include what some disapprove or to omit what others think essential, and to give off different overtones as it takes on different accents or interpretations. If official power exists to coerce acceptance of any patriotic creed, what it shall contain cannot be decided by courts, but must be largely discretionary with the ordaining authority, whose power to prescribe would no doubt include power to amend. Hence validity of the asserted power to force an American citizen publicly to profess any statement of belief or to engage in any ceremony of assent to one, presents questions of power that must be considered independently of any idea we may have as to the utility of the ceremony in question....

It was said that the flag-salute controversy confronted the Court with "the problem which Lincoln cast in memorable dilemma: 'Must a government of necessity be too *strong* for the liberties of its people, or too *weak* to maintain its own existence?'" and that the answer must be in favor of strength....

We think these issues may be examined free of pressure or restraint growing out of such considerations.

It may be doubted whether Mr. Lincoln would have thought that the strength of government to maintain itself would be impressively vindicated by our confirming power of the State to expel a handful of children from school. Such oversimplification, so handy in political debate, often lacks the precision necessary to postulates of judicial reasoning. If validly applied to this problem, the utterance cited would resolve every issue of power in favor of those in authority and would require us to override every liberty thought to weaken or delay execution of their policies.

Government of limited power need not be anemic government. Assurance that rights are secure tends to diminish fear and jealousy of strong government, and by making us feel safe to live under it makes for its better support. Without promise of a limiting Bill of Rights it is doubtful if our Constitution could have mustered enough strength to enable its ratification. To enforce those rights today is not to choose weak government over strong government. It is only to adhere as a means of strength to individual freedom of mind in preference to officially disciplined uniformity for which history indicates a disappointing and disastrous end.

The subject now before us exemplifies this principle. Free public education, if faithful to the ideal of secular instruction and political neutrality, will not be partisan or enemy of any class, creed, party, or faction. If it is to impose any ideological discipline, however, each party or denomination must seek to control, or failing that, to weaken the influence of the educational system. Observance of the limitations of the Constitution will not weaken government in the field appropriate for its exercise....

The case is made difficult not because the principles of its decision are obscure but because the flag involved is our own. Nevertheless, we apply the limitations of the Constitution with no fear that freedom to be intellectually and spiritually diverse or even contrary will disintegrate the social organization. To believe that patriotism will not flourish if patriotic ceremonies are voluntary and spontaneous instead of a compulsory routine is to make an unflattering estimate of the appeal of our institutions to free minds. We can have intellectual individualism and the rich cultural diversities that we owe to exceptional minds only at the price of occasional eccentricity and abnormal attitudes. When they are so harmless to others or to the State as those we deal with here, the price is not too great. But freedom to differ is not limited to things that do not matter much. That would be a mere shadow of freedom. The test of its substance is the right to differ as to things that touch the heart of the existing order.

If there is any fixed star in our constitutional constellation, it is that no official, high or petty, can prescribe what shall be orthodox in politics, nationalism, religion, or other matters of opinion or force citizens to confess by word or act their faith therein. If there are any circumstances which permit an exception, they do not now occur to us.

We think the action of the local authorities in compelling the flag salute and pledge transcends constitutional limitations on their power and invades the sphere of intellect and spirit which it is the purpose of the First Amendment to our Constitution to reserve from all official control.[13]

* * *

---

13. W.Va. Bd. of Educ. v. Barnette, 319 U.S. 624 (1943) (Jackson, J.).

Justice Brennan had a way with words, always interweaving his opinions with the perfect blend of sobriety and emotiveness, regardless whether he wrote about habeas, free speech or religion. An excerpt from each of those areas follows:

> But while our appellate function is concerned only with the judgments or decrees of state courts, the habeas corpus jurisdiction of the lower federal courts is not so confined. The jurisdictional prerequisite is not the judgment of a state court but *detention simpliciter*. The entire course of decisions in this Court elaborating the rule of exhaustion of state remedies is wholly incompatible with the proposition that a state court *judgment* is required to confer federal habeas jurisdiction. And the broad power of the federal courts under 28 U.S.C. § 2243 summarily to hear the application and to "determine the facts, and dispose of the matter as law and justice require," is hardly characteristic of an appellate jurisdiction. Habeas lies to enforce the right of personal liberty; when that right is denied and a person confined, the federal court has the power to release him. Indeed, it has no other power; it cannot revise the state court judgment; it can act only on the body of the petitioner.[14]

The following excerpt shows a master at work. Justice Brennan selected and edited passages with exquisite care to match the rhythm of his prose that leads to the crescendo "that debate on public issues should be uninhibited, robust, and wide-open...."

> The general proposition that freedom of expression upon public questions is secured by the First Amendment has long been settled by our decisions. The constitutional safeguard, we have said, "was fashioned to assure unfettered interchange of ideas for the bringing about of political and social changes desired by the people." *Roth v. United States*, 354 U.S. 476, 484. "The maintenance of the opportunity for free political discussion to the end that government may be responsive to the will of the people and that changes may be obtained by lawful means, an opportunity essential to the security of the Republic, is a fundamental principle of our constitutional system." *Stromberg v. California*, 283 U.S. 359, 369. "(I)t is a prized American privilege to speak

---

14. Fay v. Noia, 372 U.S. 391 (1963) (Brennan, J.).

one's mind, although not always with perfect good taste, on all public institutions," *Bridges v. California*, 314 U.S. 252, 270, and this opportunity is to be afforded for "vigorous advocacy" no less than "abstract discussion." *N.A.A.C.P. v. Button*, 371 U.S. 415, 429. The First Amendment, said Judge Learned Hand, "presupposes that right conclusions are more likely to be gathered out of a multitude of tongues, than through any kind of authoritative selection. To many this is, and always will be, folly; but we have staked upon it our all." *United States v. Associated Press*, 52 F. Supp. 362, 372 (S.D.N.Y. 1943). Mr. Justice Brandeis, in his concurring opinion in *Whitney v. California*, 274 U.S. 357, 375–376, gave the principle its classic formulation:

Those who won our independence believed ... that public discussion is a political duty; and that this should be a fundamental principle of the American government. They recognized the risks to which all human institutions are subject. But they knew that order cannot be secured merely through fear of punishment for its infraction; that it is hazardous to discourage thought, hope and imagination; that fear breeds repression; that repression breeds hate; that hate menaces stable government; that the path of safety lies in the opportunity to discuss freely supposed grievances and proposed remedies; and that the fitting remedy for evil counsels is good ones. Believing in the power of reason as applied through public discussion, they eschewed silence coerced by law—the argument of force in its worst form. Recognizing the occasional tyrannies of governing majorities, they amended the Constitution so that free speech and assembly should be guaranteed.

Thus, we consider this case against the background of a profound national commitment to the principle that debate on public issues should be uninhibited, robust, and wide-open, and that it may well include vehement, caustic, and sometimes unpleasantly sharp attacks on government and public officials.[15]

———————

A too literal quest for the advice of the Founding Fathers upon the issues of these cases seems to me futile and misdirected for several reasons: First, on our precise problem the historical record is at best ambiguous, and statements can readily be found to support either

———————

15. N.Y. Times v. Sullivan, 376 U.S. 254 (1964) (Brennan, J.).

side of the proposition. The ambiguity of history is understandable if we recall the nature of the problems uppermost in the thinking of the statesmen who fashioned the religious guarantees; they were concerned with far more flagrant intrusions of government into the realm of religion than any that our century has witnessed. While it is clear to me that the Framers meant the Establishment Clause to prohibit more than the creation of an established federal church such as existed in England, I have no doubt that, in their preoccupation with the imminent question of established churches, they gave no distinct consideration to the particular questions whether the clause also forbade devotional exercises in public institutions.

Second, the structure of American education has greatly changed since the First Amendment was adopted. In the context of our modern emphasis upon public education available to all citizens, any views of the eighteenth century as to whether the exercises at bar are an "establishment" offer little aid to decision. Education, as the Framers knew it, was in the main confined to private schools more often than not under strictly sectarian supervision. Only gradually did control of education pass largely to public officials. It would, therefore, hardly be significant if the fact was that the nearly universal devotional exercises in the schools of the young Republic did not provoke criticism; even today religious ceremonies in church-supported private schools are constitutionally unobjectionable.

Third, our religious composition makes us a vastly more diverse people than were our forefathers. They knew differences chiefly among Protestant sects. Today the Nation is far more heterogeneous religiously, including as it does substantial minorities not only of Catholics and Jews but as well of those who worship according to no version of the Bible and those who worship no God at all.... In the face of such profound changes, practices which may have been objectionable to no one in the time of Jefferson and Madison may today be highly offensive to many persons, the deeply devout and the nonbelievers alike.

Whatever Jefferson or Madison would have thought of Bible reading or the recital of the Lord's Prayer in what few public schools existed in their day, our use of the history of their time must limit itself to broad purposes, not specific practices. By such a standard, I am persuaded, as is the Court, that the devotional exercises carried on in the Baltimore and Abington schools offend the First Amendment because they sufficiently threaten in our day those substantive evils the fear of which called forth the Establishment Clause of the First Amendment. It is "*a constitution* we are expounding," and our interpretation of the First Amendment must necessarily be responsive to the much more highly charged nature of religious questions in contemporary society.[16]

* * *

Justice Hugo Black had the enviable and unparalleled ability to infuse his prose with expressiveness and emotion, a style that underscored the weighty topics with which he often grappled. Here are a few of my favorites:

> The petitioner, a Negro, was indicted in the Circuit Court of Lauderdale County, Mississippi, by an all-white grand jury, charged with the murder of a white man. He was convicted by an all-white petit jury and sentenced to death by electrocution. He had filed a timely motion to quash the indictment alleging that, although there were Negroes in the county qualified for jury service, the venires for the term from which the grand and petit juries were selected did not contain the name of a single Negro. Failure to have any Negroes on the venires, he alleged, was due to the fact that for a great number of years previously and during the then term of court there had been in the county a "systematic, intentional, deliberate and invariable practice on the part of administrative officers to exclude negroes from the jury lists, jury boxes and jury service, and that such practice has resulted and does now result in the denial of the equal protection of the laws to this defendant as guaranteed by the 14th amendment to the U.S. Constitution."....

> Sixty-seven years ago this Court held that state exclusion of Negroes from grand and petit juries solely because of their race denied Negro defendants in criminal cases the equal protection of the laws required by the Fourteenth Amendment. *Strauder v. West Virginia*, 100 U.S. 303 (1880). A long and unbroken line of our decisions since then has reiterated that principle, regardless of whether the discrimination was embodied in statute or was apparent from the administrative practices of state jury selection officials, and regardless of whether the system for depriving defendants of their rights was "ingenious or ingenuous."

> Whether there has been systematic racial discrimination by administrative officials in the selection of jurors is a question to be determined from the facts in each particular case. In this case the

---

16. Abington Sch. Dist. v. Schemp, 374 U.S. 203, 237 (1963) (Brennan, J.).

Mississippi Supreme Court concluded that petitioner had failed to prove systematic racial discrimination in the selection of jurors, but in so concluding it erroneously considered only the fact that no Negroes were on the particular venire lists from which the juries were drawn that indicted and convicted petitioner. It regarded as irrelevant the key fact that for thirty years or more no Negro had served on the grand or petit juries. This omission seriously detracts from the weight and respect that we would otherwise give to its conclusion in reviewing the facts, as we must in a constitutional question like this.

It is to be noted at once that the indisputable fact that no Negro had served on a criminal court grand or petit jury for a period of thirty years created a very strong showing that during that period Negroes were systematically excluded from jury service because of race. When such a showing was made, it became a duty of the State to try to justify such an exclusion as having been brought about for some reason other than racial discrimination.[17]

––––––––––––

We are asked to decide whether the President was acting within his constitutional power when he issued an order directing the Secretary of Commerce to take possession of and operate most of the Nation's steel mills. The mill owners argue that the President's order amounts to lawmaking, a legislative function which the Constitution has expressly confided to the Congress and not to the President. The Government's position is that the order was made on findings of the President that his action was necessary to avert a national catastrophe which would inevitably result from a stoppage of steel production, and that in meeting this grave emergency the President was acting within the aggregate of his constitutional powers as the Nation's Chief Executive and the Commander in Chief of the Armed Forces of the United States....

The President's power, if any, to issue the order must stem either from an act of Congress or from the Constitution itself. There is no statute that expressly authorizes the President to take possession of property as he did here. Nor is there any act of Congress to which our attention has been directed from which such a power can fairly be implied. Indeed, we do not understand the Government to rely on statu-

––––––––––––

17. Patton v. Mississippi, 332 U.S. 463 (1947) (Black, J.).

tory authorization for this seizure. There are two statutes which do authorize the President to take both personal and real property under certain conditions. However, the Government admits that these conditions were not met and that the President's order was not rooted in either of the statutes. The Government refers to the seizure provisions of one of these statutes (§ 201 (b) of the Defense Production Act) as "much too cumbersome, involved, and time-consuming for the crisis which was at hand."

Moreover, the use of the seizure technique to solve labor disputes in order to prevent work stoppages was not only unauthorized by any congressional enactment; prior to this controversy, Congress had refused to adopt that method of settling labor disputes....

It is clear that if the President had authority to issue the order he did, it must be found in some provision of the Constitution. And it is not claimed that express constitutional language grants this power to the President. The contention is that presidential power should be implied from the aggregate of his powers under the Constitution. Particular reliance is placed on provisions in Article II which say that "The executive Power shall be vested in a President ..."; that "he shall take Care that the Laws be faithfully executed"; and that he "shall be Commander in Chief of the Army and Navy of the United States."

The order cannot properly be sustained as an exercise of the President's military power as Commander in Chief of the Armed Forces....

Nor can the seizure order be sustained because of the several constitutional provisions that grant executive power to the President. In the framework of our Constitution, the President's power to see that the laws are faithfully executed refutes the idea that he is to be a lawmaker. The Constitution limits his functions in the lawmaking process to the recommending of laws he thinks wise and vetoing of laws he thinks bad. And the Constitution is neither silent nor equivocal about who shall make laws which the President is to execute....

The Founders of this Nation entrusted the lawmaking power to the Congress alone in both good and bad times. It would do no good to recall the historical events, the fears of power and the hopes for freedom that lay behind their choice. Such a review would but confirm our holding that this seizure order cannot stand.[18]

---

18. Youngstown Sheet & Tube Co. v. Sawyer, 343 U.S. 579 (1952) (Black, J.).

Petitioner was charged in a Florida state court with having broken and entered a poolroom with intent to commit a misdemeanor. This offense is a felony under Florida law. Appearing in court without funds and without a lawyer, petitioner asked the court to appoint counsel for him, whereupon the following colloquy took place:

"The COURT: Mr. Gideon, I am sorry, but I cannot appoint Counsel to represent you in this case. Under the laws of the State of Florida, the only time the Court can appoint Counsel to represent a Defendant is when that person is charged with a capital offense. I am sorry, but I will have to deny your request to appoint Counsel to defend you in this case.

"The DEFENDANT: The United States Supreme Court says I am entitled to be represented by Counsel."

Put to trial before a jury, Gideon conducted his defense about as well as could be expected from a layman. He made an opening statement to the jury, cross-examined the State's witnesses, presented witnesses in his own defense, declined to testify himself, and made a short argument, "emphasizing his innocence to the charge contained in the Information filed in this case." The jury returned a verdict of guilty, and petitioner was sentenced to serve five years in the state prison. Later, petitioner filed in the Florida Supreme Court this habeas corpus petition attacking his conviction and sentence on the ground that the trial court's refusal to appoint counsel for him denied him rights "guaranteed by the Constitution and the Bill of Rights by the United States Government." Treating the petition for habeas corpus as properly before it, the State Supreme Court, "upon consideration thereof" but without an opinion, denied all relief....

The Sixth Amendment provides, "In all criminal prosecutions, the accused shall enjoy the right ... to have the Assistance of Counsel for his defence." We have construed this to mean that in federal courts counsel must be provided for defendants unable to employ counsel unless the right is competently and intelligently waived.... [R]eason and reflection require us to recognize that in our adversary system of criminal justice, any person hauled into court, who is too poor to hire a lawyer, cannot be assured a fair trial unless counsel is provided for him. This seems to us to be an obvious truth. Governments, both state and federal, quite properly spend vast sums of money to establish machinery to try defendants accused of crime. Lawyers to prosecute are everywhere deemed essential to protect the public's interest in an orderly society. Similarly, there are few defendants charged with crime, few indeed, who fail to hire the best lawyers they can get to prepare and present their defenses. That government hires lawyers to prosecute and defendants who have the money hire lawyers to defend are the strongest indication of the widespread belief that lawyers in criminal courts are necessities, not luxuries. The right of one charged with crime to counsel may not be deemed fundamental and essential to fair trials in some countries, but it is in ours. From the very beginning, our state and national constitutions and laws have laid great emphasis on procedural and substantive safeguards designed to assure fair trials before impartial tribunals in which every defendant stands equal before the law. This noble ideal cannot be realized if the poor man charged with crime has to face his accusers without a lawyer to assist him.[19]

* * *

Judge Albert Branson Maris of the United States Court of Appeals for the Third Circuit, born in the 19th century, died at the age of 95 in 1989. He served for 52 years as a federal judge. The following are examples of his excellent style, including one excerpt of an opinion written when he was 94 years old:

An action arises under the laws of the United States if and only if the complaint seeks a remedy expressly granted by a federal law or if it requires the construction of a federal statute or a distinctive policy of a federal statute requires the application of federal legal principles for its disposition.... If, on the other hand, the action is not expressly authorized by federal law, does not require the construction of a federal statute and is not required by some distinctive policy of a federal statute to be determined by the application of federal legal principles, it does not arise under the laws of the United States even if federal law furnishes some necessary ingredient of the claim. Moreover, the fact that a contract is subject to federal regulation does not, in itself, demonstrate that Congress meant that all aspects of its performance or nonperformance are to be governed by federal law rather than by the state law applicable to similar contracts in businesses not under federal regulation.... Here the dispute between the parties is purely one as to the correct interpretation and effect of certain contractual documents, an ordinary contract dispute to be determined by the application of the

---

19. Gideon v. Wainwright, 372 U.S. 335 (1963) (Black, J.).

principles of Pennsylvania contract law. The fact that these documents were subject to the regulations of the FHA is not significant, since we know of no federal statutory policy which would require federal law to determine their operation and effect. The case is, therefore, not one arising under the laws of the United States.[20]

Little need be said with respect to the plaintiff's argument that the statute authorizes the lien to be enforced to secure payment of a judgment recovered in a suit brought against a driver of a motor vehicle who is not its owner. The short answer to this argument is that there is not a word in the statute with respect to the institution of such a suit. On the contrary, as we have pointed out, the lien is tied in with and its existence conditioned upon the commencement of an action against the owner. Thus, the lien would not even come into existence if suit were brought solely against the non-owning driver of the vehicle. Moreover, it would require explicit language to authorize the taking of a motor vehicle and the application of the proceeds of its sale to the payment of a judgment recovered against a third party for whose negligence the owner is not responsible. While it is not uncommon for statutes to visit upon the owner of property the unpleasant consequences of the unauthorized action of one to whom he had entrusted it ... such statutes, since they provide for the forfeiture of the property of an innocent owner, must be strictly construed.[21]

This appeal presents us with the question whether an amount received in settlement of the claim of James Edward Bent, the petitioner in the Tax Court and herein referred to as the taxpayer, for damages for violation of his rights under the First Amendment to freedom of speech is deductible from his taxable income under section 104(a)(2) of the Internal Revenue Code of 1954. The Tax Court in a well-reasoned opinion by Judge Chabot, 87 T.C. 236 (1986), held that the sum in question was so deductible. The Commissioner of Internal Revenue ... has appealed. Finding ourselves in accord with the reasoning and conclusions of Judge Chabot, we will affirm his decision.[22]

20. Lindy v. Lynn, 501 F.2d 1367, 1369 (3d Cir. 1974) (Maris, J.).
21. Smith v. Hertz Rent-A-Car, 377 F.2d 885, 888 (3d Cir. 1967) (Maris, J.).
22. Bent v. Comm'r, IRS, 835 F.2d 67, 68 (3d Cir. 1987) (Maris, J.).

* * *

Former Chief Judge William H. Hastie of the Third Circuit was our country's first black federal judge (District Court of the Virgin Islands), first black governor (governor-general of the U.S. Virgin Islands) and first black Article III judge. Judge Hastie, as did Judge Maris, had the rare ability to express complex legal concepts in clear prose:

> In the present case, the cause of action for indemnity arose when Mack satisfied the judgment, an event evidenced by formal entry of record in the Florida court on June 30, 1960.
>
> The Pennsylvania borrowing statute utilizes this concept of the arising of a cause of action in relation to place rather than time in order to specify the circumstances in which a Pennsylvania court shall apply another state's statute of limitations and to identify the appropriate state. We think the concept of when a cause arises and the concept of where a cause arises, both used to aid in the application of statutes of limitations, are *in pari materia*. In other words, the cause arises where as well as when the final significant event that is essential to a suable claim occurs. *Bank of Nova Scotia v. San Miguel*, 1st Cir. 1952, 196 F.2d 950; *Orschel v. Rothschild*, 1925, 238 III. App. 353; *Runkle v. Pullin*, 1912, 49 Ind. App. 619. In this case the cause of action arose when a judgment was entered against and later satisfied by Mack in Florida. By the same token, Florida is the state where the cause of action for indemnity arose.[23]

In this case we are asked to enforce an order of the National Labor Relations Board which accords bargaining rights to a labor union.

The controversy involves a small plant and a group of eight workers. For a long time management successfully, and apparently lawfully, opposed unionization. However, in the summer of 1963, the union advised management that seven of the eight employees had elected to be represented by it and presented signed union application cards in token of that fact. The eighth employee signed shortly thereafter. In the immediately ensuing discussions, apparently preliminary to bargaining, management expressed no doubt and demanded no

---

23. Mack Trucks, Inc. v. Bendix-Westinghouse Auto Air Brake Co., 372 F.2d 18, 20–21 (3d Cir. 1966) (Hastie, J.).

further proof concerning the unionization of its employees. However, three days later, the employer requested the Board to conduct an election on the question of representation. Shortly thereafter, the union consented to such an election.

The union and the employer conducted vigorous campaigns for and against union representation during the weeks immediately preceding the election. Most of the things said and done were lawful. However, the Board has found that two conversations of the proprietor, each with a separate employee, amounted to "coercive interrogation" and "a promise of benefit" in return for deserting the union. We think the evidence concerning these conversations warrants the finding that they constituted unfair labor practices.[24]

A detailed labor contract promotes economic stability by defining terms and conditions of employment, usually for a term of several years. After most strikes, whether legal or illegal, that occur while a labor contract is in effect, work is resumed with a large part, if not all, of the labor contract intact. Certainly such continuity in the mutually agreed terms and conditions of employment is in the public interest and should be encouraged. On the other hand, fairness to an employer confronted by an illegal strike may dictate judicial recognition of contract abrogation or damages as alternative available remedies. But it is neither necessary nor desirable to encourage the termination of labor contracts by allowing both remedies. From this viewpoint, the loss of the right it otherwise would have to collect damages for a breach is not an unfair price for an employer to pay if it insists upon total and permanent relief from the obligations it accepted under a labor contract.[25]

* * *

On occasion, even the most straitlaced of jurists can be found having some fun with what would otherwise be a staid and sober statement of the case. Here's Chief Justice Roberts in a dissent from a denial of certiorari, trying his hand at writing a crime thriller:

------

24. NLRB v. Frank C. Varney Co., 359 F.2d 774, 775 (3d Cir. 1966) (Hastie, J.).

25. Children's Rehab. Ctr., Inc v. Serv. Emp. Int'l Union., Loc. 227, 503 F.2d 1077, 1079 (3d Cir. 1974) (Hastie, J.).

North Philly, May 4, 2001. Officer Sean Devlin, Narcotics Strike Force, was working the morning shift. Undercover surveillance. The neighborhood? Tough as a three-dollar steak. Devlin knew. Five years on the beat, nine months with the Strike Force. He'd made fifteen, twenty drug busts in the neighborhood.

Devlin spotted him: a lone man on the corner. Another approached. Quick exchange of words. Cash handed over; small objects handed back. Each man then quickly on his own way. Devlin knew the guy wasn't buying bus tokens. He radioed a description and Officer Stein picked up the buyer. Sure enough: three bags of crack in the guy's pocket. Head downtown and book him. Just another day at the office.

That was not good enough for the Pennsylvania Supreme Court, which held in a divided decision that the police lacked probable cause to arrest the defendant. The court concluded that a "single, isolated transaction" in a high-crime area was insufficient to justify the arrest, given that the officer did not actually see the drugs, there was no tip from an informant, and the defendant did not attempt to flee. 941 A.2d 671, 679 (Pa. 2007). I disagree with that conclusion, and dissent from the denial of certiorari. A drug purchase was not the only possible explanation for the defendant's conduct, but it was certainly likely enough to give rise to probable cause.[26]

* * *

This next case, written by the brilliant Judge Terence Evans, proves that even the most mundane of cases can be made into jurisprudential gold when placed in the hands of a master opinion crafter:

Toilet paper. This case is about toilet paper. Are there many other things most people use every day but think very little about? We doubt it. But then again, only a select few of us work in the rarefied air inhabited by top-rate intellectual property lawyers who specialize in presenting and defending claims of unfair competition and trademark infringement under the Lanham Act, 15 U.S.C. § 1051 *et seq.* And the lawyers on both sides of this dispute are truly first-rate. Together they cite some 119 cases and 20 federal statutes (albeit with a little overlap) in their initial briefs. We are told that during the "expedited" discovery period leading up to the district court decision we are called upon

---

26. Pennsylvania v. Dunlap, 129 S. Ct. 448, 448 (2008) (mem.) (Roberts, C.J., dissenting).

to review, some 675,000 pages of documents were produced and more than a dozen witnesses were deposed. That's quite a record considering, again, that this case is about toilet paper.

We'll start by introducing the combatants. In the far corner, from an old cotton-producing state (Dixie: "I wish I was in the land of cotton, old times there are not forgotten.") and headquartered in the area (Atlanta) where Scarlett O'Hara roamed Tara in Margaret Mitchell's epic *Gone With the Wind*, we have the Georgia-Pacific Company. Important to this case, and more than a bit ironic, is that the name of Georgia-Pacific's flagship toilet paper is Quilted *Northern*. In the near corner, headquartered in the north, in Neenah, Wisconsin (just minutes away from Green Bay), and a long way from the land of cotton, we have the Kimberly-Clark Corporation. Ironically, its signature toilet paper brand is called *Cotton* elle.

The claim in this case is that a few of Kimberly-Clark's brands of toilet paper are infringing on Georgia-Pacific's trademark design. But again, this case is about toilet paper, and who really pays attention to the design on a roll of toilet paper? The parties, however, are quick to inform us that in a $4 billion dollar industry, designs are very important. Market share and significant profits are at stake. So with that, we forge on.[27]

* * *

Opinion-writing legend Richard Posner was recently described as someone who "evidently writes the way other men breathe."[28] This excerpt highlights his punchy, straightforward and provocative style:

[Appellees'] first argument is that conduct by a corporation or any other entity that doesn't have a heartbeat (we'll use "corporation" to cover all such entities) can never be a violation of customary international law, no matter how heinous the conduct. So, according to Firestone, a pirate can be sued under the Alien Tort Statute but not a pirate corporation (Pirates of the Indian Ocean, Inc., with its headquarters and principal place of business in Somalia; *cf*. U.N. Security Council, "Report of the Monitoring Group on Somalia Pursuant to

---

27. Ga.-Pac. Consumer Prods. LP v. Kimberly-Clark Corp., 647 F.3d 723, 725–26 (7th Cir. 2011) (Evans, J.).

28. Robert M. Solow, *How to Understand the Disaster*, N.Y. Rev. Books, May 14, 2009 (reviewing Richard A. Posner, A Failure of Capitalism: The Crisis of '08 and the Descent into Depression (2009)).

Security Council Resolution 1853 (2008)" 99 (Feb. 26, 2010).) Firestone argues that because corporations, unlike individuals, have never been prosecuted for criminal violations of customary international law, there cannot be a norm, let alone a "universal" one, forbidding them to commit crimes against humanity and other acts that the civilized world abhors.

The issue of corporate liability under the Alien Tort Statute seems to have been left open in an enigmatic footnote in *Sosa*, 542 U.S. at 732 n. 20 (but since it's a Supreme Court footnote, the parties haggle over its meaning, albeit to no avail). All but one of the cases at our level hold or assume (mainly the latter) that corporations can be liable.... The outlier is the split decision in *Kiobel v. Royal Dutch Petroleum Co.*, 621 F.3d 111 (2d Cir. 2010), which indeed held that because corporations have never prosecuted, whether criminally or civilly, for violating customary international law, there can't be said to be a principle of customary international law that binds a corporation....

We have to consider why corporations have rarely been prosecuted criminally or civilly for violating customary international law; maybe there's a compelling reason. But it seems not; it seems rather that the paucity of cases reflects a desire to keep liability, whether personal or institutional, for such violations within tight bounds by confining it to abhorrent conduct—the kind of conduct that invites criminal sanctions. It would have seemed tepid to charge the Nazi war criminals with battery, wrongful death, false imprisonment, intentional infliction of emotional distress, fraud, conversion, trespass, medical malpractice, or other torts. And it was natural in light of the perceived effect of the Nuremberg trials on German and international opinion concerning the type of practices in which Hitler's government had engaged that a tradition would develop of punishing violations of customary international law by means of national or international criminal proceedings; it was a way of underscoring the gravity of violating customary international law.[29]

* * *

Here are two excerpts showcasing Chief Judge Alex Kozinski's "trademarked" combination of colloquial style, biting wit, and tongue-in-cheek humor:

---

29. Flomo v. Firestone National Rubber Co., LLC, 643 F.3d 1013, 1017 (7th Cir. 2011) (Posner, J.).

After Mattel filed suit [for trademark infringement], Mattel and MCA employees traded barbs in the press. When an MCA spokeswoman noted that each album included a disclaimer saying that Barbie Girl was a "social commentary [that was] not created or approved by the makers of the doll," a Mattel representative responded by saying, "That's unacceptable.... It's akin to a bank robber handing a note of apology to a teller during a heist. It neither diminishes the severity of the crime, nor does it make it legal." He later characterized the song as a "theft" of "another company's property."

MCA filed a counterclaim for defamation based on the Mattel representative's use of the words "bank robber," "heist," "crime" and "theft." But all of these are variants of the invective most often hurled at accused infringers, namely "piracy." No one hearing this accusation understands intellectual property owners to be saying that infringers are nautical cutthroats with eyepatches and peg legs who board galleons to plunder cargo. In context, all these terms are nonactionable "rhetorical hyperbole," *Gilbrook v. City of Westminster*, 177 F.3d 839, 863 (9th Cir. 1999). The parties are advised to chill.[30]

According to our dissenting colleagues, "non-satirical and non-theatrical knowingly false statements of fact are always unprotected" by the First Amendment. Not "often," not "sometimes," but always. Not "if the government has an important interest" nor "if someone's harmed" nor "if it's made in public," but always. "Always" is a deliciously dangerous word, often eaten with a side of crow.

So what, exactly, does the dissenters' ever-truthful utopia look like? In a word: terrifying. If false factual statements are unprotected, then the government can prosecute not only the man who tells tall tales of winning the Congressional Medal of Honor, but also the JDater who falsely claims he's Jewish or the dentist who assures you it won't hurt a bit. Phrases such as "I'm working late tonight, hunny," "I got stuck in traffic" and "I didn't inhale" could all be made into crimes. Without the robust protections of the First Amendment, the white lies, exaggerations and deceptions that are an integral part of human intercourse would become targets of censorship, subject only to the rubber stamp known as "rational basis review."

---

30. Mattel, Inc. v. MCA Records, Inc., 296 F.3d 894, 908 (9th Cir. 2002) (Kozinski, J.).

What the dissenters seem to forget is that Alvarez was convicted for pure speech. And when it comes to pure speech, truth is not the sine qua non of First Amendment protection.... Alvarez's conviction is especially troubling because he is being punished for speaking about himself, the kind of speech that is intimately bound up with a particularly important First Amendment purpose: human self-expression.... Speaking about oneself is precisely when people are most likely to exaggerate, obfuscate, embellish, omit key facts or tell tall tales. Self-expression that risks prison if it strays from the monotonous reporting of strictly accurate facts about oneself is no expression at all.

Saints may always tell the truth, but for mortals living means lying. We lie to protect our privacy ("No, I don't live around here"); to avoid hurt feelings ("Friday is my study night"); to make others feel better ("Gee you've gotten skinny"); to avoid recriminations ("I only lost $10 at poker"); to prevent grief ("The doc says you're getting better"); to maintain domestic tranquility ("She's just a friend"); to avoid social stigma ("I just haven't met the right woman"); for career advancement ("I'm sooo lucky to have a smart boss like you"); to avoid being lonely ("I love opera"); to eliminate a rival ("He has a boyfriend"); to achieve an objective ("But I love you so much"); to defeat an objective ("I'm allergic to latex"); to make an exit ("It's not you, it's me"); to delay the inevitable ("The check is in the mail"); to communicate displeasure ("There's nothing wrong"); to get someone off your back ("I'll call you about lunch"); to escape a nudnik ("My mother's on the other line"); to namedrop ("We go way back"); to set up a surprise party ("I need help moving the piano"); to buy time ("I'm on my way"); to keep up appearances ("We're not talking divorce"); to avoid taking out the trash ("My back hurts"); to duck an obligation ("I've got a headache"); to maintain a public image ("I go to church every Sunday"); to make a point ("Ich bin ein Berliner"); to save face ("I had too much to drink"); to humor ("Correct as usual, King Friday"); to avoid embarrassment ("That wasn't me"); to curry favor ("I've read all your books"); to get a clerkship ("You're the greatest living jurist"); to save a dollar ("I gave at the office"); or to maintain innocence ("There are eight tiny reindeer on the rooftop").

And we don't just talk the talk, we walk the walk, as reflected by the popularity of plastic surgery, elevator shoes, wood veneer paneling, cubic zirconia, toupees, artificial turf and cross-dressing. Last year, Americans spent $40 billion on cosmetics—an industry devoted almost entirely to helping people deceive each other about their appearance. It doesn't matter whether we think that such lies are despicable or cause more harm than good. An important aspect of personal autonomy is the right to shape one's public and private persona by choosing when to tell the truth about oneself, when to conceal and when to deceive. Of course, lies are often disbelieved or discovered, and that too is part of the pull and tug of social intercourse. But it's critical to leave such interactions in private hands, so that we can make choices about who we are. How can you develop a reputation as a straight shooter if lying is not an option?

Even if untruthful speech were not valuable for its own sake, its protection is clearly required to give breathing room to truthful self-expression, which is unequivocally protected by the First Amendment. *See New York Times Co. v. Sullivan*, 376 U.S. 254, 271–72 (1964). Americans tell somewhere between two and fifty lies each day. *See* JOCHEN MECKE, CULTURES OF LYING 8 (2007). If all untruthful speech is unprotected, as the dissenters claim, we could all be made into criminals, depending on which lies those making the laws find offensive. And we would have to censor our speech to avoid the risk of prosecution for saying something that turns out to be false. The First Amendment does not tolerate giving the government such power.[31]

* * *

Judge Margaret McKeown, of the U.S. Court of Appeals for the Ninth Circuit, writing eloquently and forcefully for the en banc circuit:

It is likely that few Americans can profess fluency in the Bill of Rights, but the Fifth Amendment is surely an exception. From television shows like "Law & Order" to movies such as "Guys and Dolls," we are steeped in the culture that knows a person in custody has "the right to remain silent." Miranda is practically a household word. And surely, when a criminal defendant says, "I plead the Fifth," it doesn't take a trained linguist, a PhD, or a lawyer to know what he means. Indeed, as early as 1955, the Supreme Court recognized that "in popular parlance and even in legal literature, the term 'Fifth Amendment' in the context of our time is commonly regarded as being synonymous with the privilege against self-incrimination." *Quinn v. United States*, 349 U.S. 155, 163 (1955); *accord In re Johnny V.*, 149 Cal. Rptr.

---

31. United States v. Alvarez, 638 F.3d 666, 673–75 (en banc) (Kozinski, C.J., concurring).

180, 184, 188 (1978) (holding that the statement "I'll take the fifth" was an assertion of the Fifth Amendment privilege). More recently, the Court highlighted that "Miranda has become embedded in routine police practice to the point where the warnings have become part of our national culture." *Dickerson v. United States*, 530 U.S. 428, 443 (2000).

We granted rehearing en banc in this appeal from the district court's denial of Jerome Alvin Anderson's petition for writ of habeas corpus. Anderson challenges his conviction of special circumstances murder on the grounds that he was denied his constitutional right to remain silent and that admission of his involuntary confession into evidence violated his right to due process. Specifically, Anderson claims that he invoked his Fifth Amendment right to terminate his police interrogation and that the police officer's continued questioning violated that right.

Anderson twice attempted to stop police questioning, stating "I don't even wanna talk about this no more," and "Uh! I'm through with this." After questioning continued, Anderson stated unequivocally, "I plead the Fifth." Instead of honoring this unambiguous invocation of the Fifth Amendment, the officer queried, "Plead the Fifth. What's that?" and then continued the questioning, ultimately obtaining a confession. It is rare for the courts to see such a pristine invocation of the Fifth Amendment and extraordinary to see such flagrant disregard of the right to remain silent.[32]

* * *

Next, consider these two gems penned by the peerless Judge Diane Wood, of the U.S. Court of Appeals for the Seventh Circuit:

> When there are three job openings and a man fills the first position, it is an uphill battle for another man to prove that his gender is the reason why he was not selected. That is the task that John Gore faces in this case. Although Gore is convinced that only invidious reasons could explain Indiana University's refusal to hire him as a lecturer, he needs more than his own conviction. The district court granted summary judgment for the University on Gore's claim of gender bias, and

---

32. Anderson v. Terhune, 516 F.3d 781, 783–84 (9th Cir. 2008) (en banc) (McKeown, J.).

we agree that he did not demonstrate any genuine issue of material fact that would require a trial. We therefore affirm.[33]

I am unpersuaded by my colleagues' assertion that expert testimony is categorically inferior to published, English-language materials. Exercises in comparative law are notoriously difficult, because the U.S. reader is likely to miss nuances in the foreign law, to fail to appreciate the way in which one branch of the other country's law interacts with another, or to assume erroneously that the foreign law mirrors U.S. law when it does not. As the French might put it more generally, apparently similar phrases might be *faux amis*. A simple example illustrates why two words might be "false friends." A speaker of American English will be familiar with the word "actual," which is defined in Webster's Third New International Dictionary as "existing in act, ... existing in fact or reality: really acted or acting or carried out—contrasted with *ideal* and *hypothetical*...." WEBSTER'S THIRD NEW INTERNATIONAL DICTIONARY 22 (1993). So, one might say, "This is the actual chair used by George Washington." But the word "actuel" in French means "present" or right now. LE ROBERT & COLLINS COMPACT PLUS DICTIONNAIRE 7 (5th ed. 2003). A French person would thus use the term "les événements actuels" or "actualité" to refer to current events, not to describe something that really happened either now or in the past.

There will be many times when testimony from an acknowledged expert in foreign law will be helpful, or even necessary, to ensure that the U.S. judge is not confronted with a "false friend" or that the U.S. judge understands the full context of the foreign provision. Some published articles or treatises, written particularly for a U.S. audience, might perform the same service, but many will not, even if they are written in English, and especially if they are translated into English from another language. It will often be most efficient and useful for the judge to have before her an expert who can provide the needed precision on the spot, rather than have the judge wade through a number of secondary sources. In practice, the experts produced by the parties are often the authors of the leading treatises and scholarly articles in the foreign country anyway. In those cases, it is hard to see why

---

33. Gore v. Ind. Univ., 416 F.3d 590, 591 (7th Cir. 2005) (Wood, J.).

the person's views cannot be tested in court, to guard against the possibility that he or she is just a mouthpiece for one party. Prominent lawyers from the country in question also sometimes serve as experts. That too is perfectly acceptable in principle, especially if the question requires an understanding of court procedure in the foreign country. In many places, the academic branch of the legal profession is entirely separate from the bar. Academic writings in such places tend to be highly theoretical and removed from the day-to-day realities of the practice of law.[34]

* * *

No discussion of opinion writing would be complete without at least one morsel from the sarcasm-filled pen of Justice Antonin Scalia, long known for his caustic style and acerbic wit:

If one assumes, however, that the PGA TOUR has some legal obligation to play classic, Platonic golf—and if one assumes the correctness of all the other wrong turns the Court has made to get to this point—then we Justices must confront what is indeed an awesome responsibility. It has been rendered the solemn duty of the Supreme Court of the United States, laid upon it by Congress in pursuance of the Federal Government's power "[t]o regulate Commerce with foreign Nations, and among the several States," U. S. Const., Art. I, §8, cl. 3, to decide *What Is Golf*. I am sure that the Framers of the Constitution, aware of the 1457 edict of King James II of Scotland prohibiting golf because it interfered with the practice of archery, fully expected that sooner or later the paths of golf and government, the law and the links, would once again cross, and that the judges of this august Court would someday have to wrestle with that age-old jurisprudential question, for which their years of study in the law have so well prepared them: Is someone riding around a golf course from shot to shot really a golfer? The answer, we learn, is yes. The Court ultimately concludes, and it will henceforth be the Law of the Land, that walking is not a "fundamental" aspect of golf.[35]

* * *

---

34. Bodum USA, Inc. v. La Cafetiere, Inc., 621 F.3d 624, 638–39 (7th Cir. 2010) (Wood, J., concurring).

35. PGA Tour, Inc. v. Martin, 532 U.S. 661, 700 (2001) (Scalia, J., dissenting).

This final opinion, written by Judge Gillis of the Michigan Court of Appeals and included here in its entirety, may be my all-time favorite:

> The appellant has attempted to distinguish the factual situation in this case from that in *Renfroe v. Higgins Rack Coating & Manufacturing Co., Inc.* (1969), 17 Mich. App. 259. He didn't. We couldn't.
>
> Affirmed. Costs to appellee.[36]

---

36. Denny v. Radar Indus., Inc., 184 N.W.2d 289, 290 (Mich. App. Ct. 1970) (Gillis, J.).

CHAPTER SEVENTEEN

WRITING STYLE: A REPRISE, OR, "WATCH YOUR LANGUAGE!"

§17.1 Citations and Authorities

Over 40 years of experience in the appellate courts tell me that the judge's burdens can be considerably lightened by adherence to the following recommendations:

- Confine citations to your jurisdiction, if possible. It makes no sense to refer to another court's decision if your own court has decided the point.
- Make sure your law clerks check meticulously:
  - that the law cited in the opinion is current and in the appropriate citation format;
  - every quotation for accuracy, word for word, punctuation mark for punctuation mark;
  - each word and symbol for consistency in style (e.g., You should not use "percent" on one page and "%" on the next); and
  - that there are no typographical errors or misspellings.
- Avoid string citations if the law is settled in the jurisdiction. You should keep in mind that a single citation, one that demonstrates similar or identical facts, may give you your most effective argument.
- Never exaggerate the holding of a citation—*never*. My late colleague William H. Hastie described such misrepresentation of case holdings as "trampling over graves."
- Avoid stating the citation in terms of a broad principle. A tight, fact-specific rule of law will serve you better.
- Where there is primary reliance upon only one precedent, summarize the holding, the reasoning and the facts.

§ 17.2 Writing to Be Clear and Interesting

Good prose, in whatever genre, must be clear. It must be active. It must be lean, as lean as possible. Above all, it must excite the reader's interest. If it does not, it produces undesirable reactions in the reader, ranging from boredom to hostility. Some simple rules may help:

- Focus on the sense and substance of the writing. Few readers of opinions care about the personal mood and temper of the writer.
- Avoid the scissors-and-paste approach to quotations. Too often, such quotations prove to be neither necessary nor pertinent. Too often, we wind up with a series of disorganized paragraphs strung together in an attempt at narrative form. The use of such quotations serves to piece together what Wigmore called "a great many semi-irrelevant propositions of law," slogging through marshes of prolixity, sometimes turning the opinion magically into a law lecture and ending with an exposition that almost seems to have been engineered for the purpose of obfuscation.
- Avoid lengthy quotations. Quote only the key words, phrases or sentences of a statute or case. (In my chambers, I set forth lengthy quotations in early drafts and then instruct the law clerks to trim away the excess fat.)
- Avoid successions of loose sentences, chained together by such links as "and," "because," "but" and "or."
- Avoid chains of prepositional phrases linked together by "or," "after," "to" or other common prepositions without intervening verbs. Avoid the monotonous drumbeat of prepositional repetition: "the essence of many of the opinions of the Court of Appeals on the subject of battery." President Lincoln, after all, used three different prepositions to define the relationship of the government to the people.
- Avoid indiscriminate use of crutches: "in terms of" and "in order to."
- Omit needless words.
- Vary sentence length. Let there be rhythm to your writing. The eminent landscape architect Garrett Ecko once confided to a client a "secret" in the patterning of stone pathways: Never put two stones the same size next to each other.
- Vary sentence structure. Introduce the sentence from time to time with a subordinate clause in order to avoid the tom-tom monotony that results from starting with the subject. This rule may be waived when trying for certain effects: "I came, I saw, I conquered."
- Observe intelligent rules of grammar and punctuation.

- Master the trick of anastrophe. You must use it sparingly, but use it you should where it will achieve the effect you want better than a straightforward construction would do. Most of us can tell which of the following two forms is preferable:

  "Gone are the days when my heart was young and gay."

  "The days when my heart was young and gay are gone."

- Let your sentence unfold in the way that serves you best. Every English sentence has a word order that cannot be improved upon. A celebrated English professor once posed this example:

  > Imagine that you are walking in the woods. You detect a rustling in a bush just ahead of you. You poke the bush with a branch. A rabbit scurries out of the bush. How would you tell that simple story? A student of mine once did it this way:
  >
  > "A rabbit scurried out of the bush with a rustle of dry leaves."
  >
  > The words the student chose are not bad, but they are not in the best order. Think how the event must have presented itself to the narrator's senses, with the great surprise at the end. This is how I would do it:
  >
  > "Out of the bush, with a rustle of dry leaves, scurried a rabbit."
  >
  > Every professional comedian knows the importance of saving the punch line for last. One of that clan compared the practice to throwing a baseball past the footlights: it flies toward the audience in a straight line—and at the last minute, it curves.

Walter Kerr, the revered drama critic, made the point in his book *How Not to Write a Play*:

> [T]he serious-minded student ... will give due attention to ... learning how to place the key word in a calculated gag in just the right rhythmic position to make the line explode. (You mustn't swallow your kicker by writing "Temptation is the one thing I can't resist"; you must swing around and write, with Oscar Wilde, "I can resist anything except temptation.")[1]

---

1. Walter Kerr, How Not to Write A Play 11–12 (1955).

Do not be disheartened by the length or scope of my list. The writing of judicial opinions, like most tasks in the law, can be improved with practice. Supreme Court Justice William J. Brennan Jr. was fond of telling this story about himself:

> In his first criminal trial, the young Mr. Brennan was appointed to defend a vehicular manslaughter case. A police officer who lived near the defendant agreed to be a character witness, but the young Brennan did not know that you may—and should—prepare a witness to testify.
>
> Armed with a manual on evidence, and bereft of formal education in trial practice (Harvard Law School had not offered him any), he rose to examine: "Sir, are you acquainted with the defendant's reputation for veracity in the vicinage where he resides?"
>
> The elderly Irish cop look puzzled and then volunteered tentatively, "Well, he is a good driver, I'd say."
>
> Shaken but undeterred, Brennan repeated his question word for word. This time, the witness simply stared at him. As the future Justice began a third time, the judge interrupted.
>
> "Officer, do you know the young man over there?" pointing to the defendant.
>
> "Yes, Your Honor."
>
> "Have you ever known him to lie?"
>
> "Why, no, Your Honor."
>
> "Well, that is what young Mr. Brennan has been asking you, but he went to Harvard Law School and has forgotten how to speak English."

§ 17.3 My Pet Peeves

Many excellent authors and academics have told us how to write clearly and forcefully. We all have our idiosyncrasies with respect to usage. I have five that I feel strongly about, in some cases regardless of what the "experts" say to the contrary:

1. The use of "since" as a substitute for "inasmuch" or "because." Such use may be permissible, but in legal writing, it can be extremely confusing, e.g., "Since he went to Harvard, he has been an unbearable snob." I resort to it only in a temporal sense: "from then until now."

2. I shudder when I see "due to" used as anything but an adjectival phrase, which every authority I know considers its sole function. Right: "The

crop failure was due to continuing drought." Wrong: "Due to the continuing drought, the crop failed." If this country had the counterpart of the French Academy, dedicated to preserving the purity of the language, I would urge that body to limit the use of "due"—at least in legal writing—to "owed" or "owing," "payable," "suitable," "fitting" and "as much as required."

3. I insist that "despite," in the gruesome "despite the fact," should be limited to use as a noun. Various dictionaries define it as "spite," "malice," "contemptuous treatment," "insult," "injury." I avoid its prepositional use as a substitute for "notwithstanding."

4. "Posit" is law school jargon. When I see it in an opinion, I feel certain that the writer is a law clerk, not a judge. If you want to say "assume as fact," say: "assume as fact."

5. When I find "said" or "aforesaid" in any legal writing, I suffer a sensation similar to that created by the sound of fingernails on blackboard.

The English playwright William Wycherley offered this advice to lawyers more than three centuries ago: "[B]luster, sputter, question, cavil; but be sure that your argument be intricate enough, to confound the Court."[2]

§ 17.4 If You Only Knew[3]

By Morton S. Freeman

(1) He thought that he would study *only* Latin.
[He would study no other language.]

(2) He thought that he would *only* study Latin.
[He would study Latin, not teach it.]

(3) He thought that he *only* would study Latin.
[He would study Latin, but not master it.]

(4) He thought that *only* he would study Latin.
[No one else would study Latin.]

---

2. WILLIAM WYCHERLEY, THE PLAIN DEALER act 2, sc. 1 (1676). Lest you be tempted to take Wycherley as a role model, remember that he spent years in debtors' prison and was one of the most vicious and licentious of the Restoration comic dramatists.

3. MORTON S. FREEMAN, THE GRAMMATICAL LAWYER 51 (1979). Reprinted by permission of the ALI-ABA Committee on Continuing Professional Education.

(5) He thought *only* that he would study Latin.
     [He thought about nothing else.]

(6) He *only* thought that he would study Latin.
     [He thought about it, but did nothing.]

(7) *Only* he thought that he would study Latin.
     [He was the only one who thought so.]

§ 17.5 Word Selection[4]

By Joyce J. George

Word Selection

Writers get into trouble with word choice. Sometimes the word chosen as a substitute does not accurately reflect what the writer is thinking, and this misleads the reader. Therefore, a writer should use the purest form of expression possible without offending the reader.

Speech is the form of communication which most nearly expresses thought. The written word should be designed to sound like speech. There is more time to construct a written sentence than a spoken one; therefore, it should be grammatically correct and free of slang. Yet the reader should have the feeling that he is listening to the writer speak.

Common Words

In selecting words, try to use the most common words possible. Some writers believe, incorrectly, that their writing is stylish if they use stylish words....

It may be proper to use "category" instead of "class" when there are several classes of items in differing categories. In such a case, the word "category" would be clearer to the reader than the word "class." Usually, stilted words make the writer sound stuffy. If the reader gets the feeling that the writer is being snobbish, he may be offended and disregard the thoughts being conveyed whether they have merit or not....

---

4. Excerpted from JOYCE J. GEORGE, JUDICIAL OPINION WRITING HANDBOOK 129–33 (2d ed. 1986) (footnotes omitted). Reprinted with permission.

[T]he formal word usually is longer than the common word. So, if only for brevity, the writer should choose the simpler words to describe his thought....

Latin

Latin is the traditional language of the law. It dominates most scholarly legal works. However, Latin creates obstacles even for the legal reader. It often requires translation or at least explanation. As a result, Latin words interrupt the reading process and should be avoided. There are, of course, exceptions to the rule. When a Latin word or phrase has an independent significance in the law, it is appropriate. Certain Latin words express in shorthand form familiar legal doctrines or principles that need no detailed explanation. Each carries a legal understanding of the development of that area of the law. Examples of such phrases include:

> habeas corpus
> res ipsa loquitur
> res judicata

Other Latin terms often used in legal writing might be better translated into English. Some examples follow:

aliunde	ita est
de minimis	justa causa
factum juridicum	mens rea
in pari materia	non obstante veredicto
in propria persona	sua sponte
inter alia	sub judice
in toto	

While it may sound sophisticated to use Latin words and phrases, the author's communication with the reader suffers. What good is it to be learned, if no one can understand what you are trying to say?

Gender Words

I have been taught that use of the masculine pronouns "he," "him," and "his" is proper where the hypothetical person referred to may be of either sex. In writing this handbook I have given considerable thought to avoiding sexism. However, for precision, brevity, continuity, and a clear understanding, I have made a conscious choice to

continue this historical practice. As a female judge and this handbook's author, I have used the male pronoun to include the female.
While I make no judgments about this custom, there are times when
it will be necessary for the judicial writer to differentiate between the
sexes....

We need to consider the occasions when judges may have to express themselves in a non-sexist manner. Neutralized writing is not
easy, because our language roots are imbedded in a patriarchal society of the past. Many common, familiar words betray an unthinking
bias in favor of men. Examples of such words include the following:

> fellowman
> forefathers
> laymen
> mankind
> man-made

We can neutralize these words by making "fellowman" inhabitant,
neighbor, citizen or resident; "forefathers," founders or forebears; "lay-
men," laity; "mankind," humankind or people; and "manmade," manufactured, artificial, synthetic or the like. Some sexist terms lack a
convenient substitute which carries the same meaning and economy.
A conscious effort to neutralize a word may also sound somewhat
awkward. Therefore, careful thought must be given to just how to
present the idea without sounding strained.

Postscript[5]

From what [has been] said ... it is not to be assumed that the writing of lawyers is worse than that of most people. Others also are
tempted at times to indulge in pompous or pretentious words. Others also fail to think through exactly what they want to say before they
try to say it, and neglect to read critically and to revise what they have
written.

What Sir Ernest Gowers has said in defense of government officials
can also be said of lawyers. Most lawyers, like most officials, "write
grammatically correct English. Their style is untainted by the silly jar-

---

5. Henry Weihofen, Legal Writing Style 301–02 (1961). Reprinted with permission
of Thomson Reuters.

gon of commercialese, the catchpenny tricks of the worse sort of journalism, the more nebulous nebulosities of politicians, or the recon-
dite abstractions of Greek or Latin origin in which men of science,
philosophers and economists often wrap their thoughts. Sometimes
it is very good, but then no one notices it. Occasionally it reaches a level
of rare excellence."[6]

The manifold faults and bad practices we have pilloried in this book
are not all characteristic of the writing of most [judges]. [A writer]
can learn to avoid errors before he puts them down. When about to
begin a sentence with "It is" or "There is," he can remember that this
is a weak start, and can look for a stronger opening word; when "very"
comes to mind, he can recall that this word is almost never a help.
But no one should expect to attain perfection in his first draft. The
key to good writing is rewriting.

If you will reread your early drafts for style, you will find intensi-
fying adverbs that you put there to add force but which you now see
merely sound like bluffing or exaggeration. You will find nouns qualified by one or more adjectives; if you think, or consult a thesaurus,
you will be able to find a single noun that will do the job by itself, and
do it more pungently. You will find loose, unharnessed sentences that
you can rearrange and tighten.

When you think you have a passable draft, read it aloud. Or have
a friend, perhaps your [spouse], read it to you. As you listen, you
will hear passages that sound flat or awkward. If the reader's voice
falters, if he stresses the wrong word, if the rhythm breaks, the passage needs reworking. Perhaps it needs to be thrown away, in favor
of a fresh start.

Finally, with much labor and perhaps a little luck, you succeed in
wiping out all evidence of the sweat and toil that went into it. You
have a paragraph that sounds easy and natural. For that is the aim of
all the labor—to make it sound unlabored. "A picture is finished,"
said the painter Whistler, "when all trace of the means used to bring
about the end has disappeared."

If you succeed, you will have the gratifying feeling as you reread
your work that the words you have used and your arrangement of
them hit just the right note to produce the effect you want. Phrases,

---

6. Ernest Gowers, Plain Words, Their ABC 291–92 (1957).

sentences, whole paragraphs, ring pleasingly in your mind and your ear. "This is good!" you will say, a little surprised and more than a little pleased. That is your reward, the sense of satisfaction with a job well done that is the ultimate reward of any craftsman.

PART FOUR

CHECKLISTS

UNDERSTANDING THE CHECKLISTS

CHAPTER EIGHTEEN

APPELLATE OPINION WRITING CHECKLIST

§ 18

Author's Note: *The Checklists in Chapters 18–20 are designed for photo-copying so that the opinion writers may have copies of their checklists at their sides as they write and edit. At appropriate places in the Checklists, we have provided open boxes that can be filled with a check mark as the work progresses.*

A. Follow a planned sequence of writing tasks.

❑ 1. **Issues.** Decide what issues are to be discussed in the opinion. In a multi-judge court, this should be a collegial decision, preferably made at the decision conference.

    a. *Issue Defined.* In a separate and discrete statement, set forth the alleged error in the trial court or administrative agency.

    b. *Context of issue.* Give the reader a flavor of the context in which the issue arose. This includes the procedural history as well as the factual history.

    c. *Be neutral.* Be sure not to slant your statement of the issue in favor of either the plaintiff or the defendant.

    d. *Recap.* Do not set forth any issue *in vacuo*; each issue must be evaluated in terms of context and primary assumptions. Above all, there must be neutrality in the expression of the issue. Beware of slanting the statement. Remember Frankfurter: "Tell me the answer you want and I will phrase the question."

❑ 2. **The Road Map.**

    a. *List the issues.* Write down all the issues presented in the case. Do not worry about order or logical development.

b. *Keep it brief.* An attorney's brief should be just that: brief. So should a judge's opinion. Ask yourself from the beginning: Is this point essential to the discussion?

c. *Standard of Review.* Take each issue and accurately state the standard of review to be followed in evaluating that issue.

    (1) <u>Questions of Fact.</u> The issue presented concerns a question of fact.

        (a) Distinguish among basic, inferred and ultimate facts.

            (i) A basic fact is a narrative or historical event described by an eye- or earwitness.

            (ii) Inferred facts are drawn from basic facts. An inference is permissible only when and to the extent that logic and human experience indicate a probability that certain consequences can and do follow from the basic fact.

            (iii) An ultimate fact is a mixed question of fact and law. The following example will help to illustrate the difference: Anne Marie was driving her car at 60 m.p.h. She was in an accident. The two statements above are basic facts. Whether Anne Marie was driving *negligently* is a mixture of fact and law, a so-called ultimate fact.

        (b) Basic and inferred facts are reviewed under the clearly erroneous standard.

        (c) When dealing with ultimate facts the reviewing court should separate the issue into respective parts, applying the clearly erroneous standard to the factual component and the plenary standard to the legal component.

        (d) Generally, findings of fact by administrative agencies should be upheld if there is substantial evidence on the record as a whole to support them.

    (2) <u>Questions of Law.</u> The issue presented concerns a question of law.

        (a) The standard of review as to selection, interpretation and application of legal precepts is plenary.

    (3) <u>Questions of Discretion.</u> The issue presented concerns a question left to the discretion of the court or administrative agency appealed from.

  (a) The standard of review for issues within the discretion of the trial court is abuse of discretion.
  (b) Administrative agency.
      (i) The Administrative Procedure Act precludes review of an action that is committed to agency discretion by law.
      (ii) The substantial evidence test is applied to formal agency rulemaking or judicial orders.
      (iii) Informal agency rule-making should be upheld unless it is arbitrary and capricious.
d. *Decide upon a theme.* Write a careful and considered statement of your presentation's major issue or issues and predominant theme. Keep this statement in front of you at all times; it will help with organization.
e. *Outline.* Prepare an outline of the opinion.
   (1) Prepare a summary statement of issues raised by the appellant that will be discussed in the opinion. This summary may be inserted in the opinion in paragraph form to alert the reader as to what will follow.
   (2) Scrutinize the order in which the issues, arguments and ideas will be presented so as to determine what is most logical, interesting and informative.
f. *Remember your theme.* Look back to it as you write.
   (1) This will help to order and focus your writing.
   (2) It will build unity, logic and conciseness into your writing.
   (3) The organizing theme may need revision and refinement as the writing progresses.
g. *Organize.* Henry M. Hart, Jr. once said, "Briefs on the merits need not only tell their story to one who takes the time to read all the way through them, but ought to be so organized that they can be used, like a book of reference, for quick illumination on any particular point of concern." Remember this.

❑ 3. **Writing the facts.**
   a. Do not begin writing until you have decided what issues you will raise. Never write the facts first.
   b. Tailor the statement of the facts so that it fits only the issues raised. Write as tersely as you can.
      (1) Be accurate. DO NOT STEAL THE FACTS! Set forth findings of fact, not evidence or assertions as your facts.

(2) Be objective.

(3) Be clear.

(4) Be concise. Include only what is necessary, not what is merely interesting.

(5) Be fascinating. Remember that what you write must compete for attention in a mountain of other communications. Try to make it rise above the surrounding peaks.

☐ 4. **Edit your work.**

a. *First draft.* Prepare a complete first draft with whatever tool helps you to work and think most effectively: pen, pencil, typewriter, word processor, whatever. Never dictate an opinion!

(1) If possible, write the draft in one sitting, however long it may take.

(2) If you cannot complete the draft in one sitting, devise a strategy that will enable you to get back to it with a minimum of wheelspin. Ernest Hemingway is said to have stopped the day's work at a point where he had clearly in his head what he was going to write on the following day. I know an author who, when he starts a day with writer's block, gets back on track by retyping the last page he wrote the day before.

(3) Do not try to imitate another writer's approach. There is no such thing as a one-size-fits-all style appropriate to every writer. Each of us sets down words in a highly distinctive, "autographic" way.

b. *Rest.* Set the first draft aside.

(1) My editor, Oscar Shefler, was a world-class writer. He reported: "It often happens that, while doing something else—driving, eating lunch, walking to the bazaars of my neighborhood—I will compose in my head whole paragraphs, even whole pages. When I get back to the typewriter, it is as if I am transcribing from a script somewhere behind my eyeballs."

(2) Approach revision as a stranger, as an outside reader and editor who is seeing the copy fresh for the first time.

c. *Begin revision.*

(1) There is no such thing as good *writing*; there is only good *rewriting*.

(2) As you read, compose a reconstructive outline of the main and subordinate ideas.

(3) Identify the main ideas, according to topics if you have not done so in the first draft, and write them out in sequence, thus composing a précis.

(4) Assess the topical sequence as though you are editing someone else's work.

    (a) See where the reconstructed outline departs from your original outline and determine which is better.

    (b) Determine whether the précis fully satisfies, in content and logic, the demands of the organizing theme.

B. How to edit your own work.

❏ 1. **Edit like a reader.** Identify problems you encounter as a reader.
   a. Determine whether the sequence of ideas flows smoothly and logically.
   b. Determine whether the ideas are adequately supported.
   c. Look for conspicuous omissions.
   d. Look for needless repetition.

❏ 2. **Edit like a writer.** Assess your writing techniques and mark up the first draft as an editor would.
   a. Read certain passages aloud, if necessary, and train your ear to detect errors reliably.
   b. Avoid the trap of falling in love with your writing. In this situation, love often blinds.
   c. Assess the "beat" of your writing. There is a difference between writing for reading and writing for speaking, even though each form has both mood and rhythm. Is the mood exaggerated? Do the words come across as a stentorian roar or as a "soft sell," soothing but nonetheless persuasive?
   d. A judge is a professional writer. Follow the practice of all professional writers and editors. Never rely entirely upon your memory. Keep a select library of the best dictionaries, handbooks and other references at your elbow—a good Webster's dictionary, Roget's Thesaurus, Webster's New Dictionary of Synonyms, a good book of quotations, and, of course, THE ELEMENTS OF STYLE by Strunk and White. You may consider also BRYAN GARNER, A DICTIONARY OF LEGAL USAGE (3d ed. 2009).

C. <u>Strive to become a better writer.</u>

❑ 1. **Read constantly.**

    a. Make outside reading a lifetime professional commitment.

    b. The best writing trains your ear, helping you to listen. The worst writing helps you to learn what to avoid.

    c. Concentrate on masters of "the plain style," such as Mark Twain, George Orwell, James Thurber, E.B. White and Jonathan Swift, who provided models and weapons against the convoluted, lumbering style of legal prose.

❑ 2. **Never become complacent with your writing.**

    a. Remember, effective writing is a lifetime goal, never a final accomplishment.

    b. Become your own best critic.

    c. Try to write so that when you finish you can look at the result and honestly say, "I have just done the very best I am capable of at this stage in my literary development."

    d. Regularly review your past writing.

        (1) Ask yourself how it appeals to you.

        (2) Assess improvement or deterioration in your writing style. Are your words as persuasive as they first seemed? Do they do a good job of expressing the thoughts you originally intended?

    e. To improve, work consciously to ensure that everything you write will be better than anything you wrote before.

    f. Keep always in mind that writing is like exercising a muscle: the more you write, the easier it becomes.[1]

---

1. I have incorporated one or two suggestions from Sondra D. Fargo's Unpublished Monograph, *Techniques of Effective Writing.*

APPELLATE OPINION TESTING CHECKLIST

§ 19

❑ **Jurisdiction.**

In the federal schema, did the District Court have jurisdiction?

❑ **Standard of Review.**

Have you stated and applied the appropriate standard of review for each issue discussed in the opinion? The three most frequently used standards of review are:

1. Clearly erroneous; the issue concerns basic or inferred facts found at a bench trial.

2. Abuse of discretion; the issue is within the discretion of the fact finder.

3. Plenary; the choice interpretation, or application of a legal precept is involved.

❑ **Opening.**

Does the opening or orientation acquaint the reader with the issues on appeal, the nature of the action below, the parties, and a preview of the court's conclusion?

❑ **Summary of Issues.**

Are there one or two paragraphs wherein the reader can find a statement of the issues to be discussed? Alternatively, can the issues be identified easily as topic sentences?

❑ **Facts.**

Is there a lean, selective, economical, succinct exposition of material facts so that the reader can understand what follows?

❑   **Analysis of Issues.**

Have you set forth the *ratio decidendi*, a systematic discussion of the issues?

    ❑ 1.   Identify the flash point of the controversy and discuss only what is essential for a resolution.

        a.   If the law and its application alike are plain, your opinion should be short and to the point.

        b.   If the law is certain and the application alone is doubtful, be sure you have explained how the law applies to the facts. Be just as sure you did not waste the reader's time justifying your choice of law.

        c.   If neither the rule nor, *a fortiori*, its application is clear, discuss:

            (1) Choice, interpretation and application of the legal precept, or

            (2) Interpretation and application of the legal precept.

    ❑ 2.   Is the discussion of the issue overwritten? Have you belabored the point or stated the obvious?

    ❑ 3.   Have you discussed the critical issues presented by the appeal? Have important contentions been discussed or swept under the rug?

    ❑ 4.   Is the logical development sound?

        a.   Is the choice of a major premise supported by the applicable law and facts of the case?

        b.   Have you followed the rules of inductive and deductive logic?

        c.   Is the opinion free of formal or material fallacies?

    ❑ 5.   Does your analysis spend too much time detailing other cases?

        a.   Is it clear *why* you are citing a case?

            (1) Are you citing a case for its holding?

            (2) Are you citing a case for its reasoning?

            (3) Are you citing a case for its facts?

        b.   Can parentheticals replace extensive description of cases?

        c.   Do you use string citations for no purpose?

    ❑ 6.   What is the gobbledygook or Jabberwocky factor?

❑   **Judgment.**

Have you done substantial justice in the case?

    1.   Is there justice between the parties?

2.   Does the decision maintain the integrity of the "body of the law" for future litigants?

Bottom Line: How thoughtfully and disinterestedly did the opinion weigh the conflicts involved in the case and how fair and durable did its adjustment of conflicting interests promise to be?

WHY USE CHECKLISTS FOR WRITING, TESTING AND SHORTENING AN OPINION?

CHECKLISTS ENSURE THAT YOU TOUCH ALL THE BASES ON YOUR WAY TO FILE A "HOME RUN" OPINION.

CHAPTER TWENTY

SHORTEN-YOUR-APPELLATE-OPINION CHECKLIST

§ 20

Satisfied with your writing and rewriting, you arrive at the final task. You must become a copy editor and examine the entire piece to see where you can tighten it. When you do this yourself, you engage in a task lonely, difficult and largely uncharted. Understandably, you may have carried on a passionate love affair with your own words, especially those that seemed, in the flush of creation, divinely beautiful or devilishly clever. Few of us have the heart to follow the implicit advice of the 17th-century French author and critic Nicolas Boileau: "No one who cannot limit himself has ever been able to write." The following steps may be helpful in determining where to make your cuts:

- ❏ 1. **Opening or Orientation Paragraph.**
  - a. State the major issue (or issues) as concisely as possible. Consider how a headnote writer at Thomson West would express it.
  - b. Pique the reader's interest with your language.

- ❏ 2. **Preview.**
  - a. Tell your reader at the onset the decision of the case.
  - b. Reveal whether you reverse or affirm unless there is something about the opinion that makes it preferable for you to disclose this later.

- ❏ 3. **Jurisdiction.**
  - a. State the basis for jurisdiction, if necessary.
  - b. Generally, only a simple citation to a statute or court rule is needed. Such a statement is essential because without jurisdiction to hear the case, your opinion stands on very shaky ground.

☐ 4. **Standard of Review.**
   a. State the basis for jurisdiction, if necessary.
   b. Combine standards on all issues in one paragraph. It may be necessary to set forth varying standards applicable to different issues. If so, have a citation for each standard. It is not necessary to set forth multiple citations. Often the latest case will do. Alternatively, in a long opinion, you may set the standard of review at the start of each issue's discussion.

☐ 5. **Statement of Issues.**
   a. Introduce this subject with a topic sentence or numeral to alert the reader that it is a separate part of the opinion.
   b. Summarize the issues as fairly and neutrally as possible.
   c. Set forth the appellant's contentions you intend to discuss, and remember that you control this part of the opinion; the appellant's counsel does not.
   d. Set forth the response to appellant's contentions by describing the theories of the trial court and the appellee. If the appellee is tracking the precise analysis of the trial court, has there been a duplication? If so, say for example, "The appellee argues, as the trial court concluded, that...."

☐ 6. **Facts.**
   a. In order to avoid the need for transitional phrases, introduce with a topic sentence or a numeral that identifies the narrative.
   b. Keep your figurative blue pencil ready. Cut any facts that are not relevant to the issues presented. Look at the facts through the eyes of a lawyer or judge in a subsequent case.
   c. Pare the narrative to exclude facts that are irrelevant or immaterial to the issues.
   d. Ask yourself whether the narrative is interesting. Remember, however, to distinguish between what is important and what is merely interesting.

☐ 7. **Major Issue.**
   a. You may list the major issue first for discussion or you may wish to discuss threshold issues before you reach it, i.e. procedure matters
   b. Pinpoint the conflict between the parties. Remember, there are three possibilities:

(1) Choosing the controlling precept from competing ones (choosing the law). Or "finding" the law by creating a legal principle from a series of rules from a number of cases.

(2) Interpreting the precept (usually a statute).

(3) Applying the precept to the facts found by the fact finder.

If it is a (1) case you must proceed to (2) and (3). If it is a (2) case, you must avoid unnecessary talk that implies a choice of competing precepts was involved. If it is only (3), you must not clutter it with discussion of competing interpretations.

c. If you refer to cases from other jurisdictions, cut the discussion to the bone as to both facts and holding.

d. If you refer to cases in your own court, distill them to a fair essence rather than doing a cut-and-paste-job with lengthy quotations. Limit your description to material facts.

e. When you choose one legal precept in preference to others, explain succinctly why you are doing so. Be specific.

❑ 8. **Citations.**

a. Whenever you cite a case, think about why you are citing it. Are you citing a particular case for its facts, its holding, its reasoning or some combination of these?

b. Once you determine why you are citing a case, use a parenthetical explanation or quotation to support your point.

c. If you have multiple or string citations, reduce these to one or two leading cases. One possibility is a single previous case of first impression where you can say, "*See Able v. Baker* (collecting cases)."

d. Always ask yourself whether the citation is necessary.

❑ 9. **Quotations.**

a. <u>Cases</u>: Limit the quotation to what is absolutely necessary. Often it is necessary to use a specific quotation because it sets forth the actual language upon which you depend. Sometimes, however, a quotation is unnecessary, and an indirect statement will suffice.

b. <u>Statutes</u>: Quote only relevant provisions.

c. <u>Court Rules</u>: Quote only the necessary paragraphs or clauses.

❑ 10. **Conclusion of the Issue.**

a. State your disposition of the issues clearly and concisely:

b. "Accordingly, the Court rejects the plaintiff's contention and holds...."

❑ 11. **Subsequent Issues.**
   a. Indicate your transition.
   b. If the issue is subordinate, treat it with an extremely condensed discussion.
   c. If it is controlled by precedent, cite the case and be done with it.
   d. Follow the steps set forth in the discussion of major issues, if applicable.

❑ 12. **Disposition.**
   a. Make the disposition understandable.
   b. Introduce it with a signal such as a topic sentence or a numeral.
   c. If you have not discussed all the issues and it is a civil case, you may wish to say, "We have considered all other contentions of the appellant and conclude they are without merit" or "We have considered all other contentions of the appellant and conclude that no discussion is necessary."
   d. If it is a "vacating and remanding" case, explain the directions to the trial court either in the discussion of issues or in the disposition.
   e. If directions were previously set forth in the issue discussions, say, "We will vacate the judgment of the district court and remand the case with a direction to proceed consistent with the foregoing opinion."
   f. Never, never say, "for proceedings not inconsistent with the foregoing" unless you are writing for the United States Supreme Court and are remanding the case to the state court system.

❑ 13. **Footnotes.**
   a. Take a hard look at each footnote and ask yourself, "Is this one necessary?"
   b. If the discussion is germane, place it in the text.
   c. Do not footnote a response to a very sophisticated argument that might have been made, but was not.
   d. Do not distinguish a case that could have been cited, but was not.
   e. If you are using a footnote to quote contents of a statute, pare the quotation and insert it in the text.
   f. If you are quoting at length from a transcript, quote only what is essential.

❑ 14. **Style Critique.**
   a. Use the active voice. Wherever you can, recast sentences that begin with "There is...."

    b.   Break long and complex sentences into short and simple statements.

    c.   Examine each sentence word for word, phrase by phrase and clause by clause to see what can be cut.

☐   **15. Response to Dissenting or Concurring Opinions.**

    a.   It is not absolutely necessary to have the last word. Even though you disagree with the separate opinion, you may be able to accept it as a reasonable view without making a response. Attempt dissent with dissension. Use the test Holmes used in another context: Write a response only after you have cooled down, but while the blood still rushes to your neck.

    b.   Do not respond to the dissent or concurrence if your colleague judge has merely exercised a different value judgment in the choice, interpretation or application of a legal precept. In a calmer moment, you will remember that there is a good reason for having multi-judge courts.

    c.   It is, however, fair game to respond when the judge:

        (1) Has "trampled over graves" (misrepresented the holding of an earlier case).

        (2) Has violated the rules of logic, *i.e.,* has violated any of the six rules of the categorical syllogism (formal fallacy) or is guilty of a material fallacy.[2] Do not simply say that the reasoning is flawed. Properly label the specific flaw.

        (3) Has stolen or misstated the facts of the instant case.

---

2. *See* Ruggero J. Aldisert, Logic For Lawyers: A Guide to Clear Legal Thinking 139-44 (3d ed. 1997).

CHAPTER TWENTY-ONE

TRIAL COURT AND HEARING TRIBUNAL CHECKLISTS

Author's Note: *The Checklists in this Chapter are designed for photo-copying so that the Opinion Writers may have copies of their checklists at their sides as they write and edit. At appropriate places in the Checklists we have provided open boxes that can be filled with a check mark as the work progresses through composing the opinion in § 21.1, testing the opinion in § 21.2 and shortening it in § 21.3.*

§ 21.1 Opinion Writing Checklist

A. <u>Follow a planned sequence of writing tasks.</u>

   ☐ 1. **Issues.** Decide what issues are to be discussed in the opinion.

        a. *Context of issue.* Give the reader a flavor of the context in which the issue arose. This includes any procedural history as well as the factual history.

        b. *Be neutral.* Be sure not to slant your statement of the issue in favor of either the plaintiff or the defendant.

        c. *Recap.* Do not set forth any issue *in vacuo*; each issue must be evaluated in terms of context and primary assumptions. Above all, there must be neutrality in the expression of the issue. Beware of slanting the statement. Remember Frankfurter: "Tell me the answer you want and I will phrase the question."

   ☐ 2. **The Road Map.**

        a. *List the issues.* Write down all the issues presented in the case. Do not worry about order or logical development.

        b. *Keep it brief.* An attorney's brief should be just that: brief. So should a judge's opinion. Ask yourself from the beginning: Is this point essential to the discussion?

    c. *Decide upon a theme.* Write a careful and considered statement of your presentation's major issue or issues and predominant theme. Keep this statement in front of you at all times; it will help with organization.

    d. *Outline.* Prepare an outline of the opinion.

        (1) Prepare a summary statement of issues raised by the parties that will be discussed in the opinion. This summary may be inserted in the opinion in paragraph form to alert the reader as to what will follow.

        (2) Scrutinize the order in which the issues, arguments and ideas will be presented so as to determine what is most logical, interesting and informative.

    e. *Remember your theme.* Look back to it as you write.

        (1) This will help to order and focus your writing.

        (2) It will build unity, logic and conciseness into your writing.

        (3) The organizing theme may need revision and refinement as the writing progresses.

    f. *Organize.* Henry M. Hart, Jr. once said, "Briefs on the merits need not only tell their story to one who takes the time to read all the way through them, but ought to be so organized that they can be used, like a book of reference, for quick illumination on any particular point of concern." Remember this.

❑ 3. **Writing the Facts.**

    a. Do not begin writing until you have decided what issues you will raise. Never write the facts first.

    b. Tailor the statement of the facts so that it fits only the issues raised. Write as tersely as you can.

        (1) *Be accurate.* DO NOT STEAL THE FACTS! Set forth findings of fact, not evidence or assertions as your facts.

        (2) *Be objective.*

        (3) *Be clear.*

        (4) *Be concise.* Include only what is necessary, not what is merely interesting.

        (5) *Be fascinating.* Remember that what you write must compete for attention in a mountain of other communications. Try to make it rise above the surrounding peaks.

❑ 4. **Edit your work.**

    a. *First draft.* Prepare a complete first draft with whatever tool helps you to work and think most effectively: pen, pencil, typewriter, word processor, whatever. Never dictate an opinion!

        (1) If possible, write the draft in one sitting, however long it may take.

        (2) If you cannot complete the draft in one sitting, devise a strategy that will enable you to get back to it with a minimum of wheelspin. Ernest Hemingway is said to have stopped the day's work at a point where he had clearly in his head what he was going to write on the following day. I know a professional who, when he starts the day with writer's block, gets back on track by retyping the last page he wrote the day before.

        (3) Do not try to imitate another writer's approach. There is no such thing as a one-size-fits-all style appropriate to every writer. Each of us sets down words in a highly distinctive, "autographic" way.

    b. *Rest.* Set the first draft aside.

        (1) My one-time editor, Oscar Shefler, was a world-class writer. He reported: "It often happens that, while doing something else—driving, eating lunch, walking to the bazaars of my neighborhood—I will compose in my head whole paragraphs, even whole pages. When I get back to the typewriter, it is as if I am transcribing from a script somewhere behind my eyeballs."

        (2) Approach revision as a stranger, as an outside reader and editor who is seeing the copy fresh for the first time.

    c. *Begin revision.*

        (1) There is no such thing as good *writing*; there is only good *rewriting*.

        (2) As you read, compose a reconstructive outline of the main and subordinate ideas.

        (3) Identify the main ideas, according to topics if you have not done so in the first draft, and write them out in sequence, thus composing a précis.

        (4) Assess the topical sequence as though you are editing someone else's work.

            (a) See where the reconstructed outline departs from your original outline and determine which is better.

        (b) Determine whether the précis fully satisfies, in content and logic, the demands of the organizing theme.

B.   <u>How to edit your own work.</u>

    ❑ 1. **Edit like a reader.**

        a. Identify problems you encounter as a reader.

        b. Determine whether the sequence of ideas flows smoothly and logically.

        c. Determine whether the ideas are adequately supported.

        d. Look for conspicuous omissions.

        e. Look for needless repetition.

    ❑ 2. **Edit like a writer.**

        a. Assess your writing techniques and mark up the first draft as an editor would.

        b. Read certain passages aloud, if necessary, and train your ear to detect errors reliably.

        c. Avoid the trap of falling in love with your writing. In this situation, love often blinds.

        d. Assess the "beat" of your writing. There is a difference between writing for reading and writing for speaking, even though each form has both mood and rhythm. Do the words come across as a stentorian roar or as a "soft sell," soothing but nonetheless persuasive?

        e. A judge is a professional writer. Follow the practice of all professional writers and editors. Never rely entirely upon your memory. Keep a select library of the best dictionaries, handbooks and other references at your elbow, a good Webster's dictionary, college edition or unabridged; Roget's Thesaurus, Webster's New Dictionary of Synonyms, a good book of quotations: Oxford, Bergen Evans, Bartlett's and, of course, THE ELEMENTS OF STYLE by Strunk and White. You may consider also B. GARNER, A DICTIONARY OF MODERN LEGAL USAGE (3d Ed. Oxford, 2009).

§21.2 Opinion Testing Checklist

❑ **Jurisdiction.**

Does the court have jurisdiction? If the trial court is a U.S. District, Magistrate, or Bankruptcy Court, the opinions should state the statute or constitutional clause vesting jurisdiction in that court. Because most state trial courts have general jurisdiction, no specific statements is necessary. Certain states have trial courts of limited jurisdiction in subject matter or size of verdict, usually in larger counties. If applicable, a statute stating its limited jurisdiction should be indicated in the opinion.

❑ **Opening.**

Does the opening or orientation acquaint the reader with the issues, the nature of the action, the parties, and a preview of the court's conclusion?

❑ **Summary of Issues.**

Are there one or two paragraphs wherein the reader can find a statement of the issues to be discussed? Alternatively, can the issues be identified easily as topic sentences?

❑ **Facts.**

Is there a lean, selective, economical, succinct exposition of material facts so that the reader can understand what follows?

❑ **Analysis of Issues.**

Have you set forth the *ratio decidendi*, a systematic discussion of the issues?

  ❑ 1. Identify the flash point of the controversy and discuss only what is essential for a resolution.

  a. If the law and its application alike are plain, your opinion should be short and to the point.

  b. If the law is certain and the application alone is doubtful, be sure you have explained how the law applies to the facts. Be just as sure you did not waste the reader's time justifying your choice of law.

  c. If neither the rule nor, *a fortiori*, its application is clear, discuss:

  (1) Choice, interpretation and application of the legal precept, or

  (2) Interpretation and application of the legal precept.

❑ 2. Is the discussion of the issue overwritten? Have you belabored the point or stated the obvious?

❑ 3. Have important contentions been discussed or swept under the rug?

❑ 4. Is the logical development sound?

    a. Is the choice of a major premise supported by the applicable law and facts of the case?

    b. Have you followed the rules of inductive and deductive logic?

    c. Is the opinion free of formal or material fallacies?

❑ 5. Does your analysis spend too much time detailing other cases?

    a. Is it clear *why* you are citing a case?

        (1) Are you citing a case for its holding,

        (2) Are you citing a case for its reasoning, and/or

        (3) Are you citing a case for its facts?

    b. Can parentheticals replace extensive description of cases?

    c. Do you use string citations for no purpose?

❑ 6. What is the gobbledygook or Jabberwocky factor?

❑ **Judgment.**

Have you done substantial justice in the case?

1. Is there justice between the parties?

2. Does the decision maintain the integrity of the "body of the law" for future litigants?

Bottom Line: How thoughtfully and disinterestedly did the opinion weigh the conflicts involved in the case and how fair and durable did its adjustment of conflicting interests promise to be?

§21.3 Shorten-Your-Opinion Checklist

Satisfied with your writing and rewriting, you arrive at the final task. You must become a copy editor and examine the entire piece to see where you can tighten it. When you do this yourself, you engage in a task lonely, difficult and largely uncharted. Understandably, you may have carried on a passionate love affair with your own words, especially those that seemed, in the flush of creation, divinely beautiful or devilishly clever. Few of us have the heart to follow the implicit advice of the 17th-century French author and critic Nicolas Boileau: "No one who cannot limit himself has ever been able to write." The following steps may be helpful in determining where to make your cuts:

❑ 1. **Opening or Orientation Paragraph.**
   a. State the major issue (or issues) as concisely as possible. Consider how a headnote writer at Westlaw would express it.
   b. Pique the reader's interest with your language.

❑ 2. **Preview.**
   a. Tell your reader at the onset the decision of the case.
   b. Reveal whether you grant or deny the requested relief unless there is something about the opinion that makes it preferable for you to disclose this later.

❑ 3. **Jurisdiction.**
   a. State the basis for jurisdiction, if necessary. Generally, only a simple citation to a statute or court rule is needed. Such a statement is essential because without jurisdiction to hear the case, your opinion stands on very shaky ground.

❑ 4. **Statement of Issues.**
   a. Introduce this subject with a topic sentence or numeral to alert the reader that it is a separate part of the opinion.
   b. Summarize the issues as fairly and neutrally as possible.

❑ 5. **Facts.**
   a. In order to avoid the need for transitional phrases, introduce with a topic sentence or a numeral that identifies the narrative.
   b. Keep your figurative blue pencil ready. Cut any facts that are not relevant to the issues presented. Look at the facts through the eyes of a lawyer or judge in a subsequent case.
   c. Pare the narrative to exclude facts that are irrelevant or immaterial to the issues.

      d. Ask yourself whether the narrative is interesting. Remember, however, to distinguish between what is important and what is merely interesting.

☐ 6. **Major Issue.**

      a. You may list the major issue first for discussion or you may wish to discuss threshold issues before you reach it, i.e., procedure matters.

      b. Pinpoint the conflict between the parties. Remember, there are three possibilities:

          (1) Choosing the controlling precept from competing ones (choosing the law). Or "finding" the law by creating a legal principle from a series of rules from a number of cases.

          (2) Interpreting the precept (usually a statute).

          (3) Applying the precept to the facts found by the fact finder.

          If it is an (1) case you must proceed to (2) and (3). If it is a (2) case, you must avoid unnecessary talk that implies a choice of competing precepts was involved. If it is only (3), you must not clutter it with discussion of competing interpretations.

      c. If you refer to cases from other jurisdictions, cut the discussion to the bone as to both facts and holding.

      d. If you refer to cases in your own court, distill them to a fair essence rather than doing a cut-and-paste-job with lengthy quotations. Limit your description to material facts.

      e. When you choose one legal precept in preference to others, explain succinctly why you are doing so. Be specific.

☐ 7. **Citations.**

      a. Whenever you cite a case, think about why you are citing it. Are you citing a particular case for its facts, its holding, its reasoning or some combination of these?

      b. Once you determine why you are citing a case, use a parenthetical explanation or quotation to support your point.

      c. If you have multiple or string citations, reduce these to one or two leading cases. One possibility is a single previous case of first impression where you can say, "*See Able v. Baker* (collecting cases)."

      d. Always ask yourself whether the citation is necessary.

☐ 8. **Quotations.**

      a. <u>Cases</u>: Limit the quotation to what is absolutely necessary. Often it is necessary to use a specific quotation because it sets forth the actual language upon which you depend. Sometimes, however, a quotation is unnecessary, and an indirect statement will suffice.

b. <u>Statutes</u>: Quote only relevant provisions.

c. <u>Court Rules</u>: Quote only the necessary paragraphs or clauses.

❏ 9. **Conclusion of the Issue.**

a. State your disposition of the issues clearly and concisely: "Accordingly, the Court rejects the plaintiff's contention and holds...."

❏ 10. **Subsequent Issues.**

a. Indicate your transition.

b. If the issue is subordinate, treat it with an extremely condensed discussion.

c. If it is controlled by precedent, cite the case and be done with it.

d. Follow the steps set forth in the discussion of major issues, if applicable.

❏ 11. **Disposition.**

a. Make the disposition understandable.

b. Introduce it with a signal such as a topic sentence or a numeral.

❏ 12. **Footnotes.**

a. Take a hard look at each footnote and ask yourself, "Is this one necessary?"

b. If the discussion is germane, place it in the text.

c. Do not footnote a response to a very sophisticated argument that might have been made, but was not.

d. Do not distinguish a case that could have been cited, but was not.

e. If you are using a footnote to quote contents of a statute, pare the quotation and insert it in the text.

f. If you are quoting at length from a transcript, quote only what is essential.

❏ 13. **Style Critique.**

a. Use the active voice. Wherever you can, recast sentences that begin with "There is...."

b. Break long and complex sentences into short and simple statements.

c. Examine each sentence word for word, phrase by phrase and clause by clause to see what can be cut.

CHAPTER TWENTY-TWO

Administrative Law Judge Checklists

Author's Note: *The Checklists in this Chapter are designed for photocopying so that the Opinion Writers may have copies of their checklists at their sides as they write and edit. At appropriate places in the Checklists we have provided open boxes that can be filled with a check mark as the work progresses through composing the opinion in §22.1, testing the opinion in §22.2 and shortening it in §22.3.*

§22.1 Opinion Writing Checklist

A. <u>Follow a planned sequence of writing tasks.</u>

❑ 1. **Issues.** Decide what issues are to be discussed in the opinion.
   a. *Context of issue.* Give the reader a flavor of the context in which the issue arose. This includes any procedural history as well as the factual history.
   b. *Be neutral.* Be sure not to slant your statement of the issue in favor of either the plaintiff or the defendant.
   c. *Recap.* Do not set forth any issue *in vacuo*; each issue must be evaluated in terms of context and primary assumptions. Above all, there must be neutrality in the expression of the issue. Beware of slanting the statement. Remember Frankfurter: "Tell me the answer you want and I will phrase the question."

❑ 2. **The Road Map.**
   a. *List the issues.* Write down all the issues presented in the case. Do not worry about order or logical development.
   b. *Keep it brief.* An attorney's brief should be just that: brief. So should a judge's opinion. Ask yourself from the beginning: Is this point essential to the discussion?

    c.   *Standard of Review* (for agency review boards). Take each issue and accurately state the standard of review to be followed in evaluating that issue.

    d.   *Decide upon a theme.* Write a careful and considered statement of your presentation's major issue or issues and predominant theme. Keep this statement in front of you at all times; it will help with organization.

    e.   *Outline.* Prepare an outline of the opinion.

      (1) Prepare a summary statement of issues raised by the parties that will be discussed in the opinion. This summary may be inserted in the opinion in paragraph form to alert the reader as to what will follow.

      (2) Scrutinize the order in which the issues, arguments and ideas will be presented so as to determine what is most logical, interesting and informative.

    f.   *Remember your theme.* Look back to it as you write.

      (1) This will help to order and focus your writing.

      (2) It will build unity, logic and conciseness into your writing.

      (3) The organizing theme may need revision and refinement as the writing progresses.

    g.   *Organize.* Henry M. Hart, Jr. once said, "Briefs on the merits need not only tell their story to one who takes the time to read all the way through them, but ought to be so organized that they can be used, like a book of reference, for quick illumination on any particular point of concern." Remember this.

❑   3.   **Writing the Facts.**

    a.   Do not begin writing until you have decided what issues you will raise. Never write the facts first.

    b.   Tailor the statement of the facts so that it fits only the issues raised. Write as tersely as you can.

      (1) *Be accurate.* DO NOT STEAL THE FACTS! Set forth findings of fact, not evidence or assertions as your facts.

      (2) *Be objective.*

      (3) *Be clear.*

      (4) *Be concise.* Include only what is necessary, not what is merely interesting.

      (5) *Be fascinating.* Remember that what you write must compete for attention in a mountain of other communications. Try to make it rise above the surrounding peaks.

❑ 4. **Edit your work.**

    a. *First draft.* Prepare a complete first draft with whatever tool helps you to work and think most effectively: pen, pencil, typewriter, word processor, whatever. Never dictate an opinion!

        (1) If possible, write the draft in one sitting, however long it may take.

        (2) If you cannot complete the draft in one sitting, devise a strategy that will enable you to get back to it with a minimum of wheelspin. Ernest Hemingway is said to have stopped the day's work at a point where he had clearly in his head what he was going to write on the following day. I know a professional who, when he starts the day with writer's block, gets back on track by retyping the last page he wrote the day before.

        (3) Do not try to imitate another writer's approach. There is no such thing as a one-size-fits-all style appropriate to every writer. Each of us sets down words in a highly distinctive, "autographic" way.

    b. *Rest.* Set the first draft aside.

        (1) My one-time editor, Oscar Shefler, was a world-class writer. He reported: "It often happens that, while doing something else—driving, eating lunch, walking to the bazaars of my neighborhood—I will compose in my head whole paragraphs, even whole pages. When I get back to the typewriter, it is as if I am transcribing from a script somewhere behind my eyeballs."

        (2) Approach revision as a stranger, as an outside reader and editor who is seeing the copy fresh for the first time.

    c. *Begin revision.*

        (1) There is no such thing as good *writing;* there is only good *rewriting.*

        (2) As you read, compose a reconstructive outline of the main and subordinate ideas.

        (3) Identify the main ideas, according to topics if you have not done so in the first draft, and write them out in sequence, thus composing a précis.

        (4) Assess the topical sequence as though you are editing someone else's work.

            (a) See where the reconstructed outline departs from your original outline and determine which is better.

        (b) Determine whether the précis fully satisfies, in content and logic, the demands of the organizing theme.

B.   <u>How to edit your own work.</u>

     ☐ 1. **Edit like a reader.**

         a. Identify problems you encounter as a reader.

         b. Determine whether the sequence of ideas flows smoothly and logically.

         c. Determine whether the ideas are adequately supported.

         d. Look for conspicuous omissions.

         e. Look for needless repetition.

     ☐ 2. **Edit like a writer.**

         a. Assess your writing techniques and mark up the first draft as an editor would.

         b. Read certain passages aloud, if necessary, and train your ear to detect errors reliably.

         c. Avoid the trap of falling in love with your writing. In this situation, love often blinds.

         d. Assess the "beat" of your writing. There is a difference between writing for reading and writing for speaking, even though each form has both mood and rhythm. Do the words come across as a stentorian roar or as a "soft sell," soothing but nonetheless persuasive?

         e. A judge is a professional writer. Follow the practice of all professional writers and editors. Never rely entirely upon your memory. Keep a select library of the best dictionaries, handbooks and other references at your elbow, a good Webster's dictionary, college edition or unabridged; Roget's Thesaurus, Webster's New Dictionary of Synonyms, a good book of quotations: Oxford, Bergen Evans, Bartlett's and, of course, THE ELEMENTS OF STYLE by Strunk and White. You may consider also BRYAN GARNER, A DICTIONARY OF MODERN LEGAL USAGE (3d ed., 2009).

§ 22.2 Opinion Testing Checklist

☐ **Jurisdiction.**

Does the court have jurisdiction?

☐ **Opening.**

Does the opening or orientation acquaint the reader with the issues, the nature of the action, the parties, and a preview of the court's conclusion?

☐ **Summary of Issues.**

Are there one or two paragraphs wherein the reader can find a statement of the issues to be discussed? Alternatively, can the issues be identified easily as topic sentences?

☐ **Facts.**

Is there a lean, selective, economical, succinct exposition of material facts so that the reader can understand what follows?

☐ **Analysis of Issues.**

Have you set forth the *ratio decidendi*, a systematic discussion of the issues?

☐ 1. Identify the flash point of the controversy and discuss only what is essential for a resolution.

   a. If the law and its application alike are plain, your opinion should be short and to the point.

   b. If the law is certain and the application alone is doubtful, be sure you have explained how the law applies to the facts. Be just as sure you did not waste the reader's time justifying your choice of law.

   c. If neither the rule nor, *a fortiori*, its application is clear, discuss:

      (1) Choice, interpretation and application of the legal precept, or

      (2) Interpretation and application of the legal precept.

☐ 2. Is the discussion of the issue overwritten? Have you belabored the point or stated the obvious?

☐ 3. Have important contentions been discussed or swept under the rug?

☐ 4. Is the logical development sound?

   a. Is the choice of a major premise supported by the applicable law and facts of the case?

        b.   Have you followed the rules of inductive and deductive logic?

        c.   Is the opinion free of formal or material fallacies?

❏ 5. Does your analysis spend too much time detailing other cases?

        a.   Is it clear *why* you are citing a case?

            (1) Are you citing a case for its holding,

            (2) Are you citing a case for its reasoning, and/or

            (3) Are you citing a case for its facts?

        b.   Can parentheticals replace extensive description of cases?

        c.   Do you use string citations for no purpose?

❏ 6. What is the gobbledygook or Jabberwocky factor?

❏ **Judgment.**

Have you done substantial justice in the case?

1. Is there justice between the parties?

2. Does the decision maintain the integrity of the "body of the law" for future litigants?

Bottom Line: How thoughtfully and disinterestedly did the opinion weigh the conflicts involved in the case and how fair and durable did its adjustment of conflicting interests promise to be?

§ 22.3 Shorten-Your-Opinion Checklist

Satisfied with your writing and rewriting, you arrive at the final task. You must become a copy editor and examine the entire piece to see where you can tighten it. When you do this yourself, you engage in a task lonely, difficult and largely uncharted. Understandably, you may have carried on a passionate love affair with your own words, especially those that seemed, in the flush of creation, divinely beautiful or devilishly clever. Few of us have the heart to follow the implicit advice of the 17th-century French author and critic Nicolas Boileau: "No one who cannot limit himself has ever been able to write." The following steps may be helpful in determining where to make your cuts:

❑ 1. **Opening or Orientation Paragraph.**
    a. State the major issue (or issues) as concisely as possible. Consider how a headnote writer at Westlaw would express it.
    b. Pique the reader's interest with your language.

❑ 2. **Preview.**
    a. Tell your reader at the onset the decision of the case.
    b. Reveal whether you grant or deny the requested relief unless there is something about the opinion that makes it preferable for you to disclose this later.

❑ 3. **Jurisdiction.**
    a. State the basis for jurisdiction, if necessary. Generally, only a simple citation to a statute or court rule is needed. Such a statement is essential because without jurisdiction to hear the case, your opinion stands on very shaky ground.

❑ 4. **Statement of Issues.**
    a. Introduce this subject with a topic sentence or numeral to alert the reader that it is a separate part of the opinion.
    b. Summarize the issues as fairly and neutrally as possible.

❑ 5. **Facts.**
    a. In order to avoid the need for transitional phrases, introduce with a topic sentence or a numeral that identifies the narrative.
    b. Keep your figurative blue pencil ready. Cut any facts that are not relevant to the issues presented. Look at the facts through the eyes of a lawyer or judge in a subsequent case.
    c. Pare the narrative to exclude facts that are irrelevant or immaterial to the issues.

     d.   Ask yourself whether the narrative is interesting. Remember, however, to distinguish between what is important and what is merely interesting.

❑ 6. **Major Issue.**
     a.   You may list the major issue first for discussion or you may wish to discuss threshold issues before you reach it.
     b.   Pinpoint the conflict between the parties. Remember, there are three possibilities:
       (1) Choosing the controlling precept from competing ones (choosing the law). Or "finding" the law by creating a legal principle from a series of rules from a number of cases.
       (2) Interpreting the precept (usually a statute).
       (3) Applying the precept to the facts found by the fact finder.
       If it is an (1) case you must proceed to (2) and (3). If it is a (2) case, you must avoid unnecessary talk that implies a choice of competing precepts was involved. If it is only (3), you must not clutter it with discussion of competing interpretations.
     c.   If you refer to cases from other jurisdictions, cut the discussion to the bone as to both facts and holding.
     d.   If you refer to cases in your own court, distill them to a fair essence rather than doing a cut-and-paste-job with lengthy quotations. Limit your description to material facts.
     e.   When you choose one legal precept in preference to others, explain succinctly why you are doing so. Be specific.

❑ 7. **Citations.**
     a.   Whenever you cite a case, think about why you are citing it. Are you citing a particular case for its facts, its holding, its reasoning or some combination of these?
     b.   Once you determine why you are citing a case, use a parenthetical explanation or quotation to support your point.
     c.   If you have multiple or string citations, reduce these to one or two leading cases. One possibility is a single previous case of first impression where you can say, "*See Able v. Baker* (collecting cases)."
     d.   Always ask yourself whether the citation is necessary.

❑ 8. **Quotations.**
     a.   <u>Cases</u>: Limit the quotation to what is absolutely necessary. Often it is necessary to use a specific quotation because it sets forth the

actual language upon which you depend. Sometimes, however, a quotation is unnecessary, and an indirect statement will suffice.
    b.   <u>Statutes</u>: Quote only relevant provisions.
    c.   <u>Court Rules</u>: Quote only the necessary paragraphs or clauses.

☐ 9. **Conclusion of the Issue.**
    a.   State your disposition of the issues clearly and concisely: "Accordingly, the Court rejects the plaintiff's contention and holds...."

☐ 10. **Subsequent Issues.**
    a.   Indicate your transition.
    b.   If the issue is subordinate, treat it with an extremely condensed discussion.
    c.   If it is controlled by precedent, cite the case and be done with it.
    d.   Follow the steps set forth in the discussion of major issues, if applicable.

☐ 11. **Disposition.**
    a.   Make the disposition understandable.
    b.   Introduce it with a signal such as a topic sentence or a numeral.

☐ 12. **Footnotes.**
    a.   Take a hard look at each footnote and ask yourself, "Is this one necessary?"
    b.   If the discussion is germane, place it in the text.
    c.   Do not footnote a response to a very sophisticated argument that might have been made, but was not.
    d.   Do not distinguish a case that could have been cited, but was not.
    e.   If you are using a footnote to quote contents of a statute, pare the quotation and insert it in the text.
    f.   If you are quoting at length from a transcript, quote only what is essential.

☐ 13. **Style Critique.**
    a.   Use the active voice. Wherever you can, recast sentences that begin with "There is...."
    b.   Break long and complex sentences into short and simple statements.
    c.   Examine each sentence word for word, phrase by phrase and clause by clause to see what can be cut.

CHAPTER TWENTY-THREE

ARBITRATOR CHECKLISTS

Author's Note: *The three Checklists in this chapter are: §23.1 Writing the Opin-ion, §23.2 Testing the Opinion, and §23.3 Shortening the Opinion. The chapter is designed for photo-copying so that the Opinion Writers may have copies of their checklists at their sides as they write and edit. At appropriate places in the Check-lists, we have provided open boxes that can be filled with a check mark as the work progresses through composing and editing the opinion.*

§23.1 Opinion Writing Checklist

A. <u>Follow a planned sequence of writing tasks.</u>

    ❏ 1. **Issues.** Decide what issues are to be discussed in the opinion.
          a. *Context of issue.* Give the reader a flavor of the context in which the issue arose. This includes any procedural history as well as the factual history.
          b. *Be neutral.* Be sure not to slant your statement of the issue in favor of either the plaintiff or the defendant.
          c. *Recap.* Do not set forth any issue *in vacuo*; each issue must be evaluated in terms of context and primary assumptions. Above all, there must be neutrality in the expression of the issue. Beware of slanting the statement. Remember Frank-furter: "Tell me the answer you want and I will phrase the question."

    ❏ 2. **The Road Map.**
          a. *List the issues.* Write down all the issues presented in the case. Do not worry about order or logical development.
          b. *Keep it brief.* An attorney's brief should be just that: brief. So should a judge's opinion. Ask yourself from the beginning: Is this point essential to the discussion?

B. <u>Preliminary Statements Before Addressing the Merits.</u>

❏ 1. **Reference the Arbitration Clause of the Parties' Agreement.**
   a. Make reference to, and even quote from, the arbitration clause of the parties' agreement because it sets forth the general powers and authority of the arbitrators.
   b. The arbitration clause may even set forth the rules in relation to the procedures and evidence receptions by the arbitrators.

❏ 2. **The Governing Arbitration Law.**
   a. Determine whether the Federal Arbitration Act (FAA) or the state's Uniform Arbitration Act (UAA) applies.
   b. Deciding which statute applies turns on the language of the arbitration provision in the parties' agreement.
   c. The default rule may be to the FAA. This presumption will be overcome only if the applicable provision in the arbitration agreement evidences a "clear intent" to impose a state statute permitting a review of the award.

C. <u>Discussion of the Merits</u>

❏ 1. **Outline the Opinion.**
   a. Prepare a summary statement of issues raised by the parties that will be discussed in the opinion. This summary may be inserted in the opinion in paragraph form to alert the reader as to what will follow.
   b. Scrutinize the order in which the issues, arguments and ideas will be presented so as to determine what is most logical, interesting and informative.

❏ 2. **Writing the Facts.**
   a. Do not begin writing until you have decided what issues you will raise. Never write the facts first.
   b. Tailor the statement of the facts so that it fits only the issues raised. Write as tersely as you can.
      (1) *Be accurate.* DO NOT STEAL THE FACTS! Set forth findings of fact, not evidence or assertions as your facts.
      (2) *Be objective.*
      (3) *Be clear.*
      (4) *Be concise.* Include only what is necessary, not what is merely interesting.

(5) *Be fascinating.* Remember that what you write must compete for attention in a mountain of other communications. Try to make it rise above the surrounding peaks.

❑ 3. **Edit your work.**
   a. *First draft.* Prepare a complete first draft with whatever tool helps you to work and think most effectively: pen, pencil, typewriter, word processor, whatever. Never dictate an opinion!
      (1) If possible, write the draft in one sitting, however long it may take.
      (2) If you cannot complete the draft in one sitting, devise a strategy that will enable you to get back to it with a minimum of wheelspin. Ernest Hemingway is said to have stopped the day's work at a point where he had clearly in his head what he was going to write on the following day. I know a professional who, when he starts the day with writer's block, gets back on track by retyping the last page he wrote the day before.
      (3) Do not try to imitate another writer's approach. There is no such thing as a one-size-fits-all style appropriate to every writer. Each of us sets down words in a highly distinctive, "autographic" way.
   b. *Rest.* Set the first draft aside.
      (1) My one-time editor, Oscar Shefler, was a world-class writer. He reported: "It often happens that, while doing something else—driving, eating lunch, walking to the bazaars of my neighborhood—I will compose in my head whole paragraphs, even whole pages. When I get back to the typewriter, it is as if I am transcribing from a script somewhere behind my eyeballs."
      (2) Approach revision as a stranger, as an outside reader and editor who is seeing the copy fresh for the first time.
   c. *Begin revision.*
      (1) There is no such thing as good *writing*; there is only good *rewriting*.
      (2) As you read, compose a reconstructive outline of the main and subordinate ideas.
      (3) Identify the main ideas, according to topics if you have not done so in the first draft, and write them out in sequence, thus composing a précis.

(4) Assess the topical sequence as though you are editing someone else's work.

    (a) See where the reconstructed outline departs from your original outline and determine which is better.

    (b) Determine whether the précis fully satisfies, in content and logic, the demands of the organizing theme.

D. <u>How to edit your own work.</u>

☐ 1. **Edit like a reader.**

    a. Identify problems you encounter as a reader.

    b. Determine whether the sequence of ideas flows smoothly and logically.

    c. Determine whether the ideas are adequately supported.

    d. Look for conspicuous omissions.

    e. Look for needless repetition.

☐ 2. **Edit like a writer.**

    a. Assess your writing techniques and mark up the first draft as an editor would.

    b. Read certain passages aloud, if necessary, and train your ear to detect errors reliably.

    c. Avoid the trap of falling in love with your writing. In this situation, love often blinds.

    d. Assess the "beat" of your writing. There is a difference between writing for reading and writing for speaking, even though each form has both mood and rhythm. Do the words come across as a stentorian roar or as a "soft sell," soothing but nonetheless persuasive?

    e. An arbitrator should be viewed as a professional writer. Follow the practice of all professional writers and editors. Never rely entirely upon your memory. Keep a select library of the best dictionaries, handbooks and other references at your elbow, a good Webster's dictionary, college edition or unabridged; Roget's Thesaurus, Webster's New Dictionary of Synonyms, a good book of quotations: Oxford, Bergen Evans, Bartlett's and, of course, THE ELEMENTS OF STYLE by Strunk and White. You may consider also B. GARNER, A DICTIONARY OF MODERN LEGAL USAGE (3d Ed. Oxford, 2009).

§23.2 Opinion Testing Checklist

❑ **Opening.**

Does the opening or orientation acquaint the reader with the issues, the nature of the action, the parties, and a preview of the arbitrator's conclusion?

❑ **Summary of Issues.**

Are there one or two paragraphs wherein the reader can find a statement of the issues to be discussed? Alternatively, can the issues be identified easily as topic sentences?

❑ **Facts.**

Is there a lean, selective, economical, succinct exposition of material facts so that the reader can understand what follows?

❑ **Analysis of Issues.**

Have you set forth the *ratio decidendi*, a systematic discussion of the issues?

❑ 1. Identify the flash point of the controversy and discuss only what is essential for a resolution.

  a. If the law and its application alike are plain, your opinion should be short and to the point.

  b. If the law is certain and the application alone is doubtful, be sure you have explained how the law applies to the facts. Be just as sure you did not waste the reader's time justifying your choice of law.

  c. If neither the rule nor, *a fortiori*, its application is clear, discuss:

    (1) Choice, interpretation and application of the legal precept, or

    (2) Interpretation and application of the legal precept.

❑ 2. Is the discussion of the issue overwritten? Have you belabored the point or stated the obvious?

❑ 3. Have important contentions been discussed or swept under the rug?

❑ 4. Is the logical development sound?

  a. Is the choice of a major premise supported by the applicable law and facts of the case?

  b. Have you followed the rules of inductive and deductive logic?

        c.   Is the opinion free of formal or material fallacies?

❑   5.   Does your analysis spend too much time detailing other cases?

        a.   Is it clear *why* you are citing a case?

           (1) Are you citing a case for its holding,

           (2) Are you citing a case for its reasoning, and/or

           (3) Are you citing a case for its facts?

        b.   Can parentheticals replace extensive description of cases?

        c.   Do you use string citations for no purpose?

❑   6.   What is the gobbledygook or Jabberwocky factor?

❑ **The Award.**

Have you done substantial justice in the case?

Bottom Line: How thoughtfully and disinterestedly did the opinion weigh the conflicts involved in the case and how fair and durable did its adjustment of conflicting interests promise to be?

§ 23.3 Shorten-Your-Opinion Checklist

Satisfied with your writing and rewriting, you arrive at the final task. You must become a copy editor and examine the entire piece to see where you can tighten it. When you do this yourself, you engage in a task lonely, difficult and largely uncharted. Understandably, you may have carried on a passionate love affair with your own words, especially those that seemed, in the flush of creation, divinely beautiful or devilishly clever. Few of us have the heart to follow the implicit advice of the 17th-century French author and critic Nicolas Boileau: "No one who cannot limit himself has ever been able to write." The following steps may be helpful in determining where to make your cuts:

❏ 1. **Opening or Orientation Paragraph.**
   a. State the major issue (or issues) as concisely as possible. Consider how a headnote writer at Westlaw would express it.
   b. Pique the reader's interest with your language.

❏ 2. **Preview.**
   a. Tell your reader at the onset the decision of the case.
   b. Reveal whether you grant or deny the requested relief unless there is something about the opinion that makes it preferable for you to disclose this later.

❏ 3. **Statement of Issues.**
   a. Introduce this subject with a topic sentence or numeral to alert the reader that it is a separate part of the opinion.
   b. Summarize the issues as fairly and neutrally as possible.

❏ 4. **Facts.**
   a. In order to avoid the need for transitional phrases, introduce with a topic sentence or a numeral that identifies the narrative.
   b. Keep your figurative blue pencil ready. Cut any facts that are not relevant to the issues presented. Look at the facts through the eyes of a lawyer or judge in a subsequent case.
   c. Pare the narrative to exclude facts that are irrelevant or immaterial to the issues.
   d. Ask yourself whether the narrative is interesting. Remember, however, to distinguish between what is important and what is merely interesting.

❑   5.   **Major Issue.**

     a.   You may list the major issue first for discussion or you may wish to discuss threshold issues before you reach it.

     b.   Pinpoint the conflict between the parties. Remember, there are three possibilities:

        (1)   Choosing the controlling precept from competing ones (choosing the law). Or "finding" the law by creating a legal principle from a series of rules from a number of cases.

        (2)   Interpreting the precept (usually a statute).

        (3)   Applying the precept to the facts found by the fact finder.

        If it is an (1) case you must proceed to (2) and (3). If it is a (2) case, you must avoid unnecessary talk that implies a choice of competing precepts was involved. If it is only (3), you must not clutter it with discussion of competing interpretations.

     c.   If you refer to cases from other jurisdictions, cut the discussion to the bone as to both facts and holding.

     d.   If you refer to cases in your own court, distill them to a fair essence rather than doing a cut-and-paste-job with lengthy quotations. Limit your description to material facts.

     e.   When you choose one legal precept in preference to others, explain succinctly why you are doing so. Be specific.

❑   6.   **Citations.**

     a.   Whenever you cite a case, think about why you are citing it. Are you citing a particular case for its facts, its holding, its reasoning or some combination of these?

     b.   Once you determine why you are citing a case, use a parenthetical explanation or quotation to support your point.

     c.   If you have multiple or string citations, reduce these to one or two leading cases. One possibility is a single previous case of first impression where you can say, "*See Able v. Baker* (collecting cases)."

     d.   Always ask yourself whether the citation is necessary.

❑   7.   **Quotations.**

     a.   <u>Cases</u>: Limit the quotation to what is absolutely necessary. Often it is necessary to use a specific quotation because it sets forth the actual language upon which you depend. Sometimes, however, a quotation is unnecessary, and an indirect statement will suffice.

     b.   <u>Statutes</u>: Quote only relevant provisions.

     c.   <u>FAA/UAA Rules</u>: Quote only the necessary paragraphs or clauses.

    d.   <u>Arbitration Clause of Parties' Agreement</u>: Quote only relevant language.

☐ 8. **Conclusion of the Discussion of the Issue.**
    a.   State your disposition of the issues clearly and concisely: "Accordingly, we reject the claimant's contention and hold...."

☐ 9. **Subsequent Issues.**
    a.   Indicate your transition.
    b.   If the issue is subordinate, treat it with an extremely condensed discussion.
    c.   If it is controlled by precedent, cite the case and be done with it.
    d.   Follow the steps set forth in the discussion of major issues, if applicable.

☐ 10. **The Award.**
    a.   Make the Award understandable.
    b.   Introduce it with a signal such as a topic sentence or a numeral.

☐ 11. **Footnotes.**
    a.   Take a hard look at each footnote and ask yourself, "Is this one necessary?"
    b.   If the discussion is germane, place it in the text.
    c.   Do not footnote a response to a very sophisticated argument that might have been made, but was not.
    d.   Do not distinguish a case that could have been cited, but was not.
    e.   If you are using a footnote to quote contents of a statute, pare the quotation and insert it in the text.
    f.   If you are quoting at length from a transcript, quote only what is essential.

☐ 12. **Style Critique.**
    a.   Use the active voice. Wherever you can, recast sentences that begin with "There is...."
    b.   Break long and complex sentences into short and simple statements.
    c.   Examine each sentence word for word, phrase by phrase and clause by clause to see what can be cut.